COLLEGE-HILL

Central Auditory and Language Disorders in Children

Edited by
Robert W. Keith, Ph.D.
University of Cincinnati Medical Center

College-Hill Press

College-Hill Press
P.O. Box 35728
Houston, Texas 77035

© 1981 by College-Hill Press

Library of Congress Cataloging in Publication Data

Main entry under title:
Central auditory and language disorders in children.

    Held in Cincinnati, Ohio, May 28-30, 1980.
    Bibliography.
    Includes index.
    1. Hearing disorders in children—Congresses.
2. Auditory perception in children—Congresses.
3. Language disorders in children—Congresses.
I. Keith, Robert W. II. Cincinnati. University. Division of Audiology and Speech
Pathology. (DNLM: 1. Auditory perception—In infancy and childhood—
Congresses. 2. Language disorders—In infancy and childhood—
Congresses. 3. Perceptual disorders—In infancy and childhood—
Congresses. WV 272 C3966 1980)

RF291.5.C45C44 618.92'855   80-24873

ISBN 0-933014-61-9

Contents

92822

Participants

Katharine G. Butler, Ph.D.
Director
Department of Special Education
  and Rehabilitation
Syracuse University
805 S. Crouse Avenue
Syracuse, New York 13210

Jan L. Culbertson, Ph.D.
Acting Head
Division of Child Development
Department of Pediatrics
Vanderbilt University
Nashville, Tennessee 37232

Peggy C. Ferry, M.D.
Head
Section of Child Neurology
Department of Pediatrics
Health Sciences Center
University of Arizona
Tucson, Arizona

Susan W. Jerger, M.S.
The Neurosensory Center of Houston
6501 Fannin Street
Mail Station NA-200
Texas Medical Center
Houston, Texas 77030

Doris J. Johnson, Ph.D.
Learning Disabilities Center
The Frances Searle Building
2299 Sheridan Rd.
Evanston, Illinois 60201

Jack Katz, Ph.D.
State University of New York at Buffalo
Department of Communicative Disorders
  and Sciences
Speech and Hearing Clinic
4226 Ridge Lea Road
Amherst, New York 14226

Norma S. Rees, Ph.D.
Dean of Graduate Studies
The Graduate School and University Center
  of the City University of New York
23 West 42nd Street
New York, New York 10036

Sylvia O. Richardson, M.D.
4141 Bayshore Blvd., #1701
Tampa, Florida 33611

Rachel E. Stark, Ph.D.
Director
Speech and Hearing Division
The John F. Kennedy Institute
707 North Broadway
Baltimore, Maryland 21205

Contributing Authors

Cornelia H. Harmon, M.S.
Speech-Language Pathologist
Atlanta Speech School
3160 Northside Parkway, NW
Atlanta, Georgia

Paula Tallal, Ph.D.
Assistant Professor
Department of Psychiatry
University of California, San Diego
San Diego, California

This publication is a report of the proceedings of a symposium held in Cincinnati, Ohio on May 28, 29, and 30, 1980. The symposium was sponsored by the Division of Audiology and Speech Pathology, University of Cincinnati Medical Center.

Dorothy H. Air, Ph.D., *Program Director*

Robert W. Keith, Ph.D., *Symposium Moderator*

Preface

The planning for this symposium began soon after May 19-20, 1977, when we finished our previous symposium on Central Auditory Dysfunction (Keith 1977). While we were satisfied with the material presented at that time, as is always true of science, it left us with questions about a number of issues related to auditory perception, language, reading, and remediation. During the intervening years, and as we began active planning of the present symposium, we have heard similar questions discussed in conversation, at professional meetings, and in the literature. Among the many issues that require discussion, at least five will be considered at this symposium. They include: (1) problems of terminology; (2) cause and effect relationships between auditory processing and language; (3) assessment of auditory processing problems; (4) effects of central auditory dysfunction on a child and the child's family; and (5) remediation.

One obstacle to understanding and discussing central auditory function is the lack of agreement about appropriate terminology. Currently, the term "central auditory function" is used interchangeably with central auditory abilities, central auditory perception, central auditory processing, auditory perceptual skills, etc. Deficiencies in central auditory function have been called central auditory dysfunction, auditory perceptual disorders, nonsensory auditory deficits, auditory language learning disorders, auditory processing problems, etc. As I have written previously (Keith 1980b), lack of agreement about what to call this clinical entity is a good indication of the uncertainty about the essence of the problem and about its remediation.

When the terminology is not precisely defined or widely accepted, practical problems occur. For example, the communication between referral sources and diagnostic services can be confused or misinterpreted, particularly if the person making the referral and the examiner have two different concepts in mind when they consider the child's "auditory processing problem." Moreover, imagine the frustration felt by the parents who have spent time bringing their child in for testing and who have paid for the evaluation, when there are no clear explanations or positive recommendations. While the use of labels without definitions or descriptions of behavior has been a subject of discussion among professionals for years, we continue to use them either unaware of or resigned to accept the unfortunate consequences that can result.

Another problem resulting from the use of undefined diagnostic terminology is that "We don't know how many of them are out there." Demographic studies which estimate that 2%-20% of the population have auditory perceptual deficiencies are difficult to believe when different definitions have been used by the various investigators. If we cannot estimate the magnitude of the problem, we cannot decide how many people should be trained to provide services, how many dollars are required for diagnosis and treatment, or what kind of and how many special facilities are required for remediation programs. In short, it is impossible to lobby effectively for a program when the exact need is unknown.

Not only is the present terminology imprecise, it is also too inclusive. The abilities listed by various authors under "central auditory processing" range from the localization of sound to the comprehension of language. Apparently, it would be folly to include such a wide range of abilities under the same name. Even as a generic term, it is simply inadequate. We must formulate definitions for and differentiate between those auditory perceptual abilities which are necessary for the development of language skills and those auditory skills which arise from the comprehension of language.

The second issue before us is the cause and effect relationships that exists between auditory processing and language. The working draft of a position statement by ASHA on language and learning disabilities (ASHA 1980) states that "Professionals understand that there is little support for the persistence of a perceptual deficit model in language and learning disabilities." For those who are unfamiliar with the term "perceptual deficit hypothesis," it assumes that auditory processing is fundamental to learning language; that auditory perceptual deficits cause disorders in areas of language, reading, and learning; that auditory perception can be readily broken down into specific skills that are amenable to training, that a hierarchy of auditory perceptual skills exists with processes moving from simple to complex, and that remediation should follow the same order (Keith 1980a).

Opponents of the perceptual deficit hypothesis claim that while auditory perceptual disorders are related to disorders of language, reading, and learning, they are not the cause of those problems. Rees (1973, 1974), for example, has written that there is little foundation for the notion that most children with reading, speech, and language disorders have a fundamental problem of auditory perception of speech, a position supported by others (Sanders 1977; Lyon 1977). These authors cite verbal mediation deficiencies as being the fundamental problem.

Marquardt and Saxman (1972) found that children with underdeveloped articulation skills also show depressed scores on auditory tests of language comprehension and tests of auditory sound discrimination. They explained their results on the basis of a general developmental lag and believed that the importance of auditory subskills to speech and language acquisition remains to be demonstrated. Note how Marquardt and Saxman use tests of language comprehension to measure auditory perception. It is the continued confusion between fundamental auditory perceptual skills and auditory language comprehension abilities that causes us so much difficulty in deciding between the validity of an auditory perceptual deficit and verbal mediation deficit hypothesis and cause and effect relationships.

As Ventry (1980) points out, at the heart of the difficulty is the fact that true experimental research on humans is nearly impossible. That is, researchers cannot cause an impairment in human subjects and study the effects of that intervention on behavior. While Ventry was discussing the link between conductive hearing impairment and language, learning and auditory dysfunction, his remarks apply to research in auditory perception as well. The implication is that as a result of necessary restrictions, most of the research on central auditory processing as it relates to language has to be descriptive.

A perceptual deficit model may be unattractive to some, however, the notion of a cause and effect relationship between auditory perceptual abilities and language and learning deficiencies is intuitively appealing to others. Although the resolution of this issue lies somewhere in the future, there is experimental evidence showing that some children with language, learning, and reading disorders have difficulty in certain non-cognitive, non-linguistic auditory abilities such as binaural fusion, binaural separation, dynamic auditory localization (Devens, Hoyer, and McGroskey 1978), two-tone auditory function (McGroskey and Kidder 1980), perception of rapid transitions in acoustic signals (Tallal 1976), word recognition at favorable signal-to-noise ratios, e.g., + 9 dB S/N (Palanker 1978), etc.

The solution to the perceptual deficit vs. verbal mediation deficit hypotheses probably lies in further definition of what is meant by each of the terms. For example, if auditory perception is defined by such abilities as auditory blending, discrimination of phonemes, auditory closure, memory, or auditory comprehension, these are language-based skills that are not fundamental to learning language but which emerge as one acquires language. However, poor performance in such fundamental auditory abilities as localization, ability to perceive rapid acoustic transitions in speech, or the inability to perform any primitive imitative speech task that does not require comprehension, manipulation of intersensory information, or abstract thought is a fundamental auditory perceptual deficiency that may have important implications for language acquisition. It is extremely useful to attempt to decide which presently available central auditory tests require simple imitation, and thus little comprehension of language, and which tests are heavily weighted by language and cognitive factors.

Identifying these relationships might eliminate problems caused by attempts to relate specific test results to specific remediation strategies. Many of the central auditory tests tell us a great deal about the maturation of the auditory pathway, the development of cerebral dominance for language, etc.;

but they do not tell us about language remediation strategies and they should not be expected to do so.

The model proposed here makes it possible to arrive at important information regarding specific auditory perceptual skills that are non-linguistic or pre-linguistic. Use of these data can demonstrate neuromaturational levels of the auditory system. This information may be useful in helping us to learn why the child is able to achieve certain levels of speech and language competence before reaching a plateau in development, and why some speech and language abilities do not emerge. Given this model, we may also be able to provide information about the child who has associated problems in reading. The neuromaturational level approach is not intended to be a site of lesion assessment in the diagnostic sense, although that could result. Usually it would imply either interference with or disorganization of function.

Another issue for audiologists is Eisenberg's (1976) call for a bona fide pediatric audiologist. She correctly points out that the audiological focus has remained essentially static over the past 30 years. Our approach to a pediatric population is geared to deafness rather than hearing, and while we can say that a child responds at normal levels, we cannot say that he hears normally. One old example of this problem is the continued use of air-bone conduction and undistorted speech discrimination tests in our pediatric caseloads. We must begin thinking about assessment from middle ear to cortex and the implications of this assessment for language development and remediation strategies.

Eisenberg points out that the nature of the clinical pediatric population is altering radically. Recently there has been a startling increase in the incidence of CNS disorders and developmental disorders of communication. Audiologists should be prepared to evaluate children who have these disorders and recommend appropriate remedial procedures.

One issue that we will not have time to deal with at this meeting is related to the short and long-term effects of early chronic otitis media on central auditory processing skills and language and learning. We plan to make that the topic for discussion at our symposium next year.

Other issues related to the evaluation of central auditory dysfunction include the effect of auditory language disorders on the child and the child's family and various approaches to remediation. Since these issues comprise the major subject of this symposium, they are better left to the guest speakers.

Undoubtedly the material presented here will leave the course participant (and the reader of the proceedings) with some old and many new questions. It is my hope that this material will help put this complicated subject into better perspective, and provide new insights into the diagnosis and remediation of central auditory dysfunction in children.

RWK

References

ASHA 1980. Position statement of the American Speech, Language and Hearing Association on language and learning disabilities. Working draft in press.

Devens, J., Hoyer, E. and McGroskey, R. 1978. Dynamic auditory localization by normal and learning disability children. *J. Amer. Audiol. Soc.* 3:172-78.

Eisenberg, R. 1976. *Auditory competence in early life: the roots of communicative behavior.* Baltimore: University Park Press.

Keith, R.W. 1980a. Tests of central auditory function. In *Auditory disorders in school children,* eds. R. Roeser and M. Downs. New York: Brian C. Decker.

Keith, R.W. 1980b. "Central auditory tests." In *Speech, hearing and language,* eds. N. Lass, L. McReynolds, J. Northern, D. Yoder. Philadelphia: W.B. Saunders.

Keith, R.W., ed. 1977. *Central auditory dysfunction.* New York: Grune and Stratton.

Lyon, R. 1977. Auditory perceptual training: the state of the art. *J. Learn. Disabil.* 10:564-72.

Marquardt, T. and Saxman, J. 1972. Language comprehension and auditory discrimination in articulation deficient kindergarten children. *J. Speech Hear. Res.* 15:382-89.

McGroskey, R. and Kidder, A. 1980. Auditory fusion among learning-disabled, reading-disabled, and normal children. *J. Learn. Disabil.* 13:18-25.

Palanker, S. 1978. A study of the effects of a competing message on normal and learning-disabled children. Unpublished Masters' thesis, University of Cincinnati.

Rees, N. 1974. The speech pathologist and the reading process. *Asha* 16:255-58.

Rees, N. 1973. Auditory processing factors in learning disorders: a view from Procruste's bed. *J. Speech Hear. Dis.* 38:304-15.

Sanders, D.A. 1977. *Auditory perception of speech. An introduction to principles and problems.* Englewood Cliffs, NJ: Prentice Hall, Inc.

Tallal, P. 1976. Rapid auditory processing in normal and disordered language development. *J. Speech Hear. Res.* 19:561-71.

Ventry, I.M. 1980. Effects of conductive hearing loss: Fact or fiction. *J. Speech Hear. Dis.* 45:143-56.

Acknowledgments

This symposium was one of a series of continuing education programs sponsored by the Division of Audiology and Speech Pathology at the University of Cincinnati Medical Center. The successful implementation of these courses requires the coordinated effort of many individuals who should be recognized.

The Program Committee for this symposium was made up of the faculty of the Division of Audiology and Speech Pathology. They were: Elaine L. Bishop, Gayle Bowyer, Sharon Ciani, John G. Clark, Micki Coppel, Jack DeBoer, Susan Farrer, Sharon T. Hepfner, Linda Huntress, Kathy Justice, Ann Kummer, Drue Lehmann, Sylvia Meek, Christine Ogden, Barbara Schnarr, Joseph C. Stemple, Joan Stephens, Dianne Stewart, Jean Strother, Tommie Webster, Nancy Willard. Members of this group were responsible for multiple details that are required in producing such a program, and their willing efforts were sincerely appreciated.

The clerical work was provided by our secretarial staff, and I would like to especially acknowledge Carol Corcoran for her assistance. Graduate students from the University of Cincinnati Speech Pathology and Audiology program assisted us during the two and a half day meeting, and we appreciate their help. Overseeing all of the details of the planning and implementaton was the program director, Dorothy H. Air, Ph.D. Her skilled organizational efforts resulted in a smoothly run meeting that was a pleasure to attend.

My secretary, Kathy Grauvogel, assisted in the preparation of the proceedings of this symposium. I am always grateful to Kathy for her capable and efficient assistance.

A special acknowledgment and note of thanks is due to a superb guest faculty whose excellent presentations resulted in a meaningful symposium. The added effort required of each speaker in preparation of manuscripts for this publication was also very much appreciated.

It is my hope that these proceedings will serve as a valuable reference for students and clinicians working in areas of auditory-language dysfunction.

1

Neurological Considerations in Children with Learning Disabilities

Peggy C. Ferry, M.D.

Brain Development, Language and Learning Disabilities

Introduction

Interest in language and learning disabilities has grown dramatically over the past decade. The increased survival rates of low birth weight and other "high-risk" infants, identification and referral of learning-disabled children, establishment of evaluation teams, federal legislation mandating special education programs, and improved remediation techniques have combined to make the topic one of major importance. Coupled with these advances, there has been a substantial increase in our knowledge about basic brain development.

A thorough understanding of brain development and function is essential if we are to develop successful diagnostic and effective treatment programs for children with developmental neurological disorders. This paper will present information about: 1) normal brain development; 2) the neurological substrates of language and learning disabilities; and 3) new methods of studying brain function which, hopefully, will lead to even further advancement in our knowledge about language and learning disabilities in the future.

Normal Brain Development

The human brain begins to develop about three weeks after conception. A primitive neural groove evolves into a neural tube which closes at 21-25 days gestation. As early as the end of the third week of gestation, the nervous system has three major subdivisons: the forebrain, the midbrain, and the hindbrain. Five major subdivisions are delineated by eight weeks gestation, and by this time the earliest evidence of the cerebral hemispheres appears (Ferry et al. 1979).

Studies on reflex development in the very young fetus have shown that the brain is truly *precocious*: reflexive physiological activity such as head turning and mouth opening in response to sensory stimulation can occur at five and one half weeks of gestation; spontaneous electroencephalographic (EEG) activity can be recorded by 7 weeks; an eye-blink reflex can be obtained at 10 weeks and knee jerk reflexes have been elicited in a 12-week-old fetus.

1

By eight and one half weeks gestation, nerve cells in the brain have begun to form and connect with other cells. This nerve cell development and "wiring" develops in a highly specialized manner, with specific spatial and temporal sequencing. Myelination, or the development of "insulation" around various nerve fibers, begins to develop in the fourth month of gestation and continues in an orderly sequence throughout pregnancy and well into postnatal life. Specific pathways develop in the brain at different times, following a phylogenetically logical temporal and spatial sequence. The principal auditory structures develop by 7 weeks gestation and myelination of the auditory system begins at the end of the fifth month. Other systems not as necessary for the survival and adaptation of the newborn infant, such as pyramidal tracts and association pathways, myelinate much later after birth.

Early evidence of temporal lobe development can be seen by 10-12 weeks. It is well-formed by 20 weeks. Specific gyri of the temporal lobe develop at precise times which can be correlated closely with gestational age. For example, the superior temporal gyrus regularly develops at 28 weeks.

Thus, the first 10 weeks of intrauterine life are particularly critical for future neurological maturation. It is during this time that the anatomical, physiological, and biochemical substrates of subsequent development are formed. All of these early phases of development are significant because the most serious neurological abnormalities in children arise during this very important first 10 weeks.

As more and more infants of very low birth weight (1500 gms.) and early gestational age (32 weeks) survive, knowledge of factors which influence early brain development and concerns about the quality of life in these infants become even more important considerations than in the past.

Hemispheric Asymmetry and Specialization

Studies on "split-brain" patients stimulated a resurgence of interest in the division of labor between the two cerebral hemispheres. In addition, recent studies have shown substantial differences between brain structure and function in males and females. Thus, it is useful to think of the concept of "four separate brains," (i.e. the *left* and *right* hemispheres in *males* and *females*). These asymmetries and specialized functions have now been shown in fetuses, as well as in infants, children, and adults.

The human brain is anatomically, physiologically, and biochemically asymmetrical. Anatomical features of the left temporal lobe show a distinctly larger language comprehension area than those of the right. This asymmetry has been found in fetuses, as well as in older children, suggesting that the anatomic substrate for language development in the left cerebral hemisphere is present well before birth. Evoked response, dichotic listening and other neurophysiological studies have shown distinct functional asymmetries between the two hemispheres. Investigations of neurotransmitters in the two sides of the brain have shown distinct bio-

2

chemical asymmetry. Studies of psychopathological states have associated schizophrenia with left hemisphere lesions while affective disorders have been associated with right hemisphere damage (Flor-Henry 1974).

Sex differences in brain function are clearly evident in the fetus and are dependent upon exposure of the fetal brain to male hormones during early development. These hormones affect the structural, physiological, and biochemical organization and function of the brain. Research on the nature of these distinctions between male and female brains is currently in progress. Descriptions of differences between the left and right "hemispheres" in males and females are currently very general; one should really speak of differences in individual neuronal pathways within the nervous system, as there are literally hundreds of different individual circuits which develop and function at different rates and in different manners in the two sides of the brain.

Clinical studies have clearly indicated the selective vulnerability of left hemisphere structures, particularly the temporal lobe, in males. Developmental langugage disorders, dyslexia, autistic syndromes, temporal lobe seizures, and other neurological syndromes are significantly more prevalent in boys than in girls. The reasons for this selective vulnerability are unclear, but they may relate to the anatomical, physiological, and biochemical differences noted above. Further studies on the normal and abnormal development of the left temporal lobe in male fetuses as well as in young infants and children are clearly needed. Perhaps these hemispheric asymmetries predispose the developing temporal lobe to the harmful effects of drugs and toxins, or to intrauterine viral infections; similarly, other rapidly developing areas of the brain may be more adversely affected by perinatal asphyxia, metabolic disturbances, hyperbilirubinemia, and intracranial hemorrhage than the slowly developing areas.

New Methods of Studying Brain Function in Infants and Children

Recent scientific and technological advances in the neurological sciences have led to a dramatic increase in our knowledge of brain function. Beginning in 1972, with the advent of computed tomographic brain scans, radiological studies have truly revolutionized the practice of pediatric neurology. Technical advances have now made it possible to obtain clear, precise images of brain anatomy with minimal risk to the child. The CT scan is particularly useful in detecting intracranial hemorrhage, hydrocephalus and other congenital anomalies, brain tumors, and other mass lesions in the neonate (Ferry 1980).

The new "PET" (positron-emission tomography) scan involves injection of radioisotope-labeled material prior to scanning, to increase the likelihood of detecting abnormalities; currently, researchers are using the technique to study sensory, motor, and mental functions. This is an exciting tool for the future.

Ultrasound techniques furnish valuable diagnostic information, especially in neonates and infants. The Octoson echoscope provides rapid, painless, and safe examination of ventricular size and hemorrhagic areas. It is particularly useful in following high-risk infants who have intraventricular hemorrhage and hydrocephalus.

Recent studies of cerebral blood flow have shown that blood volume is significantly greater in the left hemisphere. Regional cerebral blood flow changes in response to specific focal tasks have been measured in human subjects during performance of various cortical functions (hand movements, stereognostic discrimination, listening, and speech). These studies identify the areas of elevated metabolic activity presumably due to locally increased neuronal activity. They permit direct analysis of patterns of activity and represent an exciting advance in our ability to study functional localization in the brain. Current investigations involving both normal and neurologically handicapped individuals will help us understand the nature of recovery processes and the activation of alternate pathways in diseased or injured brains (Halsey et al. 1974).

Studies of local brain glucose utilization have shown marked variations in the metabolic rates of various anatomical structures in the brain. The results have generally shown a higher metabolic rate in gray matter than in white matter. Interestingly, the components of the auditory system are among the most metabolically active areas of the brain, with the inferior colliculus showing the highest rate of glucose utilization. This method offers a powerful new tool with which to study the functional organization of the central nervous system, in both normal and abnormal conditions (Kennedy et al. 1978).

Electron microscopic and audioradiographic studies (in which specific fiber pathways can be traced) have revealed exciting new information about the microscopic anatomy of the brain. At the cellular level, these investigations have helped us understand the precise functions of the developing human brain (Jacobson 1978).

The evaluation of visual and auditory evoked responses of infants has increased recently. Investigations of auditory brain-stem evoked responses (ABR) from low-birth-weight infants in neonatal intensive care units suggest that as many as 20% of these infants have ABR abnormalities (Marshall et al. 1980). While evoked responses may be intriguing for the researcher and the neurophysiologist, their precise clinical usefulness remains to be determined; however it is possible that these responses, elicited by safe, non-invasive techniques, may help us follow high-risk infants in the future.

A number of other research studies are currently underway to evaluate the developing fetal brain. As noted earlier, we are still hampered by lack of detailed knowledge about the various processes that occur in the "critical" first 10 weeks of gestation. Further information is sorely needed about the effects of viruses, drugs, toxins (i.e. alcohol), and environmental hazards on the developing brain. Such knowledge will help us to prevent serious neurological damage in the fetus, and clinical application of this basic information will provide an improved outlook for neurologically handicapped children.

Neurological Evaluation of Children with Language and Learning Disabilities

Principles of Neurological Evaluation of Children

The neurological evaluation of children is not an easy task. Special expertise, training, and competence are required, particularly when assessing young children. Examiners must possess patience, flexibility, a genuine love for children, sound knowledge of normal behavior and development, and experience with a large number of children and with a wide variety of disorders.

Many children with developmental language disorders are "hard to test." Any of us who has spent time in an examining room with a two-year-old, non-verbal, crying, autistic child knows how difficult the situation can be (Rapin 1978). It is usually necessary to get down on the floor and simply play with the child, rather than attempt to perform a formal, detailed neurological examination in such situations. Observations of the child's motor function, cranial nerves, affective behavior, and other neurological attributes can be made informally. Repeated examinations may be necessary to fully evaluate the individual child's neurological findings. It is important to remember that the pediatric neurologist does more than just a "physical" examination and that, in fact, his expertise lies in a full interpretation of the child's neurological functioning. This includes not only motor development, but cognitive, linguistic, social, affective, and sensory aspects of brain function.

The pediatric neurologist can help in the evaluation of language or learning-disabled children in the following ways (Rapin 1978):

1. By helping to determine the cause of the child's problem;
2. By investigating which particular areas of the brain are involved and to what extent;
3. By evaluating whether the disorder is static or progressive and what the prognosis is for future neurological development;
4. By deciding whether additional diagnostic tests are needed (EEG, CT scan, spinal tap, etc.);
5. By working with other team members in formulating an appropriate treatment program;
6. By prescribing specific medical therapies (i.e. anticonvulsant drugs) when appropriate;
7. By explaining the medical aspects of the child's condition to the parents.

Certain basic premises about brain functioning and language disorders should be kept in mind. These include the following:

1. Delay or deviation in language development is due to disordered brain functioning. To put it simply, the child does not learn to talk with his

5

liver or big toe; normal speech and language development is a reflection of an intact, functioning brain. The only exception to this rule may occur in the extremely uncommon circumstance when a child suffers severe environmental deprivation or emotional neglect. Conditions of "elective mutism" are vastly over-diagnosed and probably occur infrequently.

2. Speech and language delay or impairment may be the *only* symptom or sign of neurological impairment. This is a reflection of functional localization in which severe damage to a circumscribed area may occur while other areas of the brain remain perfectly intact. Thus, although a child with delayed speech development may have a perfectly normal general neurological examination, this should not rule out the possibility that his delayed speech development is due to a neurological problem.

3. Neurological dysfunction and behavior disorders may co-exist; the presence of one or the other does not imply equal causation. For example, a child who suffers viral encephalitis affecting his left temporal lobe may be left with severely impaired auditory perceptual skills and may have associated behavioral problems (hyperactivity, aggression, autistic features). These behavioral symptoms may be partly due to the neurological injury; they may also be a reflection of the child's frustration at the loss of the ability to speak; or they may be associated with other emotional problems. In most children, the neurological and emotional behaviors *exist together*, and it may be a futile intellectual exercise to try to separate them. In fact, the therapy is often identical for both disorders. Similarly, some children with developmental or acquired language disorders may have prominent emotional symptoms in response to their frustration and inability to communicate with important persons in their lives (parents, siblings, playmates). In time, with the appropriate treatment and following improvement of the basic language disorder, the secondary emotional symptoms may disappear. Conversely, other children, even those who have sympathetic and understanding parents, may display increased emotional symptoms even with appropriate therapy. Each child, in each family, is different; no assumptions can be made about the proportion of neurological or beavioral features in individual cases.

4. Multiple syndromes of neurological dysfunction may co-exist in the same child, but the presence of motor or sensory abnormalities does not automatically imply that other areas of the brain are not functioning properly.

Training and Qualifications of Pediatric Neurologists

Pediatric neurology training programs encompass postdoctoral training following the standard four years of medical school. A general internship year of either pediatrics or internal medicine is followed by a residency for one or two years in general pediatrics or general neurology. During this time the prospective pediatric neurologist learns the fundamentals of neurology as a clinical science and of pediatrics as the science of medical care for children. A three-year pediatric neurology fellowship program follows in which the doctor further refines his skills. Basic scientific training in neuroanatomy, neuropathology, neurochemistry, and neurophysiology is incorporated into this three year training program. In addition, the pediatric neurology trainee becomes familiar with basic neurodiagnostic procedures such as electroencephalography (EEG), electromyography (EMG), neuroradiology (including CT brain scans), and other diagnostic tests.

While most pediatric neurology training programs provide exposure to the majority of acute clinical pediatric neurological problems, the programs do not require experience with developmental disabilities. Pediatric neurology trainees may work in cerebral palsy clinics, in mental retardation facilities, or in programs for hearing or visually impaired children, but these opportunities are quite variable across the country. Although efforts are now underway to encourage specific training in developmental disabilities for all pediatric neurology trainees, presently there are no uniform training requirements in this area.

Following completion of the trainining program, the doctors are eligible for board certification, "with Special Competence in Child Neurology," by the American Board of Psychiatry and Neurology. They may also apply for certification by The American Board of Pediatrics, but they are not obliged to do so. There are currently just over 500 board-certified pediatric neurologists in the United States. Thus, the majority of children with neurological problems receive their medical care from pediatricians and family practitioners, not from pediatric neurologists.

Components of the Neurological Examination

There are three primary components to the neurological evaluation of any child: the history, the physical examination, and the use of ancillary diagnostic tests. Of these three, the history is by far the most crucial, particularly in children with developmental language and learning disorders. Therefore, the examiner should carefully investigate the child's developmental history. Parents or the child's caretaker should be interviewed in a quiet location where privacy can be assured. I use no specific history form, preferring instead a blank sheet of paper and the opportunity to carefully interview the parents. If the child is young and distractible, babysitting services should be available during the interview. The prenatal period should be carefully reviewed with special attention to the nature and frequency of prenatal care, the possibility of maternal infections, the use of drugs, the nutritional status of the mother, and fetal movements (infants with neurological damage may have diminished fetal movements, particularly in the later months of pregnancy). The labor, delivery, and perinatal period should be reviewed thoroughly, and pertinent hospital records should be requested. Nurses' notes may be particularly valuable in assessing the child's early neurological status. The time at which the parents first saw the infant

7

after birth may provide a useful clue to his neurological integrity — if any serious problem had been observed in the immediate neonatal period, it is unlikely that the parents would have been allowed to see the child immediately. Particular problems which might predispose the child to language delay, such as hyperbilirubinemia, asphyxia, use of ototoxic drugs, low birth weight, and poor nutrition should be explored. Postnatally, any pertinent medical conditions, such as meningitis or recurrent otitis media, should be assessed. Developmental milestones should be evaluated, and it may be useful to review the family photograph album or "baby book" at this time. The presence or absence of seizures, especially after some language has developed, is important. A family history of hearing, speech, language, reading, or school problems should be noted. Autopsy findings of any family members who have died of suspicious neurological disease should be requested.

A general pediatric physical examination should be performed prior to the specific neurological examination. The child's physical growth and head circumference should be carefully measured and plotted on standard growth charts. These charts can be completed by audiologists and speech/language pathologists, as well as physicians and nurses. Ideally, the speech and hearing evaluation of every child should include completion of the growth chart. Copies are available in standard pediatric textbooks, from several companies manufacturing infant formulas, and from local public health well-child clinics.

The standard neurological evaluation consists of examining the cranial nerves, the motor system, the deep and superficial reflexes, the gait, and the mental status. The orofacial examination should evaluate the tongue diadokinesis rate, the gag reflex, the snout reflex, and the jaw jerk carefully. Evaluation of "soft signs," or minor neurological abnormalities, is not useful in children with language and learning problems.

In many children with language disorders, no additional diagnostic procedures are necessary. The selection of any additional tests rests heavily on careful evaluation of the data obtained during the history and physical examination. The one test which is mandatory in all cases of delayed language development is a careful hearing test. This should be performed by a skilled pediatric audiologist; if any question arises about the initial results, the child should be retested. An electroencephalogram may be useful in cases of an acquired language disorder or when clinical or subclinical seizures are suspected. If the child is receiving anticonvulsant drug therapy, serum drug levels may be helpful. In other cases, thyroid function, metabolic, or chromosome studies may be indicated. A computed tomographic (CT) brain scan is unncessary in children with language and learning disabilities because it is usually normal. Auditory evoked response studies may be useful in assessing the integrity of the brain stem auditory pathway; however, their clinical value in children with language disorders remains to be determined.

Rational Use of Pediatric Neurology Consultations

With just over 500 pediatric neurologists in the United States, it is clearly not possible, nor is it probably necessary, for every child with language disorders to be evaluated by a pediatric neurologist. This is particularly true in view of the limitations in the training of many pediatric neurologists, which may not include extensive experience with language-delayed children. Indications for consideration of referral to a pediatric neurologist include:

1. Any acquired language disorder in a previously normal child.
2. The presence of language disorder associated with seizures.
3. Any progressive neurological disorder with associated language impairment.
4. Language disorder with an associated hemiparesis.

This list is not meant to be restrictive, but is meant to serve as a guideline for the types of problems in which a pediatric neurologist might be useful. In many other instances, if the child's physical health is known to be normal and if he is followed regularly by a pediatrician, a pediatric neurology consultation is probably not necessary. Minor motor findings or "soft" neurological signs are not a reason for referral to a neurologist, nor are the ill-defined symptoms of hyperactivity or short attention span. Similarly, it is inappropriate to refer a child "for and EEG," "for a CT scan," or "for a Ritalin prescripton;" the specific diagnostic tests and therapy ordered by a physician should be determined by the doctor, not by a referring agency or professional. Referral agencies should keep in mind the cost of various neurologic procedures and consultations so that such consultations are used judiciously, but not excessively.

More and more neurologically handicapped children are being identified and referred for accurate diagnosis — the critical first step in planning appropriate therapy. By applying his knowledge of the developing nervous system and its disorders, the pediatric neurologist can collaborate with other professionals and can offer these children precise diagnosis, careful management, and, in many cases, an improved outlook for the future.

References

Brown, S.B., Sher, P.K. 1975. The neurologic examination of children. In *The practice of pediatric neurology*, eds. K.F. Swaiman and F.S. Wright. St. Louis: C.V. Mosby Co.

Ferry, P.C. 1980. Computed cranial tomography in children.*J. Pediatr.* 96:961.

Ferry, P.C., Culbertson, J.L., Fitzgibbons, P.M., and Netsky, M.G. 1979. Brain function and language disabilities. *Int. J. Pediatr. Otorhinolaryngol.* 1:13-24.

Flor-Henry, P. 1974. Psychosis, neurosis and epilepsy.*Brit. J. Psychiat.* 124:144-50.

Halsey, J.H., Blauenstein, U.W., Wilson, E.M., and Wills, E.H. 1979. Regional cerebral blood flow: comparison of right and left hand movement.*Neurol.* 29:21-28.

Jacobson, M. 1978.*Developmental neurobiology.* New York:Plenum Press.

Kennedy, C., Sakurada, O., Shinohara, M., et al. 1978. Local cerebral glucose utilization in the normal conscious macaque monkey.*Ann. Neurol.* 4:294.

Marshall, R.E., Reichert, T.J., Kerley, S.M., Davis, H. 1980. Auditory function in newborn intensive care unit patients revealed by auditory brain-stem potentials. *J. Pediatr.* 96:731-35.

Rapin, I. and Wilson, B.C. 1978. Children with developmental language disability: neurological aspects and assessment. In *Developmental dysphasia*, ed. M.A. Wyke. New York: Academic Press.

Swaiman, K.F. 1975. Neurologic history in childhood. In *The practice of pediatric neurology*, eds. K.F. Swaiman and F.S. Wright. St. Louis: C.V. Mosby Co.

423   Questions and Answers

Q: With all the new information about brain development, is it possible to relate this to prenatal care?

A: Yes, in many ways. For example, children born to alcoholic mothers may be afflicted with the "fetal alcohol syndrome" in which their brain is smaller than normal and they usually persist in being mildly mentally retarded. In addition to maternal alcoholism, hypertension, infections, drug ingestion, and severe malnutrition have also been associated with defects in brain development.

Q: Would you ever treat an abnormal EEG?

A: No, not in most cases. The EEG is a very nonspecific test, and it should be used only in conjunction with the history of the child and the findings on neurological examination. On occasion, if we see subclinical seizures on an EEG, particularly in association with an acquired language disorder, anticonvulsant drug therapy might be tried to see if any improvement occurs. However, in most cases this is not the situation and it is inappropriate simply to treat an abnormal EEG unless there are associated clinical indications.

Q: Would you discuss convulsive disorders in relation to language function?

A: There is an interesting clinical situation, called acquired auditory agnosia and seizures, in which the child has seizures and stops talking around two years of age. The seizures may precede, coincide with, or follow the onset of delayed speech. It is thought that this is a form of viral encephalitis which selectively affects the temporal lobes. An EEG may be helpful in these children to demonstrate temporal lobe discharges, either unilaterally or bilaterally. As I mentioned before, the trial of anticonvulsant drugs may be useful in this situation. These children should also be referred promptly for neurological evaluation, which probably would include spinal tap (to obtain viral cultures), EEG studies, and possibly a CT scan to look for temporal lobe abnormalities.

Q: Do you have a sense of time frame in which the EEG will normalize and the child will start talking?

A: No, it is quite variable. The EEG may return entirely to normal and the child may remain non-verbal. In other cases, clincal recovery of speech and language functions occurs and the EEG remains abnormal. It probably would be encouraging in an individual case if the EEG did improve, but one cannot predict language development on that basis alone.

Q: When a child is born prematurely, how long is it before he catches up?

A: Generally, we give premature infants about one year to "catch up" in their development. However, there is a lot of variation from child to child, and one must be careful when predicting the child's ultimate developmental outcome. Generally, however, the prognosis for low-birth-weight infants has been improving over the years, and 75%-80% of them are normal at five to six years of age.

Q: When should the speech pathologist press for a CT scan?

A: I really don't think a speech pathologist *should* press for a certain neurological test, just as I think it inappropriate for a physician to suggest to the speech pathologist or audiologist that a specific diagnostic test be performed. I know it is tempting to want to see what the scan might show, but in view of the expense ($250.00), the need for sedation or general anesthesia in small children, and some discomfort (an intravenous injection in some cases), it is a test which should be reserved only for certain clinical indications. I see an unfortunate tendency across the country to order unnecessary CT scans in many children with developmental problems, such as mental retardation, cerebral palsy, or delayed speech development. In the vast majority of cases this test adds nothing to the treatment program and the abnormalities seen are very nonspecific.

Q: When should an audiologist consider referring a patient whose peripheral hearing is intact but whose behavior suggests the presence of a central auditory disorder to a neurologist?

A: I haven't the faintest idea. I am afraid that most neurologists are not familiar with central auditory disorders, particularly in young children, but if you are fortunate enough to work with a neurologist who is interested in this disorder, you might ask him if he would be interested in seeing a particular child. One of the challenges to the future will be for all of us to determine the clinical indications for central auditory tests and the specific situations in which they are useful.

Q: Discuss CMV (Cytomegalovirus Infection).

A: This is one of the viral infections I mentioned that can damage the developing brain, particularly the auditory system. It is probably much more common than we had recognized in the past, and it appears likely that many asymptomatic infections occur, both in pregnant women and in children. Signs and symptoms in the newborn period may include lethargy, jaundice, a peculiar rash, and seizures, but very often there are no symptoms at all. Infection during pregnancy may produce microcephaly, congenital heart disease, and other birth defects.

Q: Discuss the effects of anticonvulsants and other drugs on processing function. Can there be permanent effects?

A: Definitely yes. Phenytoin (Dilantin) particularly, has been shown to have some permanent effects on the cerebellum. We really don't know functionally what the long-term effects of other drugs are. It is preferable for children to be on as few drugs as possible. If they are having seizures, properly monitored levels can be very helpful. Other drugs which can be widely abused are stimulants. I think these are used far too widely considering that we don't know the long-term effects. The child's behavior, language, and cognitive skills should be evaluated carefully before he is given stimulant drugs.

2

Psychological Evaluation and Educational Planning for Children with Central Auditory Dysfunction

Jan L. Culbertson, Ph.D.

Children with central auditory dysfunction are part of an often undiagnosed or mislabeled group of children with communication disorders who may experience learning and behavioral/emotional problems in school. Although tests which are effective in assessing central auditory disorders have been developed recently (Keith 1977), they are not yet widely used or understood by professionals. Even when central auditory problems are diagnosed, there is often a wide gap between obtaining the diagnosis and implementing an appropriate educational program for the child.

Careful diagnosis and educational planning for children with central auditory dysfunction requires an interdisciplinary effort, involving the expertise of audiologists, speech and language pathologists, psychologists, educators, and physicians. From this cadre of professionals, several issues have begun to be and should continue to be addressed: (1) Which evaluation tools are the most reliable and valid? (2) How early can a diagnosis be made? (3) How do the evaluation results obtained by various disciplines intercorrelate or complement each other? (4) How can interdisciplinary evaluation results be translated into effective remediation?

These issues provide a basis for ongoing exploration, and should be central to our discussion in this conference. My specific goal, however, will be to address the role of the psychologist in the interdisciplinary effort to diagnose and treat central auditory dysfunction in children. Specifically, I will discuss methodological problems in the psychological assessment of children with central auditory dysfunction, an overview of the dimensions through which learning disorders may be examined, a neuropsychological model for evaluating children with central auditory dysfunction, a method of integrating test data to form the basis of educational planning, and, finally, the evaluation of behavioral or adjustment problems in these children.

Role of the Psychologist

There are several basic assumptions to be made when discussing the role of the psychologist in evaluating all children, including those with central auditory dysfunction. First, a careful history including medical in-

13

formation from the perinatal period, past significant illnesses, social/familial data, records of school performance, and descriptive behavioral information will alert the psychologist to "red flags" in the child's development which could relate to current problems. Data obtained from the history should help the psychologist form hypotheses or questions which he/she will then attempt to answer through specific assessment methods. Initiating the assessment process with working hypotheses is an extremely important concept, because it implies that the psychologist will adapt his/her evaluation to the presenting symptoms of the child rather than attempting to "fit" the child to a particular test or test battery.

A second major assumption of psychological testing is that the end result of the assessment should not be a score; rather, the evaluation results should provide a profile of documented strengths and weaknesses for each child which could then form the basis of future educational planning. A child is not described by a score. Rather, a test score is often merely an average of many strengths and weaknesses which the child may have across various skill areas. It is the subtleties of the child's performance in these various skills which provide the most useful information for programming (Wilson and Wilson 1978).

Finally, the third major assumption in psychological evaluation is that sensory deficits should be ruled out prior to performing elaborate, detailed psychological batteries. In a child with suspected central auditory dysfunction, for instance, an evaluation of hearing levels should always be included prior to further diagnostic evaluation. Failure to obtain this information can result in wasted effort by the psychologist and both emotional stress and financial expense to the child and his family.

Methodological Issues in Psychological Evaluation

The psychologist has a myriad of standardized instruments available for evaluating cognitive and learning deficits in children. However, use of psychological tests has been criticized due to the inherent cultural and socioeconomic bias of the tests (Mercer 1973), the overuse of summary IQ scores without careful analysis of the strengths and weaknesses of the individual skills which comprise the IQ score (Wilson and Wilson 1978), and the inappropriate test selection for evaluating children with communication or sensory disorders (Rutter 1972; Culbertson, Norlin, and Ferry 1981). The criticism has served to alert psychologists to the need for careful analysis of adaptive as well as cognitive skills in cultural minorities. However, training programs for psychologists have yet to systematically emphasize alternative assessment strategies for children with sensory deficits, communication disorders, or central auditory processing disorders. For example the Stanford-Binet Intelligence Scale is commonly administered to children with communication disorders. These children are often subsequently mislabeled as mentally deficient when their abilities are at or above the average level if measured by techniques which de-emphasize the use

14

or understanding of oral language. The use of a summary IQ score, as provided by the Stanford-Binet, also may mask the individual strengths and weaknesses of the child in various skills. Psychological training could be improved by greater emphasis on the characteristics of sensory deficits, communication disorders, and central auditory disorders in children so that assessment methodology may be improved. Psychologists also need to be acquainted with assessment methods of audiologists and speech pathologists, in order to appropriately share information and refer clients to these specialists.

Goals of the Psychological Evaluation

The specific goals for psychological evaluation of children with central auditory dysfunction are similar to those for children with any type of communication or learning disorder. They include:

1. Determining cognitive ability. Specific tasks should be administered which help the examiner detect deficiencies and strengths in memory functioning, abstract thinking, and verbal versus nonverbal problem-solving skills.
2. Examining perceptual modes of learning. Tasks should be presented which require the child to process information through auditory, visual and motor modalities. It is important to include tasks which combine these modalities, since most classroom instruction occurs in this manner.
3. Observing the child's communication style. The psychologist can help to determine the need for referral to an audiologist or speech pathologist by careful observations of the child's use and understanding of oral language.
4. Evaluating academic strengths and weaknesses. Knowledge of the child's level of functioning in reading, spelling, writing, and arithmetic is essential to the planning of an effective educational program based on evaluation results.
5. Examining social/emotional adaptation. Secondary behavioral or emotional problems frequently accompany learning problems in children. As part of each psychological evaluation, a careful history regarding the child's behavior at home and at school should be obtained so that appropriate anticipatory counseling or recommendations for therapy may be included in the evaluation results.

Indications for Referral to a Psychologist

Referral to a psychologist should be made when there is any question regarding the child's level of cognitive functioning, when there is a need for sorting out verbal versus nonverbal problem-solving strategies, when there is a need for determining the relation between academic deficiencies and problem-solving strategies, and when there is a question of a primary versus a secondary emotional component to the child's learning problem.

Classification of Learning Disorders

Learning disorders in children are not classified neatly into discrete categories. However, Little (1978) has described various dimensions through which learning disorders can be examined, dimensions which provide the conceptual basis for planning an evaluation strategy. Children with central auditory dysfunction may be viewed within the same framework, which evaluates disorders of verbal versus nonverbal learning, disorders of input versus output, and disorders within specific learning modalities. I will present an overview of each of these areas, along with brief examples of ways in which a child may display these disorders.

Disorders of Verbal and Nonverbal Learning

Disorders of verbal learning may include oral language expression or comprehension. As most psychological tests require verbatim recording of the child's verbal responses to questions, the examiner may attend to the child's expressive ability by noting whether his/her definitions seem like circumlocutions, whether he/she perseverates on specific ideas or grammatical constructions, whether his/her sentences are devoid of expected vocabulary items, or whether sentence structure seems simplistic, perhaps with only noun-verb or noun-verb-noun format. A child's comprehension of language would be suspect if, for instance, he/she appears not to hear stimulus items, misunderstands stimulus items, verbalizes very little or with obvious physical effort, has trouble remembering verbal input, or is echolalic (Culbertson, Norlin, and Ferry 1981). Often discrepancies in functioning on the verbal and performance sections of intelligence tests are a clue to a child's verbal disorder. Verbal disorders may also be manifested in specific academic tasks such as reading, spelling, and writing.

Disorders of nonverbal learning may be detected in tasks of time orientation, spatial orientation, directionality, picture interpretation and social perception. A child with poor time orientation may have difficulty remembering his classroom routine and orientation problems might occur when a child is completing addition or multiplication problems which require aligning numbers appropriately. Directionality problems may occur on a gross motor level, with a child who has difficulty following a map or difficulty planning his/her motor movement through space. Picture interpretation is often required as part of academic tasks. The child who is disordered in this skill fails to perceive subtle visual cues which give meaning to the picture and provide information for problem-solving. Finally, disorders in social perception are often overlooked as a type of learning disorder. If children have difficulty perceiving visual information from pictures, it is conceivable that they may not perceive subtle facial/bodily cues which would alert them to the feelings of others. Thus, they may not perceive the unspoken social rules which would enable them to be accepted in their peer group. This may lead to serious problems in communication with peers or adults.

Disorders of Input and Output

Disorders of input involve decoding information, and include skills such as recognition, discrimination, figure-ground perception, and spatial relations. A child with poor recognition skills may have difficulty learning a sight-vocabulary in reading. Visual discrimination skills involve distinguishing between similar letters and words while auditory discrimination skills involve hearing differences between phonemes that are acoustically similar. Auditory figure-ground discrimination occurs frequently in the classroom when the child is asked to focus on the teacher's voice amid background noise from other sources. A child with visual figure-ground problems may have difficulty directing his attention to only one math problem from a page of several problems. A child with disordered spatial relations skills may confuse upper case and lower case letters.

Disorders of output involve encoding of information, and may be expressed in speaking, writing, or body movement. Examples of peripheral speech disorders are impaired articulation, dysarthria or dysfluency, while examples of central speech disorders are impaired phonology, morphology, syntax, or semantics. Disorders of writing may be observed in the speed with which a child completes a written task, in the accuracy of written tasks such as copying material from a blackboard, or in the fine motor coordination needed to execute the writing task clearly. Disorders of body movement may be seen in children with poor "motor-planning" ability (i.e., poor ability to plan movements through space).

Disorders Within Specific Learning Modalities

Disorders may occur within perceptual modalities, memory functioning, thinking, and perceptual-motor learning. Perceptual disorders may occur in the auditory modality (for which the newer tests of central auditory dysfunction are helpful in diagnosis), the visual modality (including disorders of visual-memory, visual-discrimination, and visual-cognitive association), and the haptic modality (including disorders of shape perception through tactile stimulation).

Memory functioning may be examined in tasks of short-term storage (including digit-repetition or sentence-repetition) or tasks of long-term storage (recollection of information after intervening material has been presented). Memory problems involving retrieval may be manifest in circumlocutions of speech or dysnomia. Sequencing difficulty may be observed when a child has difficulty completing a long division problem because he confuses the order of the steps, or, when a child forgets the beginning of a story he/she has heard, but remembers the middle.

Disorders of thinking may be described broadly as problems in categorizing objects of information, difficulty in perceiving associations between objects or ideas (e.g., inability to describe or contrast two items), and difficulty in conceptualizing size, shape, time, etc.

17

Finally, disorders of perceptual-motor learning may be observed in tasks involving the combination of a sensory modality with the motor modality. A child with visual-motor difficulty may not be able to copy words from the blackboard in class, whereas a child with an auditory-motor problem may not be able to write spelling words from dictation.

A Neuropsychological Model for Evaluation

Having discussed general goals of a psychological evaluation and an overview of learning dimensions which may be evaluated in a child with suspected central auditory dysfunction, I would like to focus now on a specific evaluation model. I prefer a neuropsychological evaluation model because of: (1) its emphasis on the analysis of behavior within the context of an understanding of brain functioning (including hemispheric specialization and localization of abilities), and (2) its emphasis on sampling a broad spectrum of abilities, so that the test data can then form the basis for educational planning.

There are numerous adult models for neuropsychological evaluation (Halstead 1947; Reitan and Davison 1974; Smith 1975; and Christenson 1975), but fewer which are useful for children, especially children of preschool age. I have found an approach developed by Dr. Barbara Wilson[1] to be useful for both preschool and school-age children, particularly children with communication disorders. Dr. Wilson uses a battery of currently available psychological tests to measure cognitive, linguistic, perceptual and memory skills in young children. This approach has proven to be quite useful in our clinic at Vanderbilt, and I propose it as a model for evaluating children with suspected central auditory dysfunction.

Wilson's neuropsychological model is based on several premises (Wilson and Wilson 1978):

1. Behavior is a function of central nervous system activity.
2. Assuming that the nervous system functions systematically and dysfunctions systematically, it should be possible to measure skills in children which reflect these systematic patterns of CNS functioning and dysfunctioning.
3. Selected subtests from standardized psychological instruments may be used to sample an adequate subset of behaviors, reflecting CNS functioning.
4. Deficits in particular skills should be demonstrated by more than one subtest.

The tests comprising the neuropsychological battery are chosen to measure cognitive, linguistic, perceptual, and memory skills in both school-age and preschool children. From these currently available standardized tests, subtests which measure similar skills are selected. To directly compare scores, the results are converted first to "z" scores and then to "cen-

1. Dr. Wilson is Chief of Neuropsychology, Department of Neurology, North Shore University Hospital, Manhasset, New York.

tile" scores which represent the median of the subtest scores used to measure a specific skill. These centile scores allow one to construct a profile for each child which represents his strengths and weaknesses in a variety of skills. An individualized educational program may then be planned for each child based on these data.

Table 1 lists the subtests which comprise the various factors used in the evaluation of preschool children. Subtests were grouped both according to clinical judgment about what they actually measure, and by a factor analysis of scores from a group of 40 three to five-year-old children (Wilson and Wilson 1978). Table 2 lists the subtests which incorporate the various

1. FM–Fine Motor
   Beads–H-N
   Fine Motor I–LAP

2. GrM–Graphomotor
   Draw-A-Person–McC
   Geometric Design–WPPSI
   Fine Motor II–LAP

3. AD–Auditory Discrimination
   Auditory Closure–ITPA
   Sound Blending–ITPA

4. AM_1–Auditory Memory I
   (Sequential)
   Auditory Sequential
   Memory–ITPA
   Numerical Memory 1–McC
   Verbal Memory I–McC
   Sentence Repetition–WPPSI

5. AM_2–Auditory Memory II
   (Retrieval)
   Verbal Memory II–McC
   Verbal Fluency–McC

6. AC–Auditory-Cognitive
   Auditory Association–ITPA
   Auditory Reception–ITPA
   Opposite Analogies–McC

7. VD–Visual Discrimination
   Form Discrimination–PTI
   Picture Identification–H-N

8. VSp–Visual-Spatial
   Puzzle Solving–McC
   Counting & Sorting–McC
   Block Patterns–H-N
   Block Designs–WPPSI

9. VM_1–Visual Memory I
   (Sequences)
   Tapping–McC
   Visual Attention Span–H-N
   Memory For Color–H-N
   Visual Sequential Memory–ITPA

10. VM_2–Visual Memory II Single Item
    Immediate Recall–PTI

11. VC–Visual Cognitive
    Picture Association–H-N
    Visual Association–ITPA
    Visual Reception–ITPA

12. A-V–Auditory-Visual Cognitive
    Peabody Picture Vocabulary Test
    Information Comprehension–PTI
    Picture Vocabulary–PTI
    Grammatic Closure–ITPA

H-N — Hiskey-Nebraska Test of Learning Aptitude
LAP — Learning Accomplishment Profile
McC — McCarthy Scales of Children's Abilities
WPPSI — Wechsler Preschool and Primary Scale of Intelligence
ITPA — Illinois Test of Psycholinguistic Abilities
PTI — Pictorial Test of Intelligence

Table 1.
Tests included in the factors for evaluation of preschool children

1. IQ
   VIQ–Verbal IQ (WISC)
   PIQ–Performance IQ (WISC)
   Rav–Raven's Coloured
      Progressive Matrices

2. FM–Fine Motor
   Purdue Pegboard
      Dominant hand
      Nondominant hand
      Both hands

3. GrM–Graphomotor
   Bender Gestalt Test
   Background Interference Procedure

4. AM$_1$–Auditory Memory
   (Sequencing-Nonverbal)
   Digit Span–WISC
   Auditory Sequential Memory–ITPA

5. AM$_2$–Auditory Memory
   (Sequencing-Verbal)
   Sentence Repetition–NCCEA
   Verbal Memory I–McC

6. AM$_3$–Auditory Memory (Retrieval)
   Vocabulary–WISC
   Verbal Memory II–McC

7. AC–Auditory Cognitive
   Auditory Association–ITPA

8. VD–Visual Discrimination
   Benton-Spreen Embedded Figures

9. VSp–Visual Spatial
   Block Design–WISC
   Object Assembly–WISC
   Block Patterns–H-N

10. VM–Visual Memory
    (Sequencing)
    Visual Sequential Memory–ITPA
    Visual Attention Span–H-N

11. Academic Achievement Tests
    WR –Work Recognition (WRAT)
    Sp –Spelling (WRAT)
    Ar –Arithmetic (WRAT)
    Gray–Gray Oral Reading Test

WISC — Wechsler Intelligence Scale for Children
ITPA — Illinois Test of Psycholinguistic Abilities
NCCEA — Neurosensory Center Comprehensive Examination for Aphasia
McC — McCarthy Scales of Children's Abilities
H-N — Hiskey-Nebraska Test of Learning Aptitude
WRAT — Wide Range Achievement Test

Table 2.
Tests included in the factors for evaluation of school-aged children

factors used to evaluate school-age children. The factors computed for school-age children are similar to those for pre-school children, although the tests which comprise them are different. Once again, subtests were grouped according to clinical judgment as to what each one actually measures.

Case Examples

Figure 1 illustrates the profile of a 3 year, 8 month old boy who presented with delayed language. To briefly describe the profile, note that tests are grouped according to specific modalities. Within the auditory modality, AD refers to tests of auditory discrimination with little cognitive content involved. AM$_1$ refers to short-term auditory sequential memory and AM$_2$ taps retrieval. AC involves tasks with both auditory input and verbal output which involve cognition. Within the visual modality, VD refers to tests of visual discrimination or matching. VSp taps skills of visual spatial anal-

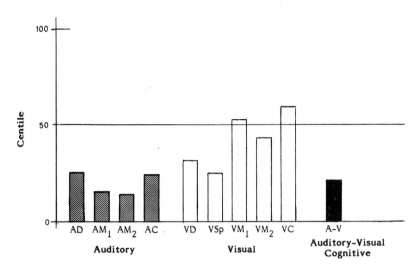

Figure 1.
Profile of a 3 year, 8 month old boy with delayed language.

ysis used in building puzzles and block designs. VM_1 taps short-term visual sequential memory whereas VM_2 requires short-term retention of single items. VC represents tasks with visual input, with a response involving some cognitive content. Finally, A-V refers to tasks involving both auditory and visual modalities, including some cognitive skills.

The profile illustrated in figure 1 indicates weaknesses in skills of auditory input and verbal output. Relative strengths are noted in visual areas, particularly where tasks involve memory and cognition. It is interesting that pairing the visual with the auditory channel did not facilitate this child's task performance.

Note also that the profile allows analysis of the various learning dimensions described earlier. From the profile and from attention to specific subtests, we can determine the child's performance on verbal versus nonverbal tasks, his performance on tasks involving individual sensory modalities or "multimodal" input, and his ability to perform different cognitive tasks (i.e., memory, discrimination) regardless of modality. We can also determine if the child's difficulties involve primarily the input/decoding of information or the output/encoding of information.

Figure 2 illustrates the profile of a 4 year, 1 month old child who also presented with a language delay. She was born prematurely at approximately 35 weeks gestation, with a birth weight of 4 lbs. 3 oz. Developmental milestones in motor and language areas were delayed. Neurological evaluation revealed fine motor and oromotor deficiencies (i.e., drooling, tongue thrust).

Profile analysis reveals relative weaknesses in fine motor (FM), graphomotor (GrM), visual spatial and visual sequencing skills. Auditory skills

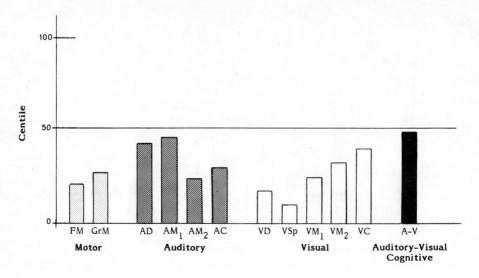

Figure 2.
Profile of a 4 year, 1 month old girl with delayed language.

are relatively intact, except for retrieving and processing complex verbal information. Auditory-visual cognitive tasks, which tapped vocabulary knowledge but did not require lengthy verbal responses, were a relative strength. This child was diagnosed as having an expressive language disorder and a mild fine motor deficiency.

The two previous case examples illustrate the differences which may be found in a profile analysis when children present with similar symptoms. Although both children presented with a language delay, the first child had primary deficiencies in decoding as well as encoding verbal/auditory information, while the second child had difficulty primarily with the encoding process. The next case will illustrate the neuropsychological evaluation model with a school aged child who presented with learning and behavior problems.

Figure 3 illustrates the profile of a 7 year, 11 month old, second grade boy who presented to a neurologist with sudden deterioration of behavior and handwriting skills in the classroom toward the end of the academic year, after having made excellent academic progress in all areas prior to that time. Both the neurological evaluation and ancillary tests, including an electro encephalogram and computed tomographic (CT) brain scan, were negative. The child was therefore referred for neuropsychological evaluation to determine if there were evidence of cognitive deterioration which would correspond with the presenting symptoms. The child had a psychological evaluation 20 months earlier, just after entering first grade, to rule

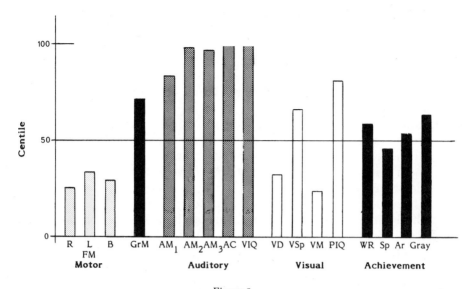

Figure 3.
Profile of a 7 year, 11 month old boy who is intellectually gifted and has a specific learning
disability with visual spatial deficits.

out a learning disorder. Results of that evaluation, using the Wechsler Intelligence Scale For Children (WISC), revealed a verbal IQ of 126 and a performance IQ of 108. When the WISC was repeated during the current evaluation, the child received a verbal IQ of 144 (above the 99th centile) and a
performance IQ of 111 (at the 77th centile). These results suggested no deterioration in cognitive abilities. However, profile analysis of this child's
performance across several modalities revealed an interesting pattern of
strengths and weaknesses.

The profile of this school-age child (fig. 3) revealed superior auditory
and cognitive abilities, particularly those involving memory for verbal information. AM$_1$, sequential memory for nonverbal information (digits), was
relatively weaker. Also, his academic achievement scores were at the average level. Since he was attending a private school and was receiving an
advanced curriculum, he was expected to perform at better than the average level in his classroom. His deficiencies were noted in fine motor skills
(FM), and in both visual discrimination and visual sequential memory skills.
He was diagnosed as being an intellectually gifted youngster who was experiencing a specific learning disability in visual perceptual skills. He had
been able to compensate for many of his visual perceptual deficiencies until the latter part of his second grade year, when academic demands increased. His sudden deterioration in behavior was probably caused by a
severe emotional reaction, secondary to the frustration he felt when attempting academic tasks.

Integration of Test Results for Educational Placement and Programming

With the advent of Public Law 94-142, placement options for children with special learning needs increased both in number and variety. Alternative classroom programs for children with learning and/or language disorders include:

1. Itinerant specialist — This program involves a teacher traveling from school to school and teaching a small group of children for a brief period each day. The itinerant specialist may also consult with the classroom teacher to provide suggestions for working with the child in the classroom.
2. The resource room — This is a classroom in a regular school, where a child with special learning needs may go for a brief period each day to receive instructions and to use special educational materials in a small group.
3. Self-contained classroom — This is a more restrictive classroom setting. It is a class with a small pupil/teacher ratio in which the child is placed full-time rather than being in a regular classroom for part of the day.
4. Full-time "special schools" — This is considered the most restrictive learning environment in which all children who attend this school require the constant programming that a full-time learning disabilities placement can provide.

Although the selection of a classroom program may depend on the severity of a child's problem, it is important to assure that each child with special learning needs has an individualized educational program, based on a careful diagnostic evaluation which describes strengths and deficiencies in various skills. The profile analysis approach lends itself clearly to the development of an educational program which would be designed to teach the child through his strengths while attempting to remediate his deficiencies.

Evaluation of Social/Emotional Adaptation

One role of the psychologist, as stated earlier, is to examine a child's emotional status during an evaluation, and to determine whether emotional symptoms are secondary to a learning problem. Silver (1979) discussed the frustrations often experienced in the classroom by children with specific learning disabilities:

"Very often the learning disabilities are not recognized or treated, and the child continues to experience repeated frustrations and failures. If the child withdraws from learning and stops trying, he or she is likely to be sent to an educational resource such as tutoring or a special class. If his emotional stress takes the form of behavioral disorders, however, he is then likely to be referred for a

24

psychiatric evaluation. To view such a child as suffering primary emotional difficulty or a character problem rather than a secondary emotional reaction to the unrecognized underlying syndrome is to miss a significant etiological factor and to plan an incomplete treatment approach" (p. 421).

A child who experiences repeated failure in the classroom may develop any of a number of different emotional reactions as he attempts to cope with the pressures and frustrations (Silver 1979):

1. Withdrawal reaction — The child avoids situations that are frustrating and becomes "unavailable for learning."
2. Regression — The child reverts to a more immature style of behavior with peers and/or adults, such as using baby talk or becoming enuretic.
3. Fear reactions — The child may develop a fear of a specific situation or person rather than displaying a generalized anxiety or depression. This specific fear may be a way of displacing his anxiety about school failure.
4. Somatic complaints — The child may develop stomachaches, headaches, or other physical symptoms, which are present only on school days and not at other times. Although the discomfort may be real, the pain often disappears when the child is allowed to stay home.
5. Paranoia — The child may attempt to avoid stress by projecting his feelings and thoughts to others, blaming them for his problems. He may feel that teachers, classmates, or others are trying to get him into trouble or show him up.
6. Diagnosis as the excuse — A child who has been tested and examined by various professionals may come to use the various labels and descriptions he has heard as an excuse. For instance, a child who had been labeled as dyslexic said, "I can't read because my eyes don't work right."
7. Depression — A child with repeated school failures, poor interaction with peers and adults, and feelings of inadequacy may feel angry and useless. Children of preschool age may express their depression by aggressive or irritable behavior, whereas an older child might exhibit the classic signs of depression. These children may internalize their anger, and often develop a poor self-image so that they feel they are worthless. Even when they are given praise, they often are unable or unwilling to accept it.
8. Passive-aggressive reaction — A child may choose to deal with his anger indirectly, in such a way that people become angry with him even when the behavior itself is not aggressive. For example, a child who dawdles may infuriate his parents, even though he is not behaving aggressively.
9. Passive-dependent reaction — A child may choose to deal with his anger by simply avoiding situations which might result in failure or unpleasant feelings. The child's helplessness and dependency may create feelings of anger in others.
10. Clowning — The child who becomes the "class clown" may be doing so to cover feelings of inadequacy and depression, or to avoid situa-

tions which create stress, such as being called upon to recite in the classroom. By disrupting the classroom, the child who is clowning may divert the teacher's attention from his academic difficulties.

11. Impulse disorder — The child acts impulsively without taking time to think about the consequences of his actions. These children may be emotionally labile, showing explosive or aggressive reactions after only a slight provocation.

Often professionals see children who have symptoms of behavioral or emotional disturbance, when, in fact, the symptoms mask learning difficulties which have created frustrating and embarrassing situations for the child. The school psychologist may feel inadequately trained to handle these problems, or may have too large a case load to become involved in long-term therapy. However, the school psychologist can play an important role in making an appropriate referral to a clinical psychologist or psychiatrist who will work with the family in therapy as needed.

Summary

I have attempted to review the role of the psychologist in the diagnostic evaluation of children with complex learning disorders, to discuss the individual skills which should be evaluated, to present a neuropsychological model for conducting the evaluation, and to review some of the secondary emotional reactions which may accompany learning disorders in children. Although these guidelines may be directed toward children with complex learning disorders, I feel that they may be generalized to include children with central auditory dysfunction as well. My hope is that this conference will serve as the impetus for further interdisciplinary collaboration, in both clinical and research areas, to improve our understanding of the special needs of children with central auditory dysfunction.

References

Christenson, A.L. 1975. Luria's Neuropsychological Investigation: text, manual and test cards. New York: Spectrum.

Culbertson, J.L., Norlin, P.F., and Ferry, P.C. 1981. Communication disorders in childhood. J. Pediatr. Psychol. In press.

Halstead, W.C. 1947. Brain and intelligence: a quantitative study of the frontal lobes. Chicago: University of Chicago Press.

Keith, R.W., ed. 1977. Central auditory dysfunction. New York: Grune & Stratton.

Little, L.J. 1978. The learning disabled. In Exceptional children and youth, ed. E.L. Meyen. Denver: Love Publishing Co.

Mercer, J. 1973. Labeling the mentally retarded. Berkeley, CA: University of California Press.

Reitan, R.M. and Davison, L.A., eds. 1974. Clinical neuropsychology: current status and applications. New York: V.H. Winston & Sons.

Rutter, M. 1972. Psychological assessment of language disabilities. In The child with delayed speech, eds. M. Rutter and J.A.M. Martin. Philadelphia: J.B. Lippincott Co.

Silver, L.B. 1979. The minimal brain dysfunction syndrome. In *Basic handbook of child psychiatry*, vol. 2, ed. J.D. Noshpitz. New York: Basic Books, Inc.

Smith, A. 1975. Neuropsychological testing in neurological disorders. In *Advances in neurology*, vol. 7, ed. W.J. Friedlander. New York: Raven Press.

Wilson, B.C. and Wilson, J.J. 1978. Language disordered children: a neuropsychologic view. In *Developmental disabilities of early childhood*, eds. B.A. Feingold and C.L. Banks. Springfield, IL: C C Thomas.

Questions and Answers

Q: Elaborate more on how I could evaluate problem solving strategies in a child.

A: Let me provide a couple of examples. The Object Assembly subtest on the WISC-R involves integrating puzzle pieces to form an object. As the child completes this task, I observe whether he is attentive to shape cues from the puzzle pieces or whether he puts them together randomly. I observe whether he attends to markings on the puzzle pieces; whether he labels certain pieces as the "top," "bottom," etc; whether he knows the label for the object he is constructing; whether he learns from his errors or repeats the same mistakes.

A second example involves a youngster who was attempting the Visual Sequential Memory subtest of the ITPA. On this test, she was required to arrange a series of geometric shapes in the correct sequence after seeing a picture of that sequence. This youngster had excellent verbal skills but weak visual perceptual skills. She had made many errors on the easier items from the Visual Sequential Memory test when suddenly she devised the strategy of labeling the geometric forms as "curly," "spider," etc. She rehearsed these verbal labels for the series of forms while examining the picture of the correct sequence. Her errors decreased and she achieved a superior score on the test. Her verbal strategy provided important information regarding the best remedial approach to use with her in school.

Q: Is the Leiter International Performance Scale the best non-verbal test to use with children who have communication disorders?

A: The Leiter Scale is one of several tests which are primarily visually motor based which I use in conjunction with more verbally loaded tests. Other tests would be the Hiskey-Nebraska Test of Learning Aptitude, which is useful for ages 3-18 years. The Pictorial Test of Intelligence is another. The Merrill-Palmer Scale, even though it has old norms and needs to be updated, is sometimes useful. It does go down to the 18-month age level. These remarks must be seen in the context of my practice which is primarily with infants and pre-schoolers up to age 5; about 2/3 of the children we see in our clinic are in that age group, and it is very difficult to find tests which are appropriate at that early age. With school age children we certainly have more to choose from and the Leiter is a good instrument. In my assessment, I try to balance tests that are more visual-motor oriented with language-oriented tests.

Q: What are some of the areas I look at when trying to separate the secondary vs. primary emotional characteristics, especially with a 3-5 year old child.

A: While taking a history I would question, for example, the timing of onset of the problems. With a 3-5 year old who is already experiencing some behavior problems, I would not expect that they are necessarily school-related problems. It is much more difficult with a 7-year old to determine whether the learning problems and inappropriate class placement are causing the behavior disorder. With older children, I would want to know if the onset of behavior problems occurred about the time the child started school or began having learning problems in school. So timing of onset is one factor.

I would also want to know the setting in which most of the behavioral problems occur. Do they mostly occur at home or at school? Sometimes that is a good clue to whether academic pressures and learning difficulties are causing the problems. Also, looking at the intensity of the problems would be another way. A child who has severe relational disorders may be destructive to animals, to himself, or to other people and would not be a child, I think, with a secondary emotional problem. I would also evaluate the child formally to rule out learning deficiencies as a cause of frustration and anxiety.

Q: In a multidisciplinary center, how is overlapping in testing avoided? For instance, between speech pathology and psychological testing?

A: That is one of the problems with most multidisciplinary teams. When you put a group of physicians, speech pathologists, psychologists, etc., together, there are more overlapping skills and training than non-overlapping skills. I now leave out significant parts of testing that I would do if I were in private practice alone. I simply do not duplicate some of the testing that the speech pathologist does. I have learned what to omit by observing the speech pathologist's testing, by having long discussions about what they are doing, and by task analyzing the subtests of our different tests. Just because my test has the same name as that of the speech pathologist's does not mean that it is actually measuring the same thing. So, we have to carefully look at what we are asking the child to do. There may be some tests which we want to duplicate in order to get a second measure of the child's performance. So, I do not mean to say that I do not duplicate ever. Sometimes it is helpful to do that, but an understanding and an awareness of where we overlap is very important.

Q: Would you be comfortable dropping out some of the verbal subtests of the WISC?

A: The literature suggests that the validity of the WISC holds up when you look at a total verbal IQ or performance IQ. The validity drops when you start leaving out subtests. I would be very uncomfortable quoting an IQ score without completing at least four of the six subtests of either the verbal or the performance section of the WISC.

Q: If you were working with a speech pathologist, would you be using the verbal IQ to give information about a child's intelligence?

A: I think the implication would be whether it would be valid to use the verbal IQ with a language disordered child. I often do get a verbal IQ to compare with the performance IQ. The discrepancy between the two scores gives me very useful information in understanding the verbal and nonverbal abilities of the child. I use the verbal section of the IQ tests descriptively, also. I use the child's verbal responses to the different items as my own language sample of how the child communicates orally with me. I must be careful, however, to interpret the verbal IQ as a measure of the child's language functioning (or dysfunctioning), rather than as a measure of the child's intelligence.

3

Evaluation of Central Auditory Function in Children

Susan Jerger, M.S.

Introduction

The evaluation of auditory function in children is concerned with two basic questions: 1) how much hearing loss, if any, exists; and 2) where is the hearing impairment located? The first question concerns the degree of loss; the second question concerns the site of loss. This latter question involves differentiating between two primary auditory sites: the peripheral auditory system and the central auditory system. Today, we are going to concentrate on procedures currently used to evaluate central auditory disorders at the level of either the brain stem or the temporal lobe. Our discussion will include three basic methodologies: pure tone audiometry, electrophysiologic techniques, and speech audiometry.

Pure Tone Audiometry

Results of pure tone audiometry in patients with central auditory disorders generally show normal pure tone sensitivity on both ears. Figure 1 documents this observation in 21 patients with surgically or radiographically confirmed brain stem or temporal lobe disorders. This figure presents average threshold hearing levels (HLs) at octave intervals between 500 and 4000 Hz for 16 patients with confirmed intra-axial brain stem lesions and 5 patients with confirmed unilateral temporal lobe lesions. The patients were 14 males and 7 females ranging in age from 6 to 57 years. The data in figure 1 are presented in terms of the ear ipsilateral (I) or contralateral (C) to the affected side of the brain. The shaded area in the figure represents the normal range.

In both groups of patients the average pure tone audiogram shows normal, bilaterally symmetrical, pure tone sensitivity, with the exception of a mild loss at 4000 Hz on both ears of the brain stem group and on the contralateral ear only of the temporal lobe group. These data confirm the general observation (Jerger 1960; Calearo and Antonelli 1968; Liden and Korsan-Bengtsen 1973; Jerger, J. and Jerger, S. 1974; Jerger, S. and Jerger, J. 1975) that patients with central auditory disorders do not have significant hearing loss. One exception to these findings may involve patients with bilat-

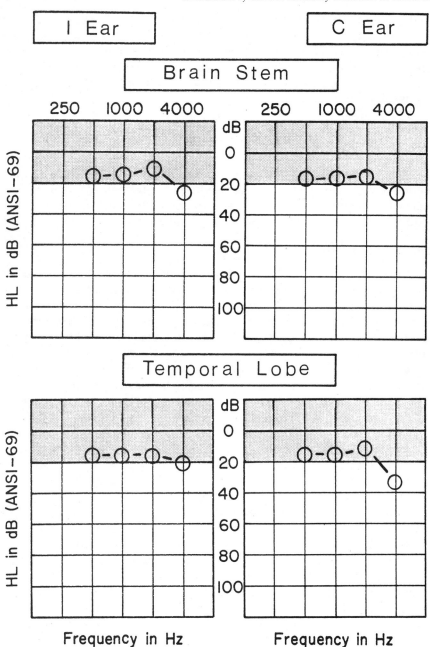

Figure 1.
Average pure tone audiogram in 16 patients with confirmed intra-axial brain stem disorders and 5 patients with confirmed unilateral temporal lobe disorders. Data are presented in terms of the ear ipsilateral (I) or contralateral (C) to the affected side of the brain. The shaded area represents the normal range.

31

eral, rather than unilateral, temporal lobe disease. In these rare patients cortical "deafness" may be observed (Jerger et al. 1969; Jerger, Lovering, and Wertz 1972). The audiogram may show a bilateral hearing loss of varying degree or, on occasion, no observable behavioral response to sound. Characteristic findings in a child with bilateral temporal lobe disease will be presented subsequently.

Electrophysiologic Techniques

During the past 10 years, two electrophysiologic techniques uniquely suited to the evaluation of young children have become available to clinicians. One technique is impedance audiometry; the other procedure is auditory brain stem evoked response (ABR) audiometry.

Impedance Audiometry

In evaluating central auditory disorders by means of impedance audiometry, acoustic reflexes provide the primary basis for differential diagnosis. Acoustic reflex thresholds are measured by presenting a sound to either ear and varying its intensity level until the lowest HL that produces a stapedial muscle contraction is determined. Results are obtained in two different ways: first, by coupling the impedance bridge probe to one ear and presenting sound to the opposite ear (crossed stimulation); and, second, by presenting both the probe and the sound to the same ear (uncrossed stimulation). Reflex thresholds are routinely measured for broadband noise signals and for pure tone signals at octave intervals between 250 and 4000 Hz.

The results of impedance audiometry are valuable in assessing hearing in young children for two reasons. First, the difference between acoustic reflex thresholds for pure tones vs. broadband noise is sensitive to the presence of any sensorineural hearing loss (Niemeyer and Sesterhenn 1974; Jerger, et al. 1974). In individuals with normal hearing, reflex thresholds are approximately 70 dB sound pressure level (SPL) for broadband noise and about 95 dB SPL (85 dB HL) for pure tones. This normal difference between pure tone and noise thresholds disappears, however, in the presence of sensorineural hearing loss. In fact, the pure tone - noise difference becomes systematically smaller as the degree of sensorineural hearing loss becomes increasingly more severe. Diagnostically, Sensitivity Prediction from Acoustic Reflexes (SPAR) may be especially helpful in children who are too young to be tested by conventional behavioral techniques.

Another value of impedance audiometry is that the relation between crossed and uncrossed reflexes is sensitive to the presence of auditory disorder at the level of the brain stem (Greisen and Rasmussen 1970; Jerger, S. and Jerger, J. 1977). For example, in individuals with normal auditory function, crossed and uncrossed reflex thresholds are both characteristically within the normal range, between about 70 to 100 dB HL, at approximately the same level. In contrast, in persons with brain stem auditory disorders, uncrossed reflexes are generally within normal limits, but crossed reflexes usually occur at abnormally elevated HLs. Normal uncrossed reflexes and abnormal crossed reflexes may be referred to as a horizontal reflex pattern abnormality (Jerger 1975).

In short, in pediatric audiologic evaluations, the SPAR measure and the relation between crossed and uncrossed reflexes (reflex pattern) provide useful diagnostic information about the presence 1) of any sensorineural hearing loss, and 2) of any auditory disorder at the level of the brain stem.

ABR Audiometry

Brain stem evoked potentials are commonly recorded by placing surface electrodes on the vertex and mastoid. A response is evoked by presenting click signals to an ear and averaging the corresponding electrical activity with a computer. Figure 2 illustrates the typical ABR waveform from a normal individual. The waveform shows six positive peaks labelled in their order of occurrence with Roman numerals. This complex, sound-induced waveform is not yet completely understood (Achor and Starr 1980).

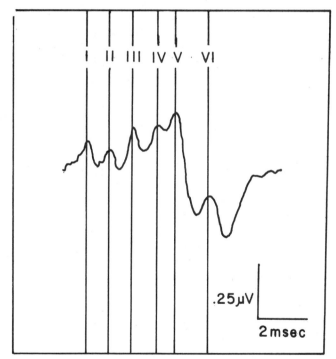

Figure 2.
Characteristic auditory brain stem evoked response (ABR) waveform from a normal individual. The waveform shows six positive peaks traditionally labeled in their order of occurrence with Roman numerals. (From Jerger, J. and Jerger, S. 1980. "Measurement of hearing in adults." In M. Paparella and D. Shumrick, eds., *Otolaryngology*, 2nd ed.. Philadelphia: W.B. Saunders Co.)

However, the electrical potentials are apparently a reflection of the activation of the eighth nerve and successive brain stem auditory nuclei and tracts. Each of the six peaks has an expected latency, or time interval between the presentation of the sound and the appearance of the peak response.

Clinically, diagnostic information from the ABR response is characteristically based on any observed change in the latency of one or more of the peaks. In general, results of ABR audiometry conform to the following rule (Stockard and Rossiter 1977; Hashimoto, Ishiyama, and Tozuka 1979): Patients with brain stem auditory disorders generally show poorly formed ABR waveforms with substantially delayed peak latencies or an absence of one or more of the expected peak responses. In contrast, patients with temporal lobe auditory disorders typically show normal ABR waveforms and normal peak latencies.

ABR audiometry and impedance audiometry add a new dimension to the audiologic evaluation of neuro-otologic disorders. The following two patients illustrate the unique contribution of these two procedures to evaluating central auditory disorder in children who cannot be tested by conventional behavioral audiometric techniques. Results in the two selected patients illustrate the diagnostic value of both abnormal and normal findings. For example, in Case 1 with brain stem disorder, abnormal acoustic reflexes and ABR responses were useful in documenting abnormal brain stem auditory function. In contrast, in Case 2 with temporal lobe disorder, normal acoustic reflexes and ABR results were important in documenting normal physiologic responses to sound.

Illustrative Patients

Case 1. The first patient is a 7-year-old girl with a brain stem contusion due to head trauma from an automobile accident. At the time of the hearing test the child was semi-comatose. No behavioral audiogram could be obtained.[1] However, impedance audiometry and ABR audiometry were carried out. Figure 3 shows the acoustic reflex pattern. In this figure the 4 boxes represent results on the probe ear for the 2 crossed and the 2 uncrossed conditions. A white box represents normal results; a black box represents abnormal results. Abnormal findings may reflect either elevated (greater than 100 dB HL) or absent (greater than 110 dB HL) acoustic reflexes. In this patient acoustic reflexes were normal to uncrossed stimulation and abnormal to crossed stimulation on both ears. For example, with sound to the right ear and the impedance bridge probe coupled to the left ear, crossed acoustic reflexes were abnormal at all frequencies. In contrast, uncrossed reflexes with both the sound and the probe to the right ear were consistently within normal limits. Sound to the left ear produced the same pattern of results. Acoustic reflexes were abnormal to crossed stimulation but normal to uncrossed stimulation. The reflex pattern was characterized by a horizontal configuration, the unique signature of intra-axial brain stem disorders.

---

1. Subsequent to this evaluation, the patient returned for behavioral audiometric testing. The audiogram showed normal pure tone sensitivity on both ears.

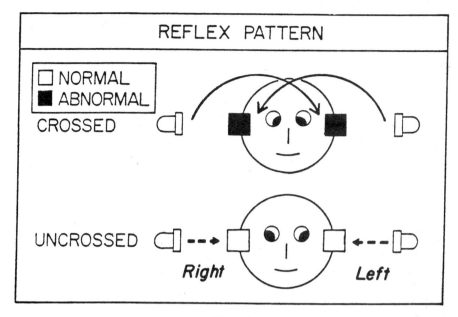

Figure 3.
Acoustic reflex pattern in a 7-year-old girl with a brain stem contusion due to head trauma. Acoustic reflexes were abnormal on both ears to crossed stimulation only. Note the horizontal configuration, the signature of intra-axial brain stem disorder. The child was semi-comatose at the time of the evaluation. A pure tone audiogram could not be obtained but was found to be normal later. ABR audiometry showed no recognizable waves I through V on either ear at the intensity limits of the equipment.

Results of ABR audiometry showed no recognizable waves I through V on either ear at the intensity limits of the equipment. This finding is consistent with a central auditory disorder at the level of the brain stem.

Findings in this child highlight the value of electrophysiologic measures in the diagnostic evaluation of children who are too ill to be tested behaviorally. The presence of a brain stem auditory disorder was supported by abnormal crossed acoustic reflex thresholds and normal uncrossed reflex thresholds and by the absence of any observable responses on ABR audiometry.

Case 2. Figure 4 presents results on a 5-year-old girl with a final medical diagnosis of auditory agnosia. The parents reported that this child seemed to develop normally until about 2-1/2 years of age. At that time she experienced a grand mal seizure, high fever, and a 24 hour period of left hemiparesis. Her parents did not notice any hearing difficulty. She was placed on medication to control the seizures.

When the child was about 4-1/2 years old, the parents noticed that she seemed to have trouble hearing. They took the child to an otologist. An audiogram showed essentially normal hearing on both ears. During the next year the child's hearing was retested on three different occasions. Results showed an apparent progressive hearing loss bilaterally. The serial audiograms in this patient are detailed elsewhere (Jerger and Hayes 1976). At 5-1/2 years of age she was brought to the Texas Medical Center for evaluation. The final medical diagnosis was bilateral temporal lobe disease and auditory agnosia.

Figure 4 shows results of her first audiologic evaluation in Houston. During behavioral observation and structured audiologic testing, the child did not appear to respond to any environmental sounds or auditory signals. Results of impedance audiometry and ABR audiometry were in striking contrast to behavioral results. For example, acoustic reflexes were present at normal HLs at all frequencies on both ears. The reflex pattern (fig. 4a) was normal. The SPAR measure predicted normal sensitivity on the left ear and, at most, a very mild sensorineural loss on the right ear. ABR audiometry (fig. 4b) showed wave V responses at normal latencies from both ears. Repeatable responses were elicited at intensity levels down to 20 dB HL on each ear. This finding is consistent with normal peripheral hearing sensitivity bilaterally.

Results in this patient illustrate the value of impedance audiometry and ABR audiometry in crosschecking the results of behavioral audiometry. The diagnosis of essentially normal hearing sensitivity in this child contributed to the accurate identification of her disorder (auditory agnosia). Had this child been diagnosed as severely hearing impaired, recommendations for rehabilitation would have been inappropriately based on the assumption of a profound hearing loss. Results in this patient emphasize that acoustic reflexes and ABR responses are independent of the cognitive processing of sounds. Although this child had no observable awareness of auditory signals or speech, she had consistently normal acoustic reflexes and ABR responses.

In summary, findings in these two patients illustrate the limitations of conventional behavioral audiometry in some children with central auditory disorders. In the above two patients, acoustic reflexes and ABR audiometry provided the primary tools for evaluating auditory function. The present results also underscore the need for a test battery approach in diagnostic audiologic evaluations. In many individuals an important contribution to the test battery may be provided by yet another technique, namely, speech audiometry.

Speech Audiometry

Presently, specific speech tests for evaluating central auditory disorder are not as standardized as speech tests for evaluating peripheral auditory sites. For example, current diagnostic speech audiometry consists of a variety of word and sentence materials that have been made difficult to understand by a variety of methods, e.g., filtering, time compression, competing messages, etc.

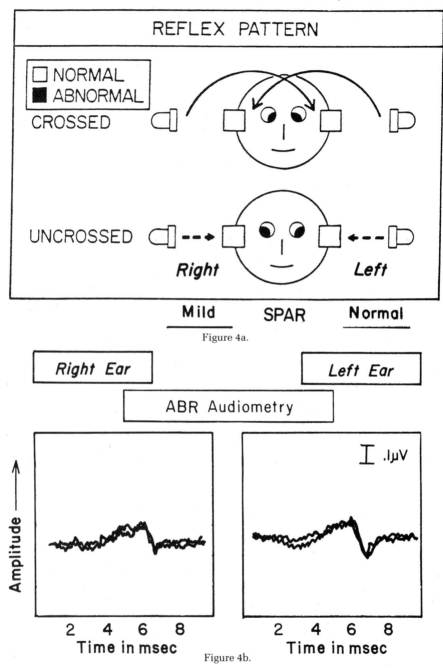

Figure 4a.

Figure 4b.

Figure 4.
Audiometric results in a 5-year-old girl with auditory agnosia. A pure tone audiogram could not be obtained. The child did not appear to respond to any sound: a) acoustic reflex pattern and SPAR results; and b) ABR waveform to click signals at 50 dB HL. Acoustic reflexes and ABR audiometry were important in documenting normal physiologic responses to sound.

37

In contrast to the variety of available test materials, the testing paradigms for presenting the materials are relatively routine. For example, in most test batteries for evaluating central auditory function, test materials are presented in two different ways. In one approach the target word or sentence is presented to one ear and a competing signal is presented to the opposite ear. This paradigm may be referred to as a dichotic listening task or a contralateral competing message (CCM) condition. A CCM task requires the listener to attend to one ear and ignore the opposite ear, a process that may be referred to as selective attention. Diagnostically, dichotic testing paradigms are particularly sensitive to the presence of any auditory disorder at the level of the temporal lobe (Katz, Basil, and Smith 1963; Jerger, J. and Jerger, S. 1975; Berlin 1976).

In the other approach the target word or sentence is presented to one ear and degraded by either filtering, temporal alterations, or a competing message to the same ear. This approach may be referred to as a monotic listening task or an ipsilateral competing message (ICM) condition. Degraded monotic speech tasks require the auditory system to code a complex, degraded acoustic signal and transmit it to the higher auditory centers for processing. Diagnostically, degraded monotic tests are particularly sensitive to the presence of any auditory disorder at the level of the brain stem (Jerger, J. and Jerger, S. 1974; Jerger, S. and Jerger, J. 1975).

Children Seven Years of Age and Older

The different patterns of speech intelligibility results that may characterize brain stem and temporal lobe sites of disorders in children at least 7 years of age may be illustrated by a test battery consisting of three procedures: the performance vs. intensity (PI) function, the staggered spondaic word (SSW) test, and the synthetic sentence identification (SSI) test.

PI Function

PI functions are obtained by presenting monosyllabic word (PB) or sentence materials at several different intensity levels. The goal is to define performance from that intensity level yielding 0% to 20% correct to a maximum speech intensity of 90 dB HL. In individuals with normal auditory function, the PI function typically rises to a maximum as intensity is increased, then levels off and maintains a plateau as the intensity is further increased above the level yielding maximum performance.

The PI function is useful in evaluating patients who might have a central auditory disorder for two reasons. First, the function may show a consistent performance difference between ears that cannot be accounted for on a peripheral sensitivity basis. This unusual performance deficit usually appears on the ear contralateral to the affected side of the brain. Second, the shape of the PI function may be abnormal. For example, as the intensity of the speech is increased above the level yielding maximum performance, there may be an unusual reduction in performance. This drop in performance at high intensity levels is called rollover of the PI function (Jerger, J. and Jerger, S. 1971).

Diagnostically, abnormal performance on PI functions is a non-specific finding. Abnormal results may be consistent with either brain stem or temporal lobe disorder. Generally, however, PI function abnormalities may be characterized as relatively more dramatic in patients with brain stem disorder and relatively more subtle in patients with temporal lobe disorder.

SSW Test

The SSW test requires the listener to repeat spondee words that are presented to both ears in competing and non-competing conditions. The time sequence of the spondee word presentation to each ear may be illustrated as follows: The first syllable is presented to the right ear in isolation; the second syllable on the right ear is simultaneous with the first syllable on the left ear, and the final syllable the left ear is presented in isolation. In patients with normal auditory function, performance is normal for competing and non-competing conditions. In contrast, in patients with temporal lobe disorder, performance is characteristically normal for the non-competing condition, but unusually depressed for the competing condition (Katz, Brasil, and Smith 1963). In patients with brain stem disorder, SSW results are unpredictable (Jerger, J. and Jerger S. 1975). Some patients may have completely normal performance. Other patients may show unusual performance deficits for the competing condition. Performance deficits in patients with either brain stem or temporal lobe sites are usually observed on the ear opposite the affected side of the brain.

SSI Test

The SSI test requires the listener to select a sentence from a list of 10 alternatives. The sentence is routinely presented with a competing speech message in the background. Performance is measured for both ICM and CCM conditions. For the ICM condition, the message-to-competition ratio (MCR) is varied from + 10 dB to -20 dB. For the CCM condition, the MCR is routinely varied from 0 dB to -40 dB. The patient's relative performance on the two conditions assists in differentiating brain stem and temporal lobe sites (Jerger J. and Jerger, S. 1975). A relatively greater performance deficit for an ICM than for a CCM suggests a brain stem site; a relatively greater deficit for a CCM than for an ICM suggests a temporal lobe site. The following patients illustrate the patterns of speech intelligibility results that may characterize brain stem and temporal lobe sites of disorder.

Illustrative Patients

Case 3. Figure 5 presents results for a 9-year-old boy with an intra-axial brain stem disorder. Pneumoencephalography revealed an intrinsic neoplasm of the pons, primarily on the right side. The final medical diagnosis was a pontine glioma. The primary clinical symptoms noted at hospitalization were ataxia, headaches, a tendency to fall to the left, and speech production difficulties. The patient did not notice hearing difficulties on either ear.

The pure tone audiogram (fig. 5a) showed normal sensitivity in the left ear and a very mild sensitivity loss at 500 Hz only in the right ear. Average pure tone threshold results at 500, 1000, and 2000 Hz (PTA) were 11 dB HL on the right ear and -2 dB HL on the left ear.

With the exception of an elevated reflex threshold HL at 500 Hz on the left ear, acoustic reflex thresholds were present at normal HLs on both ears. Although absolute reflex threshold HLs were within the normal range, results on both ears showed an unusual rising configuration with poorer thresholds in the low and mid frequency region than in the high frequency region.

The PI function for PB words (PI-PB) was within normal limits bilaterally. However, maximum scores showed slightly poorer performance on the left ear than on the right ear. The PB max scores were 100% on the right ear, but only 88% on the left ear. Poorer speech intelligibility performance on the left ear was unusual in view of the poorer pure tone sensitivity results on the right ear.

Speech thresholds from the PI-PB function (PBT scores) were 15 dB HL on both ears. The PBT score agreed with pure tone sensitivity measures on the right ear, but was slightly elevated relative to pure tone results on the left ear.

The possibility of central auditory disorder was explored in this patient with the SSI procedure (fig. 5b) and the SSW test. SSI-ICM performance on the right ear was within the normal range as illustrated by the shaded area. In contrast, SSI-ICM results on the left ear showed a marked performance deficit. Average performance was 77% on the right ear, but only 37% on the left ear. Performance for the SSI-CCM procedure was completely normal (100%) on both ears at all MCRs. SSW results were normal bilaterally. Average SSW scores for the competing condition were 88% on the right ear and 82% on the left ear.

The overall configuration of results was consistent with a disorder of the auditory pathways at the level of the brain stem. A brain stem site was supported by relatively normal pure tone sensitivity, asymmetric PI-PB functions, normal SSW results, and abnormal performance for the SSI-ICM procedure coupled with normal performance for the SSI-CCM test. Notice that all speech intelligibility deficits appeared on the left ear, the ear opposite the affected side of the brain stem.

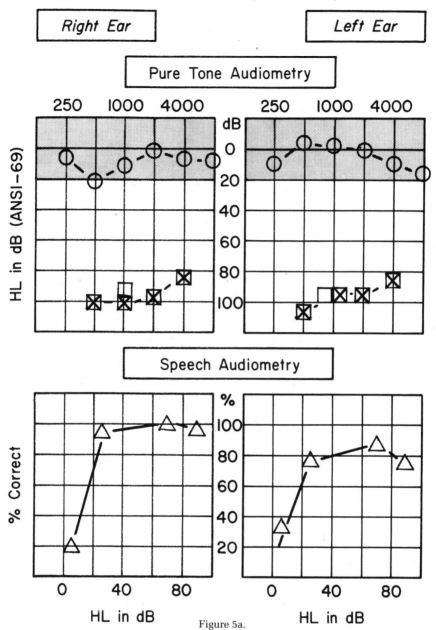

Figure 5a.

Figure 5.
Audiometric results in a 9-year-old boy with an intra-axial brain stem disorder primarily on the right side: a) pure tone audiometry, acoustic reflex thresholds, and PI-PB functions; and b) SSI test in the presence of an ipsilateral competing message (SSI-ICM) and a contralateral competing message (SSI-CCM). Notice the abnormal performance for the SSI-ICM procedure coupled with normal performance for the SSI-CCM test. All speech intelligibility deficits are observed on the left ear. (KEY: Pure Tone Audiometry, ◯ air conduction; ⊠ crossed acoustic reflex; ☐ uncrossed acoustic reflex; Speech Audiometry, △ PB.)

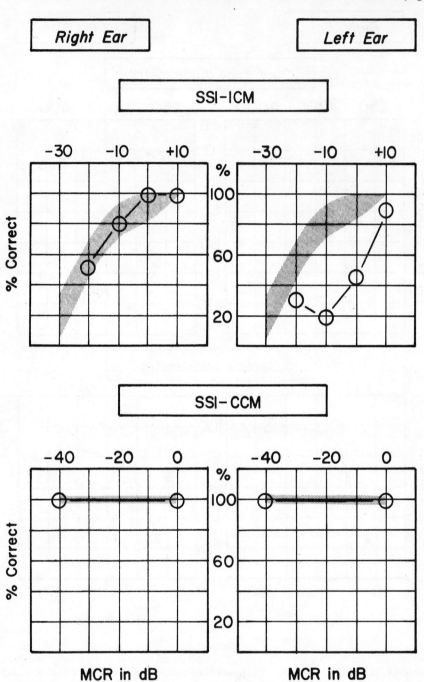

Figure 5b.

Case 4. Figure 6 shows results on a 12-year-old boy with a final diagnosis of cerebral dysfunction manifested by dyslexia, dyscalculia, hyperactivity, and shortened attention span.

The child's antenatal and neonatal history may be briefly summarized as follows: During the latter period of pregnancy, the mother received medical treatment for a kidney infection, hypertension, and swelling. At birth, the baby appeared to be in severe distress and was not expected to live. He weighed 4-1/2 lbs. His head appeared grossly misshapen. The cranial abnormality was described as a prominence in the occipital region and a ridge across the area of the coronal suture. His head had a prominent scar due to an abnormal forceps delivery. The baby remained in the hospital for medical treatment after the mother was dismissed. At 6 weeks of age, his birth difficulties seemed to subside. Subsequently, developmental milestones appeared to proceed normally.

The patient was initially referred for medical evaluation 4 years ago. According to school reports, he was not developing academic skills satisfactorily. However, estimates of his full scale IQ score were consistently within normal limits, about 100 to 110. He was 8 years old and in the second grade. He could not spell, could not read, and could not recite the alphabet, the days of the week, the months of the year, or numbers up to 50. He did not know his address, phone number, or birthday. With the exception of impaired intellectual function, the neurologic evaluation and physical examination were within normal limits. Skull X-rays were normal. EEG findings were consistent with a nonspecific abnormality characterized by poorly regulated and slow activity in all areas. An excess of slow fused activity was particularly apparent in the occipital region.

At the time of the hearing test, the child was in a class for brain injured children with learning disability. He was referred for audiologic evaluation because the mother thought he had difficulty hearing. She had noticed a hearing problem for as long as she could remember.

A pure tone audiogram could not be obtained in this patient because of inconsistent responses. However, speech thresholds for spondee words were within normal limits bilaterally. The spondee thresholds were 15 dB HL on the right ear and 20 dB HL on the left ear. This finding suggests normal hearing sensitivity for at least some frequencies in the range important for speech understanding.

Crossed and uncrossed acoustic reflex thresholds were present at normal HLs at all test frequencies on both ears. The reflex pattern (fig. 6a) was normal. PI-PB functions (fig. 6b) showed relatively normal maximum intelligibility scores bilaterally. The PB max scores were 92% on the right ear and 80% on the left ear. No rollover was observed on either ear. Although maximum performance was within the normal range on both ears, an unusually slow rise to maximum performance was observed, especially on the right ear. For example, the intensity range corresponding to the performance range from 40% to 92% correct on the right ear was a startling 60 dB.

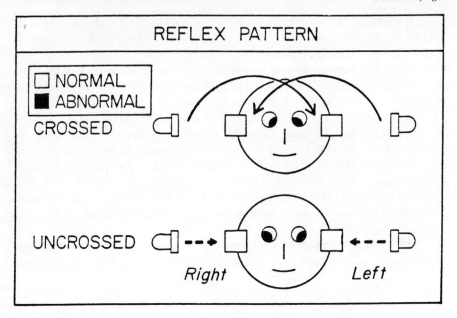

Figure 6a.

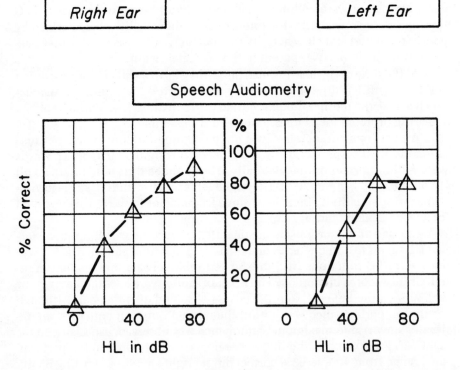

Figure 6b.

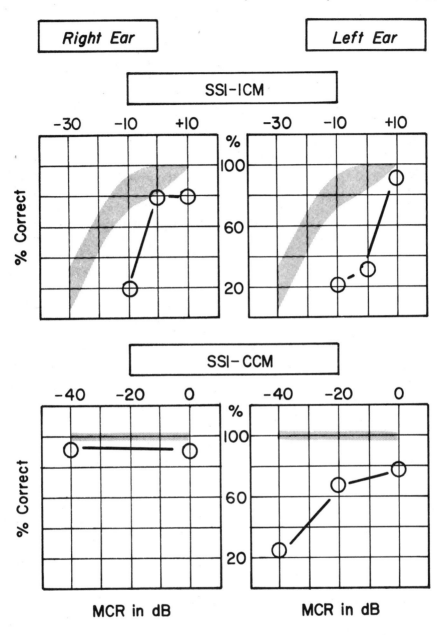

Figure 6c.

Figure 6.
Audiometric results for a 12-year-old boy with cerebral dysfunction. A pure tone audiogram could not be obtained due to unusual inconsistency in responding to pure tone signals: a) acoustic reflex pattern; b) PI-PB functions; and c) the SSI procedure. Notice that SSI-ICM results were abnormal on both ears and that SSI-CCM results were abnormal on the left ear only.

The SSI-ICM procedure (fig. 6c) was abnormal on both ears. The SSI-CCM procedure was performed without difficulty on the right ear, but showed a large performance deficit on the left ear. The SSW test showed a large performance difference between ears. Average scores for the competing condition were 80% on the right ear, but only 15% on the left ear.

The overall pattern of diagnostic test results was consistent with a temporal lobe site. The presence of a temporal lobe disorder was supported by the large performance difference between ears on the SSW test and a relatively greater loss on the SSI-CCM procedure than on the SSI-ICM procedure. Notice that the SSI test yielded poor performance on both ICM and CCM tasks. ICM scores were abnormal for both ears; CCM scores were abnormal for the left ear only. Exceptions to the temporal lobe pattern of this patient are abnormal ICM scores for one ear only or normal ICM performance on both ears. However, in our experience, bilateral deficits on ICM testing and unilateral deficits on CCM testing (fig. 6c) are the most characteristic results. In the interpretation of SSI results, the overriding principle that characterizes temporal lobe disorders is relatively more difficulty on CCM tasks than on ICM tasks.[2]

In summary, results in these patients illustrate the diagnostic value of PI functions, the SSI test, and the SSW procedure in differentiating patients with brain stem and temporal lobe auditory disorders. We want to emphasize the particular importance of speech audiometry in evaluating patients with unilateral temporal lobe disorders and brain stem disorders rostral to the inferior colliculi. In these individuals, results of diagnostic speech audiometry frequently show substantial abnormalities in the presence of completely normal findings on ABR audiometry and acoustic reflex testing (Jerger, J., Neely, G., and Jerger, S. 1980). Results in Case 2 (fig. 4) highlight the normal responses to ABR audiometry and impedance audiometry in patients with temporal lobe pathology.

Children Six Years of Age and Younger

Existing procedures for speech audiometry have two serious limitations when applied to children 6 years of age and younger. First, current tests are traditionally not applicable in children below 4-1/2 or 5 years old (Willeford 1976; Young and Tracy 1976; Costello 1977; Pinheiro 1977; Elliott 1979; Elliott, et al. 1979). Second, results may be influenced by differences in receptive language ability rather than by true central auditory deficits (Pfau and Albrecht 1976; Battin 1979). The contaminating influence of variable receptive language skills on speech audiometry in young children has been emphasized by several investigators (Mills 1977; Elliott, et al. 1979).

2. Because this child had a diagnosis of dyslexia, we determined that he could correctly identify the 10 SSI sentences presented in quiet before testing began.

For these reasons, several laboratories are presently developing more suitable materials for speech audiometry in young children. Today, I want to describe briefly our own work in this area. During the past few years, we have developed a new Pediatric Speech Intelligibility (PSI) test appropriate for children as young as 3 years of age. In our approach (Jerger, S. et al. 1980), we incorporate the normal differences in receptive language function that characterize children between 3 and 7 years old. To do this, the test items were generated by a group of 87 normal children in this age range. Our goal was to develop both monosyllabic word and sentence messages. Previous findings in adults (Jerger and Hayes 1977) have demonstrated that the relation between performance for words and sentences is of unique value in detecting central auditory disorder, even in the presence of peripheral hearing loss.

Generation of Test Materials

Sixty (60) pictures were drawn onto 5" x 8" index cards. Of these pictures, 30 represented different monosyllabic words and 30 represented different actions that could be described with a sentence. The children were asked to name the object of each "word" card and to describe the action of each "sentence" card. Our goal was to select "word" and "sentence" pictures that normal children identified consistently and correctly.

Elicited Responses to Sentence Stimulus Pictures

The responses of the normal children to the sentence stimulus pictures fell into three different patterns, as shown in Table 1. The response patterns were associated with differences in chronological age, vocabulary skills as measured by the Peabody Picture Vocabulary Test (PPVT) (Dunn 1965), and receptive language ability as defined by the Northwestern Syntax Screening Test (NSST) (Lee 1971). For example, the younger children, about 3-1/2 years, consistently responded in one of 2 ways: 1) with a pronoun substituted for the subject of the sentence (example: He's brushing his

Response Pattern	Test Sentence	Terminology
1. He's brushing his teeth.	omitted	
2. A bear brushing his teeth.	Show me a bear brushing his teeth.	Format I
3. A bear is brushing his teeth.	A bear is brushing his teeth.	Format II

Table 1.
The three patterns characterizing the responses of 87 normal children to 30 sentence stimulus pictures. Two different types of test sentences were constructed to represent the differences in the childrens' responses. The 2 different sentence formats were termed I and II. Notice that the pronominal response (pattern 1) was not selected for inclusion in the new test for reasons discussed in the text.

teeth), or 2) by omitting the auxiliary verb "be" in forming the present pro-gressive verb tense of the sentence (example: A bear brushing his teeth). In contrast, the older children, approximately 5-1/2 years, always responded with complete, adult-like sentences (example: A bear is brushing his teeth).

Determination of Sentence Construction for Test Materials

To represent the differences in the children's responses, two different types of test sentences were formed as illustrated in Table 1. In one con-struction, termed Format I, the test sentence consists of "noun phrase/verb + 'ing'/noun phrase" (pattern 2). The sentence is preceded by the car-rier phrase, "show me." An example of a Format I sentence is "Show me a bear brushing his teeth." In the other construction, termed Format II, the test sentence is composed of "noun phrase/auxiliary verb + 'ing'/noun phrase" (pattern 3). Sentences are not preceded by a carrier phrase. An ex-ample of a Format II sentence is "A bear is brushing his teeth."

Notice, in Table 1, that we did not select pronominal sentence con-structions for inclusion in the test battery. We rejected pronominal con-structions for several reasons. First, children in the pronominal response group consistently used a pronoun plus the contracted form of the auxil-iary verb, e.g., "He's." Menyuk (1969) has stressed that the construction "He's," in the absence of examples of "He is" utterances, probably reflects a memorized construction, and is not considered an independent use of the auxiliary verb "be". Second, children with a pronominal response (pattern 1) did not differ from children with a pattern 2 response in terms of chron-

Format I	Format II
1. Show me a rabbit painting an egg.	1. A rabbit is painting an egg.
2. Show me a bear brushing his teeth.	2. A bear is brushing his teeth.
3. Show me a horse eating an apple	3. A horse is eating an apple.
4. Show me the rabbit putting on his shoes.	4. The rabbit is putting on his shoes.
5. Show me the bear combing his hair.	5. A bear is combing his hair.
6. Show me the bear drinking milk.	6. The bear is drinking milk
7. Show me a rabbit reading a book.	7. A rabbit is reading a book.
8. Show me the fox rollerskating.	8. The fox is rollerskating.
9. Show me a bear eating a sandwich.	9. A bear is eating a sandwich
10. Show me a rabbit kicking a football.	10. A rabbit is kicking a football.

Table 2.
The 10 sentences comprising the pediatric speech intelligibility test. Notice that the sen-tences are presented in 2 different formats to represent the different speech patterns of a group of normal children.

48

ological age, vocabulary skills, and receptive language abilities. Consequently, we reasoned that a pattern 2 sentence construction may represent appropriate speech materials for children in both pattern 1 and pattern 2 groups. This opinion is supported by our retrospective observation that all children in the pattern 1 response group used a pattern 2 construction on at least 11% of their utterances.

PSI Sentence and Word Materials

Tables 2 and 3 present the 10 sentences and 20 words selected for the PSI test. These items represent the sentence and word stimulus pictures that the normal children identified most consistently and correctly. In subsequent test situations, the sentences are presented as two lists of five sentences each; the words are presented as four lists of five words each. The equivalency of the different sentence and word lists was established in a group of 20 normal children.

1. bear	6. dog	11. frog	16. pig
2. bird	7. duck	12. hat	17. spoon
3. boat	8. fish	13. house	18. sun
4. book	9. flag	14. key	19. train
5. car	10. fork	15. knife	20. tree

Table 3.
The 20 monosyllabic words comprising the pediatric speech intelligibility test. The responses of a group of normal children to the selected word items did not differ as a function of chronological age, vocabulary skills, or receptive language ability.

Validity of Different Sentence Formats as a Means of Equating Differences in Language Development Among Children

The purpose of developing Format I and Format II sentences was to control the influence of receptive language ability on speech audiometric results. To establish the validity of the different sentences as a means of equating performance in young children with differences in developmental language skills, both Format I and Format II sentence materials were administered to 24 normal children. Subjects were 14 boys and 10 girls ranging in age from 3 years 4 months (3-4) to 9-0 years.

Each child was seated at a table containing a picture identification response card (a 38-1/2 cm x 39-1/2 cm card with five pictures). After each sentence had been presented, the child was instructed to point to the picture corresponding to the sentence that he heard. The test sentences were presented at 50 dB SPL, a level yielding 100% correct response from all

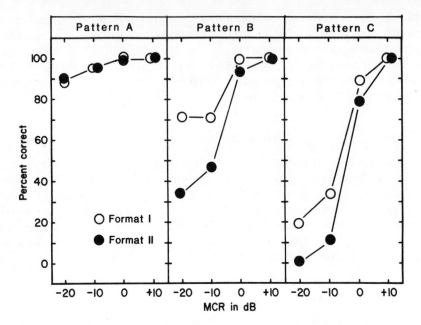

Figure 7.
Average results for the three different patterns characterizing performance for Format I and Format II sentences in the presence of an ipsilateral competing message. The message to competition ratio (MCR) varied from + 10 dB to -20 dB. Ages ranged from 3-4 to 9-0 years.

children. In order to make the listening task sufficiently difficult, performance for the sentences was measured with a competing speech message in the background. The intensity of the competing message was varied from a MCR of + 10 dB to a MCR of -20 dB.

In the 24 children, the relation between performance for Format I vs Format II sentence materials showed three different results. Figure 7 shows average performance for each pattern. In one pattern (labeled A), performance for both Format I and Format II sentences remained unusually good, between 85 to 100%, at all MCRs. In the second pattern (labeled B), performance for Format II sentences systematically declined as the MCR became increasingly more difficult. However, in this pattern, performance for Format I materials was relatively good (55%-85%) at the most difficult MCR, -20 dB. In the third pattern (labeled C), performance for both Format I and Format II materials declined as a function of the MCR. However, performance for Format I sentences was relatively poor (0%-35%) at the most difficult MCR. The difference between performance for Format I vs. Format II sentences was statistically significant (p < .01) in both pattern B and C groups.

Effect of Chronological Age and Receptive Language Age

Chronological age did not consistently distinguish among the children yielding the three different results for Format I and Format II sen-

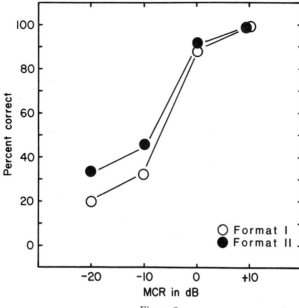

Figure 8.
Average performance for Format I sentences in the pattern C group (see fig. 7) and Format II sentences in the pattern B group. The difference between Format I and Format II sentences is syntactic construction. The difference between children with pattern C vs pattern B performance is receptive language ability, but not necessarily chronological age. Apparently, "language equivalent" data may be generated by varying the syntactic format of sentence materials according to the listener's receptive language age.

tences (fig. 7). For example, 5-1/2-year-old children were present in both pattern B and C groups. In contrast to overlapping chronological ages, however, receptive language age as measured by the NSST sharply differentiated the 3 groups. Receptive language scores were always greater than or equal to 37 (about 6-10 years) in children with pattern A performance, were between 32 to 36 (about 5-8 to 6-7 years) in children with pattern B performance, and were always less than or equal to 31 (about 5-4 years) in children with pattern C performance.

Sentence Format and Receptive Language Ability

The data for figure 7 suggest that for children with receptive language ages of less than about 6-10 years, both Format I and Format II sentence constructions appear necessary. In children with relatively high receptive language scores (32-36), Format I sentences are too easy (pattern B). In children with relatively low receptive language scores (less than or equal to 31), Format II sentences are too difficult (pattern C). Further, as shown in figure 8, performance for Format II sentences in the pattern B group and performance for Format I sentences in the pattern C group are equivalent.[3] In other words, if the sentence format is varied as a function of a child's receptive

3. Results were statistically equivalent at 0 dB MCR (t = 0.77, p = 0.54), -10 dB MCR (t = 1.38, p = 0.19) and at -20 dB MCR (t = 1.82, p = 0.09) (Hebbler 1979).

51

language ability, performance for Format I and Format II materials is comparable. In this sense, the data of figure 8 may be viewed as language equivalent.

In summary, the importance of the PSI test is that diagnostic speech audiometry may now be carried out in children as young as 3 years of age. Further, PSI results do not appear to be compromised by the pronounced differences in receptive language skills characterizing children between 3 and 7 years old.

Normative data for the PSI test materials have been defined in a group of 81 normal children between the ages of 3 and 7 years. Presently, we are in the process of defining the different patterns of PSI results associated with central auditory abnormality. To this end, the PSI central test battery (performance for words vs. sentences, in quiet vs. in competition, and in an ipsilateral competing mode vs. a contralateral competing mode) is being administered to children with well-documented, circumscribed brain stem or temporal lobe disorders.

Test-Retest Reliability of the PSI Procedure

In order to establish the reliability of the new PSI speech materials, we tested a series of normal children on two separate occasions. The ages of the children ranged from 3-0 to 6-10 years. Test-retest data were obtained in 35 children for the sentence materials and in 32 children for the word items. The average time interval between tests was 29 days for sentences and 3 days for words.[4]

The distribution of test-retest difference scores (initial test minus retest) had a mean of -2.5% for sentence materials and -1.2% for word items. The standard deviation of the difference scores was 10% for the sentences and 9.5% for the words. The coefficient of stability (Downie and Heath 1959) between test-retest measures was 0.82 for sentences and 0.92 for words.

Non-Auditory Factors Influencing PSI Test Results

Figure 9 presents a simplified model of the different cognitive processes affecting the PSI test. The first line of the figure briefly outlines the basic components involved in responding to an auditory signal. More specifically, after the presentation of an auditory signal, the child is required to code the sensory signal; to process the transformed information and extract the critical features; to decode and interpret the information; and to produce a motor response. These components of the listening task are processed both physically (a bottom-up sensory analysis) and conceptually (a top-down internal analysis). Norman (1976) emphasizes that physical processing is triggered by the arrival of sensory information, and conceptual processing is triggered by a person's expectations based on the context of the sensory event. The physical and conceptual processing functions interact and operate simultaneously throughout the listening task.

4. The difference in inter-test intervals would ordinarily be expected to favor reliability of words over sentences. In fact, however, reliability was similar for the 2 sets of materials.

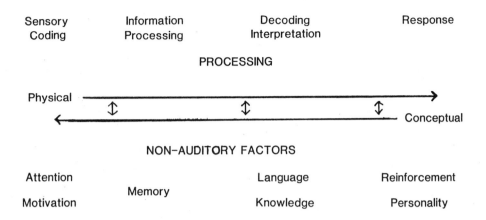

Figure 9.
A simplified model of the cognitive processes affecting the PSI test. In this figure, we associate each non-auditory factor with a specific component of the signal-response process. Please note, however, that this arbitrary structuring is oversimplified and that a non-auditory function may affect several component skills, rather than a single component skill as we imply.

In addition to the status and functioning of the auditory system, at least 7 non-auditory factors, shown in the last line of figure 9, may affect a child's performance on the PSI task. Drs. Culbertson and Johnson have talked about many of these factors in their presentations at this meeting. To date, the non-auditory factors that may influence auditory test results do not appear to have received primary attention from audiologists. However, in young children with different maturational levels, these non-auditory abilities assume a critical role. For example, before we can interpret test results as consistent with abnormal auditory function, the non-auditory factors that may affect performance in the testing situation should be controlled. For many years, cognitive psychologists (Flavell 1977; Bourne, Dominowski, and Loftus 1979) have cautioned against inferring competence or incompetence from performance on a test when the non-targeted skills required in the task are not specified and controlled.

We should emphasize at this point that we realize that behavioral auditory test results will always be influenced to a greater or lesser extent by a person's non-auditory cognitive skills. In fact, we agree with Klahr and Wallace's (1970) suggestion that it may be impossible to develop a test that yields a perfect correlation between test results and competence vs. incompetence on a selected skill. With these qualifications in mind, we have tried to minimize the effect of non-auditory factors in the following manner.

In an attempt to focus a child's attention, four different controls are built into the PSI test. First, the listening task consists of a closed message set of five items. A specified, restricted task domain defines what the child may expect to hear. Second, the primary and secondary messages are spoken by different male voices. Third, the target items are presented first in quiet and then in the presence of a competing message. The intensity level of the competing message is slowly varied from an MCR of + 10 dB (the competing message is less intense than the target message) to the test condition MCR which is + 4 dB for words and 0 dB for sentences. The purpose of the second and third control mechanisms is to provide a vocal contrast and an initial loudness discrepancy between the two speech messages. Theoretically, these two mechanisms should help focus and maintain a child's attention to the target. Finally, for word items and for Format I sentences, a carrier phrase, "Show me," differentiates the target item from the competition. Recently, Flavell (1977) and Bourne, Dominowski, and Loftus (1979) have pointed out the different peripheral (e.g., loudness) and central (closed message set) factors that may aid attention in children. In an attempt to maintain a child's motivation at a relatively constant level for as long as possible, candy or raisins are offered at selected intervals as a reward for cooperation.

In figure 9, memory refers to the echoic and short-term memories that are critical to the processing of auditory signals. For the PSI test, the child's memory capacity and function is controlled in three ways. First, as previously discussed, the listening task involves a closed message set of five pictured items. Theoretically, a pictorial representation of each test item reduces the necessity of independently storing and retrieving a target message in the memory device. Kobasigawa (1974) and Bransford and Johnson (1972) have documented the beneficial effect of contextual cues on memory function. For example, Bransford and Johnson found that the memory functioning of high school students improved from 3.6 to 8.0 correct items when pictures of the messages were available to the students at the time of input. Kobasigawa noted that structured (cued) recall with pictures, in contrast to unstructured recall condtions, doubled the memory performance of first graders and eliminated the unstructured-recall performance differences between first graders and sixth graders.

Second, the meaningfulness of the PSI speech materials, in contrast to nonsense words and synthetic sentences, is an aid to memory in children. Slobin (1971) and Muma (1978) have previously discussed the fact that meaningful materials are easier to code, store, and retrieve than nonmeaningful messages. Finally, as an aid to both memory and depth of processing, we require that each child name and briefly discuss the target items before the testing begins. The effectiveness of verbal labeling and elaboration as a mnemonic device has been documented in the literature (Miller and Johnson-Laird 1976; Luszcz and Bacharach 1980).

As discussed previously in this chapter, the influence of receptive language ability on PSI results is controlled 1) by a carefully restricted vocabulary for word and sentence messages, and 2) by varying the format of the sentence messages to match the child's language functioning. In figure 9, the term "knowledge" refers to the child's past experiences, intelligence, and expectations. To control for the possibility that substandard

54

knowledge will yield abnormal PSI results, we determine, before testing begins, that the child can correctly point to all the target items. For this pre-test condition, the items are presented in quiet either via the tape recorder or in a live-voice- plus-lip-reading condition.

The effect of reinforcement is quasi-controlled by positive verbal remarks, such as "good listening," and by the previously mentioned candy or raisin treats as reinforcements for cooperation. Finally, the effect of personality traits on the PSI test is presently under investigation. Each child's rate of information processing (cognitive tempo) and his processing strategy (analytic or synthetic) is currently being defined by the Muma Assessment Program (Muma and Muma 1979). Results of this investigation will determine the effect of selected personality traits on the PSI performance.

In addition to the procedures described above, two other techniques that control the influence of non-auditory factors on the interpretation of PSI results are the use of 1) relative performance measures and 2) ear asymmetry. Specifically, in the interpretation of results, one criterion defining normal vs. abnormal auditory function is based on relative differences between performance measures 1) for words vs. sentences, 2) in quiet vs. in competition, and 3) in an ipsilateral competing mode vs. a contralateral competing mode. In many patients, these performance differences are observed on one ear only. The observation of a relative performance deficit and/or an asymmetric performance on the two ears strengthens our ability to interpret abnormal performance as an auditory-specific dysfunction, rather than a generalized non-auditory cognitive disability.

In summary, performance on the PSI test is necessarily influenced by a complex interaction of auditory and cognitive skills. Although we have attempted to control the influence of non-auditory factors on PSI performance with facilitative task conditions, we should stress that a complete understanding of a child's performance is possible only through the coordinated efforts of a team approach, involving specialities such as psychology, speech-language pathology, and audiology.

The Following Points Were Stressed in This Chapter

1. Pure tone sensitivity is characteristically within normal limits on both ears in individuals with central auditory disorder. However, it should be noted that pure tone audiometry cannot be carried out in some patients with central auditory disorder due to illness (case 1), limited cognitive awareness of sound (case 2), or unusual threshold inconsistency (case 4).

2. Impedance audiometry and auditory brain stem evoked response (ABR) audiometry are of unique diagnostic value in those patients with central auditory disorders who cannot be tested by conventional behavioral audiometric techniques. Patients with brain stem disorders characteristically show abnormal results on acoustic reflexes and ABR

audiometry (case 2). Patients with temporal lobe disorders usually show normal physiologic responses to sound (case 4).

3. Speech audiometry is of unique diagnostic value in the differentiation of individuals with brain stem and temporal lobe sites of disorder. In particular, we want to stress the unique value of speech audiometry in the evaluation of patients with unilateral temporal lobe disorders or brain stem disorders rostral to the inferior colliculi. In these individuals, results of speech audiometry frequently show substantial abnormality in the presence of normal findings on impedance and ABR audiometry.

4. Results of speech audiometry in children below 7 years of age may be compromised by differences in receptive langugage ability.

5. The new Pediatric Speech Intelligibility (PSI) Test controls the influence of receptive language ability on speech audiometry by incorporating the normal differences in receptive language function that characterize children between 3 and 7 years of age. The PSI test may be administered to children as young as 3 years of age.

Acknowledgments

The preparation of this chapter was supported, in part, by Public Health Service Research Grant NS-10940 from the National Institute of Neurological and Communicative Disorders and Stroke. Patient data presented in this chapter were obtained in the Audiology Laboratories, Baylor College of Medicine and the Neurosensory Center, under the direction of Dr. James Jerger.

References

Achor, J. and Starr, A. 1980. Auditory brain stem responses in the cat. I. Intracranial and extracranial recordings. II. Effects of lesions. *Electroencephal. Clin. Neurophysiol.* 48:154-90.

Battin, R. 1979. Willeford battery in children. *Corti's Organ*, 4:4.

Berlin, C. 1976. New developments in evaluating central auditory mechanisms. *Ann. Otol.* 85:833-41.

Bourne, L., Dominowski, R. and Loftus, E. 1979. *Cognitive processes.* Englewood Cliffs, NJ: Prenti :e-Hall, Inc.

Bransford, J. and Johnson, M. 1972. Contextual prerequisites for understanding: some investigations of comprehension and recall. *J. Verb. Learn. Verb. Beh.* 11:717-26.

Calearo, C. and Antonelli, A. 1968. Audiometric findings in brain stem lesions. *Acta Otolaryngol.* 66:305-19.

Costello, M. 1977. Evaluation of auditory behavior of children using the Flowers-Costello test of central auditory abilities. In *Central auditory dysfunction*, ed. R.W. Keith. New York: Grune & Stratton.

Downie, N. and Heath, R. 1959. *Basic statistical methods.* New York: Harper and Brothers.

Dunn, L. 1965. *Expanded manual for the Peabody picture vocabulary test.* Minneapolis, MN: American Guidance Service.

Elliott, L. 1979. Performance of children 9 to 17 years on a test of speech intelligibility in noise using sentence material with controlled word predictability. *J. Acoust. Soc. Amer.* 66:651-53.

Elliott, L., Connors, S., Kille, E., Levin, S., Ball, K. and Katz, D. 1979. Children's understanding of monosyllabic nouns in quiet and in noise. *J. Acoust. Soc. Amer.* 66:12-21.

Flavell, J. 1977. *Cognitive development.* Englewood Cliffs, NJ: Prentice-Hall, Inc.

Greisen, D. and Rasmussen, P. 1970. Stapedius muscle reflexes and otoneurological examinations in brain stem tumors. *Acta Otolaryngol.* 70:366-70.

Hashimoto, I., Ishiyama, Y., and Tozuka, G. 1979. Bilaterally recorded brain stem auditory evoked responses. Their asymmetric abnormalities and lesions of the brain stem. *Arch. Neurol.* 36:161-67.

Hebbler, S. 1979. *Advanced statistical analysis.* Radio Shack TRS-80 Microcomputer System. Fort Worth, TX: Radio Shack.

Jerger, J. 1975. Diagnostic use of impedance measures. In *Handbook of clinical impedance audiometry,* ed. J. Jerger. New York: Amer. Electromedics Corp.

Jerger, J. 1960. Audiological manifestations of lesions in the auditory nervous system. *Laryngoscope* 70:417-25.

Jerger, J., Burney, P., Mauldin, L., and Crump, B. 1974. Predicting hearing loss from the acoustic reflex. *J. Speech Hear. Dis.* 39:11-22.

Jerger, J. and Hayes, D. 1977. Diagnostic speech audiometry. *Arch. Otolaryngol.* 103:216-22.

Jerger, J. and Hayes, D. 1976. The cross-check principle in pediatric audiometry. *Arch. Otolaryngol.* 102:614-20.

Jerger, J. and Jerger, S. 1975. Clinical validity of central auditory tests. *Scand. Audiol.* 4:147-63.

Jerger, J. and Jerger, S. 1974. Auditory findings in brain stem disorders. *Arch. Otolaryngol.* 99:342-50.

Jerger, J. and Jerger, S. 1971. Diagnostic significance of PB word function. *Arch. Otolaryngol.* 93:573-80.

Jerger, J., Lovering, L., and Wertz, M. 1972. Auditory disorder following bilateral temporal lobe insult: report of a case. *J. Speech Hear. Dis.* 37:523-35.

Jerger, J., Neely, G., and Jerger, S. 1980. Speech, impedance, and auditory brain stem response audiometry in brain stem tumors. Importance of a multiple test stretegy. *Arch. Otolaryngol.* 106:218-23.

Jerger, J., Weikers, N., Sharbrough, F., and Jerger, S. 1969. Bilateral lesions of the temporal lobe. A case study. *Acta Otolaryngol.,* suppl. 258:1-51.

Jerger, S. and Jerger, J. 1977. Diagnostic value of crossed vs uncrossed acoustic reflexes. Eighth nerve and brain stem disorders. *Arch. Otolaryngol.* 103:445-53.

Jerger, S. and Jerger, J. 1975. Extra- and intra-axial brain stem auditory disorders. *Audiol.* 14:93-117.

Jerger, S., Lewis, S., Hawkins, J. and Jerger, J. 1980. Pediatric speech intelligibility test. I. generation of test materials. *Int. J. Pediat. Otorhinolaryngol.* 2:217-30.

Katz, J., Basil, R., and Smith, J. 1963. A staggered spondaic word test for detecting central auditory lesions. *Ann. Otol. Rhinol. Laryngol.* 72:908-17.

Klahr, D. and Wallace, J. 1970. An information processing analysis of some Piagetian experiental tasks. *Cog. Psychol.* 1:358-87.

Kobasigawa, A. 1974. Utilization of retrieval cues by children in recall. *Child Develop.* 45:127-34.

Lee, L. 1971. *The Northwestern syntax screening test.* Evanston, IL: Northwestern Univ. Press.

Lee, L. 1977. Reply to Arndt and Byrne. *J. Speech and Hear. Dis.* 42:323-27.

Liden, G. and Korsan-Bengtsen, M. 1973. Audiometric manifestations of retrocochlear lesions. *Scand. Audiol.* 2:29-40.

Luszcz, M. and Bacharach, V. 1980. Preschoolers' picture recognition memory: the pitfalls of knowing how a thing shall be called. *Canad. J. Psychol. Rev.* 34:155-60.

Menyuk, P. 1969. *Sentences children use.* Cambridge, MA: MIT Press.

Mills, J. 1977. Noise and children: a review of literature. *J. Acoust. Soc. Amer.* 58:767-79.

Miller, G. and Johnson-Laird, P. 1976. *Language and perception.* Cambridge, MA: Harvard Univ. Press.

Muma, J. 1978. *Language handbook. Concepts, assessment, intervention.* Englewood Cliffs, NJ: Prentice-Hall, Inc.

Muma, J. and Muma, D. 1979. *Muma assessment program. Descriptive assessment procedures: cognitive-linguistic-communicative systems.* Lubbock, TX: Natural Child Pub. Co.

Niemeyer, W. and Sesterhenn, G. 1974. Calculating the hearing threshold from the stapedius reflex threshold for different sound stimuli. *Audiol.* 13:421-27.

Norman, D. 1976. *Memory and attention. An introduction to human information processing.* 2nd ed. New York: John Wiley & Sons, Inc.

Pinheiro, M. 1977. Tests of central auditory function in children with learning disabilities. In *Central auditory function,* ed. R. W. Keith. New York: Grune and Stratton.

Pfau, E. and Albrecht, R. 1976. Sprachentwicklung und sprachaudiometrie bei vorchulkindern. *Folia Phoniat.* 28:112-18.

Slobin, D. 1971. *Psycholinguistics.* Glenview, IL: Scott, Foresman, and Co.

Stockard, J. and Rossiter, V. 1977. Clinical and pathologic correlates of brain stem auditory response abnormalities. *Neurology* 27:316-25.

Willeford, J. 1976. Central auditory function with learning disabilities. *Audiol. Hear. Ed.* 2:12-20.

Young, E. and Tracy, J. 1976. An experiment short form of the staggered spondaic word list for learning disabled children. *Audiol. Hear. Ed.* 3:7-11.

Questions and Answers

Q: What materials do you use for the competing message? How did you select the message to competition ratio? On the PI function, is the competing message presented ipsilaterally or contralaterally?

A: The competing messages for the word and sentence test items are the normal children's responses to the rejected sentence stimulus pictures. In other words, we had a pool of 30 sentence stimulus pictures as I previously described. Out of this pool we selected the 10 pictures that the normal children identified consistently and correctly for the test sentences. We had 20 sentence cards remaining. The responses to these 20 rejected cards became the competing sentences.

To select the message-to-competition ratio (MCR) for the performance vs. intensity (PI) functions, we defined performance in normal children as a function of the MCR. To do this, we presented the word and sentence test items at 50 dB SPL and varied the MCR from + 10 to -10 dB. Our goal was to find the elbow of the MCR function, that point where the normal children could just get about 90% correct. Above that point, the task was too easy; below that point, the task was too hard. On the basis of these data, we selected an MCR of 0 dB for sentence materials and + 4 dB for word materials. For the PI functions, the competing sentence is presented to the same ear that receives the test word or sentence; in other words, we use an ipsilateral competing message (ICM) for the PI functions.

58

Q: Are the PSI speech materials tape recorded and, if so, by whom?

A: The PSI materials were tape recorded by two male talkers with general American dialect. One talker recorded the word and sentence test items. The other talker recorded the competing sentences.

Q: Why did you use the NSST? Do you use any of the Goldman-Fristoe-Woodcock battery?

A: When we began this project to have children generate the speech materials, we called colleagues around the U.S. and explained what we were trying to do and asked their advice. They routinely advised us to use the Peabody Picture Vocabulary Test and the Northwestern Syntax Screening Test. Our friends were perhaps noting that we needed to quantify expressive language ability, as well as receptive language and vocabulary skills. Anyway, after we got the data, we went back and looked at what correlated best with our results and it was the NSST. I realize that the NSST norms are based on a restricted socioeconomic range of children. However, this test worked best for us.

     About the Goldman-Fristoe-Woodcock battery, we are not using this test at the present time. In a personal conversation that I had with Dr. Goldman, he told me that he thought his standardization sample was limited below about 3 1/2 years of age. Since we were testing children less than 3 1/2 years old, we decided not to use the GFW test. However, Dr. Goldman and I have discussed some possible collaborative projects for the future.

Q: Susan Jerger, will your test be commercially available and has it been published anywhere?

A: First, we have written one article so far on the generation of the test materials. It is in press in the *International Journal of Pediatric Otorhinolaryngology*.

     Second, the PSI test is not commercially available. After we have developed the norms to our satisfaction and have gained some clinical experience with it, perhaps we can find a way to distribute it to people who are interested.

Q: Would you comment on the implications of your new test for education, habilitation, etc.

A: I would say that poor performance on any of the available auditory tests may be attributable to many different kinds of abnormalities as elucidated by Drs. Johnson and Culbertson. They have pointed out that you can't answer "Why" by just administering one test in isolation. You need to look at strategy and other underlying sources of test behavior. I can just say at this point that my goal was to try to document reliably auditory function in children with normal hearing and with hearing loss. If these children have evidence of central auditory disorder on the PSI test, particularly those with normal hearing, then we can refer them for further, appropriate testing, such as psychological and speech/language evaluations. After we have reliably documented that something is wrong, we and the other resource people who have been helping us can consider the "Why" question.

4
Audiological and Auditory Language Tests of Central Auditory Function

Robert W. Keith, Ph.D.

The evaluation of central auditory function in children is a complex task requiring a great deal of information in many areas, including anatomy of the auditory pathways, auditory abilities, and speech and language development. In addition, knowledge of auditory tests, including their administration and interpretation, factors that can affect auditory test results, and application of test findings to remediation programs are necessary. While this list is not inclusive, it helps to emphasize that evaluation of central auditory function cannot be approached simplistically and without adequate preparation.

In my introductory remarks to the symposium, I commented on the problems caused by lack of agreement on terminology and lack of consensus on cause and effect relationships between auditory perceptual disorders and language learning problems. These issues are posed by perceptual deficit versus verbal mediation deficit hypotheses that are discussed in the preface. Nevertheless, as debate persists, it is necessary for us to continue to evaluate children with communication disorders and to initiate remediation programs. The purpose of this brief communication is to evaluate some of the procedures being used and to provide a framework for clinicians to use in evaluating central auditory function.

Preliminary Evaluation

History

The approach to auditory evaluation should reflect fundamental clinical skills and not be totally test bound. Our clinical skills include especially careful history taking and observation of child, parent, and child-parent interactions. I will not dwell on fundamentals of history taking, since that subject should be familiar to everyone at this conference.

Every history should include questions about possible middle ear problems. Special areas of concern in the historic evaluation of auditory perceptual abilities include the following:

1. Auditory attention (does the child listen? for how long? does he say "huh" and "what" frequently?);

2. Auditory memory (can he remember things said, and in the proper sequence?);
3. Auditory performance in the presence of background noise (can he listen selectively and ignore background sound? is he abnormally sensitive to noise?);
4. Latency of response to verbal command or questions (does he require a long time to respond appropriately?).

Various authors have suggested formats for taking auditory histories that can be adapted for use in evaluating central auditory function (Katz and Strickman 1972; Myklebust 1954), and others have made specific recommendations for this child population (Cole and Wood 1978; Keith 1980b). In addition, Fisher (1980) has designed an auditory problem screening checklist for parents and teachers that can also be used as a basis for organizing a history-taking interview. Whether an examiner uses a blank piece of paper to record the history, as Dr. Ferry does, or uses the structured format of a questionnaire, the history should be systematic, complete, and informative.

Another part of the evaluation includes observation of the child's total behavior, including his auditory responses. These observations can serve both to verify and to add to information gained through the history interview. While it is preferable to observe the child in his normal home and school environment, observation of behavior in a clinic situation can be extremely valuable. It may also be useful to keep anecdotal notes of behavior observed during formal testing to help interpret test results.

Peripheral Hearing Tests

The auditory evaluation should always begin with an assessment of auditory sensitivity and middle-ear function. Pure tone air-conduction thresholds must be obtained in a quiet environment meeting ANSI standards for acceptable background noise during audiometric testing. Persons doing tests of central auditory abilities in schools should remember that pure tone screening tests and even pure tone threshold testing done in noisy environments fail to identify children with mild but educationally disadvantageous conductive hearing losses. In such situations, the addition of immitance tests, especially tympanometry, will help identify middle-ear dysfunction that may contribute to the child's poor auditory responses. A conductive or sensorineural hearing loss can have profound effects on central test battery interpretation. The importance of adequate preliminary assessment of middle-ear and cochlear function cannot be overemphasized.

An undistorted speech intelligibility test in a quiet environment should also be done as a baseline for interpreting other tests that utilize a speech signal. While this test usually has minimum diagnostic value, it is important to know whether performance is reduced. The addition of performance-intensity (PI) testing for undistorted words can give additional information. The PI function of some children with impaired auditory perception shows abnormal growth, requiring additional intensity for good intelligibility.

Following these preliminary tests, the central auditory battery can take two different directions. These include what I prefer to call (until better terminology is suggested) (1) tests of auditory neuromaturational level and (2) tests of auditory language function. While both approaches probably will be used with a given child, they should be recognized as being distinctly different.

Tests of Auditory Neuromaturational Level

Many currently used tests of central auditory function are able, if properly interpreted, to tell us about auditory maturational levels. These results may provide insight into the auditory neurological system and yield information about why an auditory language learning problem exists. In her previous remarks, Dr. Ferry stated a basic premise about brain and language function, i.e., that, with some exceptions, "delay or deviation in language development is due to disordered brain function." This disordered brain function may be reflected in several ways, including failure to develop normal asymmetry of cerebral function, i.e., no hemispheric dominance of language; inability to localize sounds; poor ability to synthesize or integrate sounds or to separate sounds presented to the two ears; poor ability to listen to a primary message in the presence of a competing background sound, etc.

In situations where the neurological structure is inadequate for processing a complex acoustic signal in an imperfect listening environment, language learning problems may result. Given an immature auditory pathway, it is reasonable to assume that language may develop to a certain degree and then reach a plateau because of structural limitations. For example, when the neurological system is not sufficiently redundant to interpret low redundancy speech signals, or not sufficiently mature to develop multiple meaningful associations, the child may have limited vocabulary and reduced intellectual abilities.

I propose that tests of auditory neuromaturational level reflect fundamental auditory abilities. These abilities could be called primary perception (as opposed to conception), or what Dr. Doris Johnson terms auditory capacity (as opposed to auditory strategy). In order to qualify as a test of auditory neuromaturational levels, therefore, a test has to meet the following criteria:

1. It cannot be loaded with language comprehension items.
2. It cannot require linguistic manipulation of the signal.
3. It should not utilize (but when necessary should minimize) cross sensory input (auditory-visual) or response modality (e.g., auditory-motor).
4. It should utilize non-linguistic signals.
5. It must be primarily a speech imitative task using non-meaningful ma-

terial or speech stimuli so familiar to the person being tested that comprehension plays no role in the response.

Given these restrictions, a number of auditory tests of neuromaturational level may be described:

1. Auditory localization

2. Binaural synthesis
   a. Binaural fusion
   b. Rapidly alternating speech perception
   c. Masking level differences

3. Binaural separation
   a. Staggered spondaic words
   b. Competing sentences
   c. Dichotic CV identification

4. Resistance to distortion
   a. Auditory figure ground
   b. Filtered speech
   c. Time compressed speech

Some specific examples of tests and interpretation follow.

Auditory Localization

Tests of auditory localization are used every day when testing infants in audiology clinics and can be easily adapted for older children. Since localization skills are established at a very early age, it is clearly abnormal for a child past infancy to be unable to localize sound sources when peripheral hearing is normal.

Binaural Synthesis

Of the various tests of binaural synthesis, both the binaural fusion and the Rapidly Alternating Speech Perception (RASP) are incorporated into the central auditory test pattern of Willeford (1977, 1980). During the binaural fusion test, a low-pass band (500-700 Hz) and high-pass band (1900-2100 Hz) of spondaic words are presented simultaneously to opposite ears. The test ear is considered to be the ear receiving the low-pass band. Although this somewhat arbitrary definition does not follow from the traditional definition of binaural tests (Matzker 1959; Smith and Resnick 1972), it is not an issue for discussion here. The RASP is administered by presenting sentences that are switched from one ear to the other in alternating bursts of 300 msec.

Available normative data on RASP tests yield excellent performance approaching 100% scores even in children down to five years of age, with little normal variability. Normal RASP scores are shown on table 1. The binaural fusion norms, given by age level, are shown on figure 1 (Willeford 1978). A fairly wide range of response is indicated at the earlier ages, with variability decreasing and mean performance increasing with age.

Age	N	LE	RE	LE	RE	LE	RE
5	25	99.2	99.2	2.6	3.9	90/100	80/100
6	25	98.3	98.0	2.2	4.6	90/100	80/100
7	25	98.3	99.5	2.2	2.2	90/100	90/100
8	25	98.8	99.5	1.4	2.2	90/100	90/100
9	25	98.8	99.8	1.4	1.4	90/100	90/100
10	25	99.8	100.0	1.4	0.0	90/100	100/100
5/10	150	98.9	99.3	1.9	2.4	90/100	80/100

Left and right ears are scored according to ear in which stimulus items are initted (lead ear). Each ear becomes the lead ear 10 times after 20 items. Lists A and B.

Table 1.
Mean percent correct, standard deviation and range of scores obtained on normal children using a test of Rapidly Alternating Speech Perception (RASP). Results are reported at each age level between 5 and 10 years (Willeford 1978).

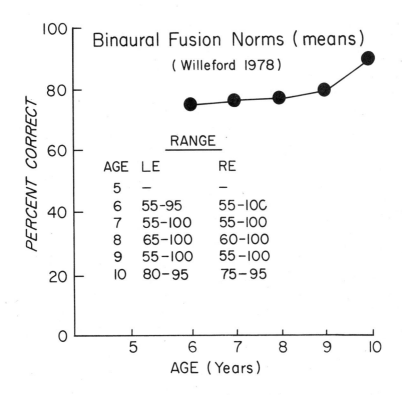

Figure 1.
Mean percent and range of correct scores obtained on normal children using a test of binaural fusion. Results are plotted at each level between 6 and 10 years. N = 40 in each age group (Willeford, 1978).

Masking level differences (MLD) are obtained by measuring speech thresholds in the presence of noise for two conditions: (1) with both speech and masker in phase at the two ears and (2) with the speech out of phase and noise in phase at the two ears. The binaural release from masking that normally results from these testing conditions is approximately 10 dB.

Normal peripheral hearing and the ability and understanding to perform the task are necessary precursors to successful binaural synthesis testing. When these conditions are met, any child who shows binaural fusion difficulties, or who cannot understand rapidly alternating speech, or who does not achieve release from masking on MLD tasks, can be assumed to exhibit compromise of brainstem integrity.

Binaural Separation

There are at least three tests of binaural separation. This group of tests is usually considered to assess function at the cortical level. The familiar Staggered Spondaic Word Test (SSW) by Katz (1968, 1977) presents overlapping spondees to the two ears, as shown:

Time Sequence

	#1	#2	#3
Right Ear	UP	STAIRS	
Left Ear		DOWN	TOWN
	non-competing	competing	non-competing

SSW test results can be interpreted according to data made available by Katz (1976) that are shown on table 2.

Note the superior performance in the right ear with competing word in the left (RC condition) at the early ages, and the gradual improvement in right and left ear performance and reduction in variability as children mature. Children with auditory processing problems score far below the average for their age, fail to show ear dominance effects, or fail to increase the left ear score with age. To determine neuromaturational age levels, one can compare a given child's scores to the age norms. For example, a 12-year-old child with an RC score of 40% and an LC score of 60% performs functionally like a 6 year-old. Also, by retesting a child over a period of two or three years, it is possible to determine whether further maturation of the auditory pathway has occurred and the rate at which maturation is taking place.

The stimulus paradigm of the binaural separation test included in the Willeford battery (1977, 1980) is shown in Figure 2. In this test, sentences are presented simultaneously to separate ears, with the primary message 15 dB lower than the competing message. The test results can be interpreted according to the normative data shown in figure 3. This figure shows a strong right ear advantage for young children, with left ear scores im-

66

Age	Right Non-Competing	Right Competing	Left Competing	Left Non-Competing
6	1.35 (10.58)	16.8 (13.16)	32.0 (16.62)	3.65 (11.02)
7	.5 (5.11)	16.0 (18.87)	28.0 (14.9)	0 (3.8)
8	−4.3 (5.0)	1.7 (8.4)	18.0 (14.89)	−1.5 (8.10)
9	−1.3 (5.75)	4.2 (5.96)	16.7 (16.24)	−.3 (4.14)
10	−2.2 (3.17)	1.8 (4.41)	9.2 (9.46)	−1.8 (3.14)
11	−1.7 (4.73)	2.3 (7.22)	3.6 (5.09)	−1.9 (1.90)

Table 2.
Mean percent error and standard deviation (in parentheses) of corrected staggered spondaic word tests obtained on normal children. Results are reported at each age level between 6 and 11 years (Katz, 1976).

DICHOTICALLY–COMPETING MESSAGES

Figure 2.
Illustration of dichotically competing messages used in the binaural separation test. (Reprinted from Willeford, 1977, with permission of Grune and Stratton).

proving with age. Note, especially, the normal wide range of scores obtained in the left ear of children between the ages of 5 and 8 years of age. Again, the neuromaturational level can be determined by comparing a given child's scores to normative data. Retesting over a period of time can establish whether maturation of central auditory function has occurred.

Dichotic CV listening tasks usually employ a set of six consonant-vowel nonsense syllables that are presented simultaneously in pairs to the two ears. The six CV syllables are /pa/, /ta/, /ka/, /ba/, /da/, and /ga/. Thirty to sixty pairs of stimuli are presented, and scores are obtained for right to left ears. Performance of normal children shows a right ear advantage from the age of 5 years (the youngest age reported in the literature). With age the performance of right and left ears improves (Mirabile et al. 1978), although the difference between ears is maintained into the adult years (Olsen 1977). As children grow older, their capacity to produce a correct response to stimuli presented to both ears also improves (Berlin et al. 1973).

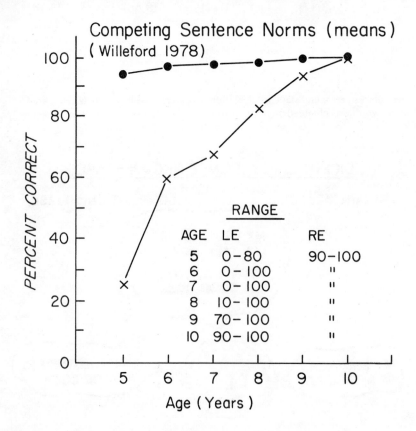

Figure 3.
Mean percent and range of correct scores obtained on normal children using a competing sentence test of binaural separation. Results are plotted at each age level between 5 and 10 years. N = 25 at age 5 and N = 40 for all other age groups.

Dichotic listening tests are used to study hemispheric dominance of language-disordered and dyslexic children (Sommers and Taylor 1972; Pettit and Helms 1979; Hynd and Obrzut 1978; Knox and Roeser 1980). In these children failure to establish hemispheric dominance for language function, as evidenced by dichotic listening results, may indicate a neurological basis for their language, reading, or learning problem.

Resistance to Distortion

Tests of a child's resistance to distortion utilize the traditional audiological diagnostic model described by Teatini (1970). This model proposes that persons with normal auditory systems have little difficulty understanding distorted speech with reduced acoustic redundancy. However, when the auditory system also has reduced redundancy because of a specific lesion or other neurological abnormality, the person has much greater difficulty understanding distorted speech.

Three speech tests with reduced redundancy are suggested here: speech in noise (auditory figure ground), filtered speech, and time compressed

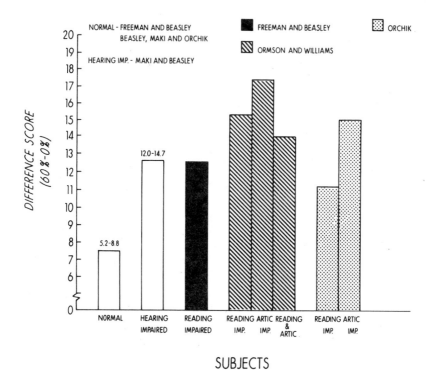

Figure 4.
Percent difference score results of 60% and 0% time compressed speech obtained on normal children and children with hearing losses, articulatory problems, and reading impairments. (Reprinted from Beasley and Freeman, 1977, with permission of Grune and Stratton).

speech. In each case it is important to refrain from distorting the speech so badly that the task becomes one of auditory closure. That is, when a great deal of the acoustic signal is absent, the task becomes a cognitive one, requiring the child to "fill in" or to guess at the entire message when part is missing. For example, speech in competing noise at favorable S/N ratios (+9 dB or so) is a distorted speech task, but speech at 0 or -6 dB S/N ratio becomes a direct masking study that assesses auditory closure abilities. Similarly, since low pass filtered speech at 500 Hz may be too difficult for young children, while low-pass filtered speech at 1000 Hz may be more suitable (Farrer 1977).

Regardless of technical details of acoustic signals, current tests that use distorted speech can separate those children who have central difficulties from those who do not. Using tests of time compressed speech, Beasley and Freeman (1977) have published data (see figure 4) showing poorer performance by children with reading and articulation difficulties when compared to normals. Although Beasley and Freeman have published some data indicating improved performance on time compressed speech tasks as a function of age, their data are not complete.

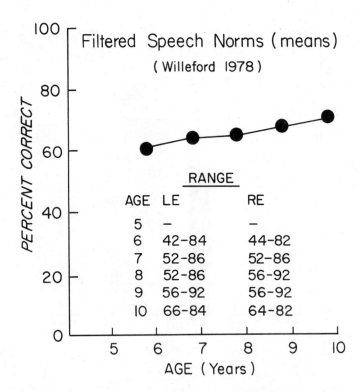

Figure 5.
Mean percent and range of correct scores obtained on normal children using a 500 Hz low-pass filtered speech test. Results are plotted at each age level between 6 and 10 years. N = 40 at each age level. (Willeford, 1978).

Normative data from the Willeford (1978) 500 Hz low-pass filtered speech test is shown in figure 5. These data show improvement in average performance with age but indicate a wide range of scores for all ages reported.

The mean error scores from the Goldman-Fristoe-Woodcock Test of Auditory Discrimination (Goldman, Fristoe, and Woodcock 1970) are shown in figure 6. Both the quiet and noise subtests show improvement in performance with age, and represent data that can be used to establish a child's level of performance. Speech testing in noise can also yield information about a child's functional auditory behavior in a noisy classroom.

Other approaches to evaluating fundamental auditory capacities using nonlinguistic or low-level cognitive tasks have been developed. For example, Devens, Hoyer, and McGroskey (1978) have demonstrated that learning-disabled children as a group were inferior in their abilities to track a moving speech signal and moving white noise. In addition, McGroskey and Kidder (1980) showed that normal children experience auditory fusion of two-tone pulses at shorter time intervals than was true for reading-disordered or learning-disabled children. Tallal (1978) also showed that temporal order imperception is present in children with abnormal language development. Further discussion of central auditory testing is available elsewhere (Keith 1977, 1980a).

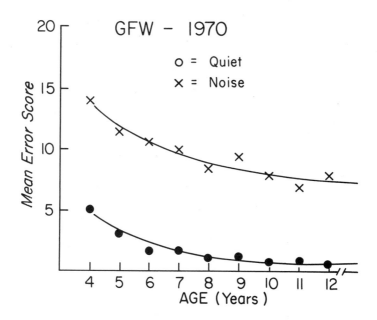

Figure 6.
Mean error scores obtained by normal subjects on the Quiet and Noise subtest of the Goldman-Fristoe-Woodcock Test of Auditory Discrimination. Results are plotted at each age level between 4 and 12 years. (Goldman et al., 1970).

In summary, all neuromaturational tests of central auditory function have the following characteristics (Keith 1980b):

1. They are applicable only after the emergence of language, requiring either pointing to a picture that represents the stimulus word or repeating a syllable, word, or sentence.
2. Many of the tests indicate substantial maturational effects. Generally, at early ages, results of these tests are highly variable, with average performance improving remarkably between 6 years and 12 years of age. No age-related data are reported for Masking Level Difference tests. Rapidly Alternating Speech Perception (RASP) is nearly as good at age 5 as at age 12.
3. They reveal that at approximately 12 years of age the auditory system of normal children has matured to the point where responses approximate those of adult listeners.
4. They show that children with speech, language, reading, and learning problems perform poorly; although some children with language or reading problems yield normal scores, others with poor auditory test results have normal language.

Finally, these tests are helpful in the following ways:

1. They may describe the maturation level of the central auditory pathways and, through longitudinal studies on a given child, demonstrate maturation of central auditory abilities.
2. They may identify progressive neurological disease.
3. They can assess improvement in auditory abilities resulting from medication.
4. They may aid in ruling out abnormalities of the central auditory pathways as contributing to a language learning problem.
5. They may describe whether cerebral dominance for language has occurred.
6. They can indicate whether the auditory channel is "weak" or "strong," and whether classroom, tutoring, or remedial material should be introduced via auditory channels when teaching through strengths.
7. They are useful for research into auditory perceptual problems.

It should be clear, however, that these tests of central auditory function cannot be expected to indicate specific language, learning or reading deficits. Nor, when used alone, can they indicate clear remediation strategies for language/learning-disordered children, although remediation can follow from a more broadly based assessment.

Auditory-Language Tests

In the previous section I have attempted to describe test procedures that may indicate a child's auditory capacity from a neurological point of view. Those I prefer to call auditory-language tests are those that have such a heavy language bias that their only resemblance to an "auditory" test is that they utilize an acoustic signal.

In a typical description of central auditory abilities, many factors listed involve language processing or cognitive manipulation of an acoustic signal. For example, the ability to store and retrieve auditory stimuli and to do it in the proper sequence (auditory memory span and sequence); the ability to identify phonemes, syllables, or morphemes embedded into words (auditory analysis); the ability to blend isolated phonemes into words (phonemic synthesis); the ability to determine the whole word when part is missing (auditory closure) - all are examples of language based tasks. Tests designed to measure these abilities do not, in fact, provide any insights into fundamental auditory capacity. Instead, they are designed to provide information about cognitive strategies, (i.e., how well the child can use language).

Cognitive factors are even more pronounced when cross modality responses are required or when a child is required to manipulate objects or pictures. When the child is directed to point to a line drawing in response to a verbal signal, for example, it is difficult to know whether visual perception or auditory perception is the problem in an abnormal response.

Some examples of tests that assess auditory-language abilities can be given. The Denver Auditory Phoneme Sequencing Test (Aten 1979) contains a sequential section subtest that requires children to point to a series of pictures in the same order in which they were heard. Aten has found that children up to the age of 12 years show a progression in ability to retain words that are minimally phonemically varied. This test may show the effects of increased memory with age. It may also differentiate children with difficulty in language learning, spelling, and other academic areas. As defined here, however, these are auditory-language deficits, and not "deficits in auditory perception," as stated by the author (Aten 1979).

The Auditory Analysis Test (Rosner and Simon 1971) requires the child to form a new word when a phoneme or syllable is removed from a longer word. For example, (g)ate without (g) is "ate," (t)rail without (t) is "rail," and g(l)ow without the (l) is "go." To do this task the child must be able to identify the phoneme in the word even though the sound spoken in isolation is acoustically different from what it is when co-articulated. Therefore, it is not a simple discrimination task. In addition, when a phoneme in the middle position has been identified and "removed" from the word, the child must blend the remaining sounds into a new word. This is clearly a complex language mediated task.

A number of tests directly or indirectly measure auditory closure. This ability occurs when the child is able to understand the whole word or message when part is missing or missed. One example is the Auditory Closure Subtest of the Illinois Test of Psycholinguistic Abilities (Kirk, McCarthy, and Kirk 1968). To administer the test, the examiner says "airpla ____" and the correct response is "airplane." Other examples are "tele/one" (telephone); "/isher/an" (fisherman); etc. In order to do an auditory closure task, it is necessary to have an adequate knowledge of the language being used.

73

Other tests measure auditory closure in different ways. The Flowers-Costello (1970) Tests of Central Auditory Abilities include a low-pass filtered speech test. When part of the word is missing acoustically, the child must know the language in order to respond correctly. In addition, speech-in-noise tests at signal-to-noise ratios that mask parts of the acoustic spectrum are also tests of auditory closure. In this case the masking of the speech signal forces the child to understand the whole word when parts are missing. Among recent tests, the Goldman-Fristoe-Woodcock Auditory Selective Attention Test (Goldman, Fristoe, and Woodcock 1974) uses competing sounds that increase from a positive to negative signal-to-noise ratio, making the listening task progressively more difficult. The authors state that this test battery identifies subjects who are "deficient in selective attention skills" (Goldman, Fristoe, and Woodcock 1974). It seems, however, that the listening task is more complex than described by the authors, and at least one language skill (auditory closure) is also assessed.

A slightly different situation exists in another test described by these authors. The Goldman-Fristoe-Woodcock Test of Auditory Discrimination (Goldman, Fristoe, and Woodcock 1970) Noise Subtest uses a constant + 9 dB Signal-to-Noise ratio that provides less direct masking than the Selective Attention test. However, this test can serve as an example of a class of tests that assess several cognitive skills simultaneously. The first cognitive skill is vocabulary, with words like "shack," "vine," "tack," or "rake" being more or less familiar to a child, depending on his circumstance. During a pre-test training procedure, the examiner helps the child learn the association between word and picture. During the test, therefore, the child is required to remember any new associations recently learned. The use of pictures obviously requires visual perception, auditory visual associations, and an auditory-visual-motor response. Finally, the tests assesses the child's ability to discriminate among speech sounds under different conditions of quiet and noise.

Many other examples of auditory-language tests can be given. These comments are not intended to detract from the usefulness of these tests in assessing children's ability to use auditory input. The point is that it is misleading to say that auditory function is being assessed when the task is primarily language oriented. The least we can do in these cases is to drop the term "auditory" in favor of "auditory-language" to more precisely describe the situation.

Remediation

The remediation approach to central auditory disorders will take different directions, depending on the outcome of the total battery of auditory perceptual and auditory-language tests, along with language tests, reading tests, and other educational observations and tests. When a child has fundamental auditory problems, remediation may attempt to compensate for the deficiencies by special placement, teaching through strengths, maximizing auditory abilities through use listening programs, teaching verbal mediation skills, etc. When children have language learning disorders, clinicians may use any of the additional approaches that will be discussed at this conference.

Summary

In summary, it seems to me (1) that central auditory function is an entity that needs increased study, understanding, and defintion; (2) that neurological dysfunction can compromise the ability of the child to process complex acoustic stimuli or to acquire the associations necessary to learn sophisticated language; (3) that tests of central auditory function can indicate when auditory-based problems may be present which contribute to the child's language learning problems; (4) that remediation programs can go a long way toward alleviating the problems caused by these auditory-based disorders; and (5) that future research should involve creative development of non-linguistically loaded stimuli that can better assess auditory abilities apart from language abilities.

References

Aten, J. 1979. *The Denver auditory phoneme sequencing test.* Houston: College-Hill Press.

Beasley, D. and Freeman, B. 1977. Time altered speech as a measure of central auditory processing. In *Central auditory dysfunction,* ed. R.W. Keith. New York: Grune and Stratton.

Berlin, C., Hughes, L. et al. 1973. Dichotic right ear advantage in children 5-13. *Cortex* 9:393-401.

Cole, P. and Wood, M. 1978. Differential diagnosis. In *Pediatric audiology,* ed. F. Martin. Englewood Cliffs, NJ: Prentice Hall, Inc.

Devens, J., Hoyer, E., and McGroskey, R. 1978. Dynamic auditory localization by normal and learning-disability children. *J. Amer. Audiol. Soc.* 3:172-78.

Farrer, S. 1977. An experimental design for a filtered word test to identify auditory learning-disabled children. Unpublished Masters' thesis, University of Cincinnati, Cincinnati, Ohio.

Fisher, L. 1980. Learning disabilities and auditory processing. In *The speech-language pathologist in the schools,* ed. R. van Hattum. Springfield, IL: C C Thomas

Flowers, A. and Costello, R. 1970. *Flowers-Costello test of central auditory abilities.* Dearborn, MI: Perceptual Learning Systems.

Goldman, R., Fristoe, M., and Woodcock, R. 1970. *GFW test of auditory discrimination.* Circle Pines, MN: American Guidance Service, Inc.

Goldman, R., Fristoe, M., and Woodcock, R. 1974. *GFW auditory selective attention test.* Circle Pines, MN: American Guidance Service, Inc.

Hynd, G. and Obrzut, J. 1978. Differential assessment of cerebral dominance and developmental reading disorders using the dichotic listening task. *Psychology* 15:1-16.

Katz, J. 1977. The staggered spondaic word test. In *Central auditory dysfunction,* ed. R.W. Keith. New York: Grune and Stratton.

Katz, J. 1976. *C-SSW Means (+ S.D.'s).* SSW short course handout, University of Cincinnati Medical Center.

Katz, J. 1968. The SSW Test: An interim report. *J. Speech Hear. Dis.* 33:132-46.

Katz, J. and Strickmann, S. 1972. A case history for children. In *Handbook of clinical audiology*, 1st ed., ed. J. Katz. Baltimore: Williams and Wilkins.

Keith, R.W. 1980a. Central auditory test battery. In *Speech, language and hearing*, eds. N.J. Lass, L.V. McReynolds, J.L. Northern, and D.E. Yoder. Philadelphia: W.B. Saunders Co.

Keith, R.W. 1980b. Tests of central auditory function. In *Auditory disorders in school children*, eds. R. Roeser and M. Downs. New York: Brian C. Decker.

Keith, R.W., ed. 1977. *Central auditory dysfunction*. New York: Grune and Stratton.

Kirk, S., McCarthy, J., and Kirk, W. 1968. *Illinois Test of Psycholinguistic Abilities*. Urbana, IL: University of Illinois Press.

Knox, C. and Roeser, R. 1980. Cerebral dominance and auditory perceptual asymmetries in normal and dyslexic children. *Seminars in speech, language and hearing* 1:181-94.

Matzker, J. 1959. Two new methods for the assessment of central auditory function in cases of brain disease. *Ann. Otol. Rhinol. Laryngol.* 68:1185-97.

McGroskey, R. and Kidder, H. 1980. Auditory fusion among learning-disabled, reading-disabled, and normal children. *J. Learn. Disabil.* 13:18-25.

Mirabile, P., Porter, R., Hughes, L., and Berlin, C. 1978. Dichotic lag effect in children 7 to 15. *Developm. Psychol.* 14:277-85.

Myklebust, H. 1954. *Auditory disorders in school children: a manual for differential diagnosis*. New York: Grune and Stratton.

Olsen, W. 1977. Performance of temporal lobectomy patients with dichotic CV test materials. Presentation at the Annual Convention of The American Speech and Hearing Association, November 2-5, Chicago.

Pettit, J. and Helms, S. 1979. Hemispheric language dominance of language-disordered, articulation-disordered, and normal children. *J. Learn. Disabil.* 12:71-6.

Rosner, J. and Simon, D. 1971. The auditory analysis test. *J. Learn. Disabil.* 4:384-92.

Smith, B. and Resnick, D. 1972. An auditory test for assessing brain-stem integrity: a preliminary report. *Laryngoscope* 82:414, 424.

Sommers, R. and Taylor, M. 1972. Cerebral speech dominance in language-disordered and normal children. *Cortex* 8:224-32.

Tallal, P. 1978. An experimental investigation of the role of auditory temporal processing in normal and disordered language development. In *Language acquisition and language breakdown*, eds. A. Caranazza and E. Zurif. Baltimore: Johns Hopkins University Press.

Teatini, G. 1970. Sensitized speech tests: results in normal subjects. In *Speech audiometry*, ed. C. Rojskjaer. Odense, Denmark: Danavox.

Willeford, J. 1980. Central auditory behaviors in learning-disabled children. *Seminars in speech, language and hearing* 1:127-40.

Willeford, J. 1978. Expanded central auditory test battery norms. Personal communication.

Willeford, J. 1977. Assessing central auditory behavior in children: a test battery approach. In *Central auditory dysfunction*, ed. R.W. Keith. New York: Grune and Stratton.

5

Considerations in the Assessment of Central Auditory Disorders in Learning-Disabled Children

Doris J. Johnson, Ph. D.

Children with learning disabilities are a complex, heterogeneous group of individuals. By definition, they have adequate sensory integrity, at least average mental ability, and no primary emotional disorders although many are frustrated because of their inability to learn normally. They are homogeneous because their potential exceeds their achievement in one or more areas of learning such as understanding or using spoken language, reading, writing, calculating, or in various aspects of nonverbal behavior such as body image and spatial orientation. Their underachievement is related to disturbances in one or more basic psychological processes such as attention, perception, memory or conceptualization. While there are problems associated with the definition of the population and with the precise assessment of various areas of learning, considerable research has been generated which has added to our understanding of their difficulties.

The primary purpose of this paper is to alert diagnosticians and researchers to factors which may interfere with the performance of learning disabled and other handicapped children. Although many tests are designed to assess a specific function, typically, many cognitive factors are involved. For example, the standardized tests of auditory memory for digits involve general comprehension of the task, attention, perception, memory, as well as both recall and reproduction of the digits. Children who perform below expectancy may fail for a variety of reasons other than poor auditory memory.

Audiologists and others who are involved in assessing auditory acuity in young children are aware that tests must be selected according to the child's age and developmental level. The procedures that can be used with the 4 year old cannot be used with children under 2 years because of various developmental and cognitive factors. Handicapped children, particularly those with specific learning disabilities, may have a variety of subtle processing disorders which interfere with their performance. Thus, the diagnostic team should be prepared to consider several factors when a child is seen for assessment or when they are interpreting the results of an evaluation.

Our orientation to the study of learning disabilities is one which views the child as an information processor, as one who has multiple modalities for input and output of information and the potential for a variety of complex integrative networks (Johnson 1977). The goals of the evaluation are to determine which input systems are intact and which may be less efficient, to ascertain which modes of response are available, and to note which types of information the children are able to process at various levels. If one looks only at broad areas of achievement such as language, reading, or spelling, the subtle processing disturbances may not be identified. For example, some children with retrieval problems have difficulty with oral reading and may substitute words which have similar meanings. Similarly, children with visual perceptual and memory disturbances may reverse letters when writing but not when reading.

There are several theoretical schema that we use in our study of learning processes (Johnson and Myklebust 1967). The first relates to the broad concept of "input- integration-output." Children may have a disturbance at one or more levels; therefore, in order to provide the most effective remediation, efforts should be made to determine the source of the problem. When a child fails a task that requires a verbal response, it may be impossible to know whether the difficulty occurs at the level of input, integration or output. Hence, we find it helpful to begin the assessment by analyzing the modes of response or output that are intact.

Response Output

With infants reflexes may be the primary mode of response; as the child matures a variety of other responses become available, such as pointing or marking. Gesturing and pantomiming require a higher level of cognition because they often involve some aspects of symbolic behavior and planned motor movements. Thus, before giving children commands such as "Show me how you comb your hair," one should note whether the child can imitate the pattern, whether he or she can comprehend the language, and whether the imagery and representation are intact.

Some tasks require an understanding of the concepts of "same" and "different" (Wepman 1958). While such tests are very useful, the diagnostician should determine whether the child is able to comprehend the idea of sameness and of difference. It also is important to note whether the child is aware of the specific attributes which he or she is to compare. Blalock (1977) reported that children with language and learning disabilities tended to fail items that involved ambiguity. For example, the child who attends to irrelevant details may note minor variations in pictures, letters or prosody rather than attending to the major content. Thus, materials and directions should be very clear and explicit.

"Yes-No" responses are used in many tests and can be helpful in determining what a child knows, particularly the child who is unable to speak. However, occasionally, handicapped children do not have a consistent "yes-no" response; thus the clinician should evaluate this concept before beginning the assessment. "Yes or no" can be demonstrated by nodding or shaking the head, by saying the words, by pointing to the printed words or by writing. Experienced diagnosticians also should be aware of guessing and perseveration resonses. Additional checks for reliability may be needed.

In our work with language impaired and learning disabled children we have found that manipulation is a valuable mode of response for determining what a child knows. For example, the school age child who has severe difficulties with oral syntax and auditory memory may be able to demonstrate his knowledge of grammar (if he can read the material selected) when he is asked to organize words in sentences. Similarly, children who have visual-motor or visual memory problems may demonstrate their ability to spell by organizing cut-out letters or anagrams.

Children may fail many tests requiring oral responses because they have input problems, comprehension, apraxia and other articulation problems, retrieval difficulties and other expressive symbolic disorders. Other tests, particularly those associated with visual memory, require written responses. Failures may be due to disturbances of visual perception and visual motor integration as well as to memory. Similarly, when researchers measure visual memory by asking the child for an oral response, failure could be due to disorders in either visual or auditory processes. Prior to using a test which requires an auditory-motor or written response the diagnostician should evaluate the child's ability to respond appropriately.

With increasing age, maturation, and school instruction, the child is able to deal with many types of information and is able to respond in a variety of ways. Handicapped children, however, may have processing deficiencies that prevent them from demonstrating what they know. By choosing a mode of response that is intact, the diagnostician may obtain results which more accurately represent the child's input and integration abilities.

Cross Modal Sensory Integration

A second major theoretical schema pertains to the semi-autonomous systems concept described by Hebb (1963). He proposed that the brain is made up of systems which may operate semi-independently or together. This concept has many implications for assessment and remediation (Johnson and Myklebust 1967). Basically we are interested in knowing how a child learns through each sensory system and how he or she integrates information from two or more modalities. We try to ascertain whether a child can perceive, remember, and interpret what he or she hears, sees, or feels; then we explore integration or crossmodal learning. One of the major objectives is to explore which learning "circuits" are operative or inoperative. A second goal is to determine which combinations of input facilitate learning. In our work we have observed that some children are overloaded by multisensory inputs. On the other hand, some children with auditory disorders cannot profit from intrasensory stimulation. They may fail an intrasensory auditory task but when given pictures, objects or other figures to accompany the auditory stimulation, they perform better.

Researchers and diagnosticians should note the number of sensory systems required to perform tasks, particularly those tasks which purport to assess some process within a single sensory channel. For example, certain auditory discrimination tests require the child to point to pictures. Often, these are very appropriate, particularly for children who cannot handle a comparison task. On the other hand, a failure may be due to auditory processing disorders, visual processing disorders such as difficulties with picture interpretation, or cross modal disorders. Similarly, when children are given confrontation naming tasks which require picture naming, the diagnostician should be aware that failure may be due either to word retrieval or to delay in interpreting the picture. While these latter problems do not occur frequently, they are observed in children who have visual nonverbal perceptual disturbances. One 6 year old who was asked to point to figures named by the examiner during a picture vocabulary test made many more errors than expected. When the examiner asked the child to name several pictures, it was evident that the errors were due to disordered visual processes rather than to a language disturbance. For example, the child called the picture of a key a "six;" "spectacles were an "eight;" a rural mail box was "a piece of toast." Another 4 year old scored above average on all auditory tasks that did not involve pictures but scored somewhat below average on those that required the integration of the auditory and visual systems.

Considerable research in intra- and intersensory learning was stimulated by Birch and Belmont (1964) who reported that poor readers were deficient in intersensory learning because they could not integrate visual-spatial patterns with auditory temporal ones. Birch's work was later criticized by Bryant (1968) and others because he had not controlled intrasensory learning processes. Nevertheless, Birch stimulated considerable research. Bryant (1968) and Ettlinger (1967) review some major theoretical issues related to research in cross modal learning. Zaporozhets and Elkonin (1971) also provide theoretical hypotheses and data pertaining to normal development of cross modal perception.

Verbal and Nonverbal Learning

In our "systems analysis" approach to the study of learning disabilities we also feel that it is important to examine the child's ability to process various types of information. Thus, a third construct pertains to verbal and nonverbal learning. Verbal learning includes oral language, reading, written language, and similar forms of behavior whereas nonverbal learning involves the perception and/or interpretation of spatial orientation, geometric figures, melodies, etc.

Studies of brain function and hemispheric specializtion in recent years have enhanced our understanding of verbal and nonverbal leaning. While more clinical investigations are needed with young children, diagnosticians should review the nature of the tasks they use in assessment. A picture vocabulary test involves visual, nonverbal information and auditory verbal input. Thus, as indicated in the previous section, a failure may occur for many reasons. Many reading comprehension tests require the child to match printed words with pictures; thus visual verbal and visual nonverbal processes are required. A very careful, systematic analysis of the entire test battery given to a child will permit the examiner to see whether there are patterns of success or failure that relate to input-integration or output, to intra- or intersensory learning, and to verbal or nonverbal learning.

Level of Disturbance

A fourth and final theoretical schema involves the *level* of the disturbance (Myklebust 1960; Johnson and Myklebust 1967). We have suggested that a processing deficiency may occur at the level of attention, perception, memory (imagery), symbolization or conceptualization. While it is sometimes difficult to draw clear distinctions between these levels, efforts are made to study processing through each sensory channel.

Attention

Attention is one of the first processes to consider when studying learning disabled children. Many in this population are distractible, disinhibited and perseverative (Strauss and Lehtinen 1947). During the preschool years normal children appear to be somewhat distractible but with maturation, socialization, and environmental controls, they steadily improve in their ability to attend (Zaporozhets and Elkonin 1971). When attention controls do not develop the children have difficulty performing at the level of their ability. Some comment on the energy that is needed "just to listen."

Because even subtle attention problems may be present among learning disabled children, diagnosticians and researchers should be aware of potential problems. The testing environment should be free from distractions and considerable structure should be provided. Kagan (1965) found that impulsive children who fail to scan the task before making decisons tend to make more errors. Other researchers found that learning disabled children were more impulsive and less reflective than those who were normal (Keogh and Donlon 1972; Hallahan and Kauffman 1976). In our clinical work we have found that many of these children function below the level of their potential (Johnson 1979). In one instance a 6 year old made 15 errors on an auditory discrimination test the first time it was given. Later, using a different form, the clinician held the child's hand, encouraging him to look at all of the pictures before responding, and the child made only one

81

error. The same child scored at a 4 year level on a picture vocabulary test which was given without structure but he achieved a 6 year level when his hand was held and he scanned each picture before responding. The child had a problem but it was one of attention rather than one of perception or comprehension.

Researchers and others also should be aware of subtle signs of perseveration, that is, the tendency to repeat the same response without being able to shift. This behavior is often observed in adult aphasics but it is found in varying degrees among children with central nervous system involvement. Their inability to shift may be observed on any task that requires rapidly changing of responses.

Perception

The second level of processing that we consider is perception which we define as those processes that require a minimal amount of interpretation (Johnson and Myklebust 1967). The goal of our assessment at this level is to deterine whether the child can detect differences in sounds, words, phonemes, pictures, and other figures that he or she hears, sees, or feels. Disturbances of both visual and auditory perception have been reported in learning disabled children (Orton 1937; Strauss and Lehtinen 1947; Myklebust 1954; Eisenson 1972). In recent years studies have indicated that the problems may not be at the level of perception but may be at higher levels of cognition. Vellutino (1977), for example, suggests that many reading problems which formerly were attributed to the inaccurate perception of letters or words may, in fact, be due to linguistic difficulties, particularly when the child is asked to read aloud. Oral reading requires the retrieval and conversion of visual material to the auditory-motor system.

Researchers who use dichotic procedures should be aware of the various cognitive factors involved in the tasks. Often the tests require intersensory integration, pointing to syllables: saying syllables, or digits, etc. While some children may have no difficulty responding to these procedures, others with processing deficiencies may not be able to perform. Some of our young adults with severe reading disorders were unable to be tested on dichotic tasks which involved pointing to "pa" and "ba" because they still tended to invert and reverse letters.

Imagery

The third level on the hierarchy of experience is imagery. Many children have adequate attention and perception but they do not retain what they hear or see. Disturbances may occur in either short term or long term memory; they may occur at the level of recognition or recall; they also may occur in some sensory systems but not in others. Hence, a comprehensive study of the child is needed. Since the research in this area is so vast, we simply want to alert clinicians and others to the need for analyzing tasks and for noting the nature and type of memory requirements of each. Many tests that purport to measure auditory or visual memory may test many other cognitive functions including picture interpretation, language, and writing. Through a systematic analysis of the child's successes and failures, the diagnostician can identify the problem more clearly.

Symbolization

Symbolization is the next level of processing to be considered. This aspect of cognition involves representation and the ability to understand that something stands for something else. Symbolic behavior involves many aspects of nonverbal communication, picture interpretation, oral language, reading, writing and arithmetic. Many children with auditory language difficulties have problems with higher levels of symbolic behavior. Some also have problems with gesture and pantomime. The goal of the evaluation is to ascertain the breadth and depth of the symbolic disorder. Even though a child may appear to have primarily an oral language disorder, every attempt should be made to determine whether the child needs remediation in other aspects of learning.

Conceptualization

Finally, some children have difficulties with higher levels of conceptualization. They may comprehend simple vocabulary items but fail to grasp the meaning of superordinate terms such as "animals" and "tools." Some have thinking disorders of the type described by Strauss and Lehtinen (1947). They tend to group items according to some insignificant detail rather than to a more general attribute. Some also appear to have generalized problems in comprehending tasks (Pistono 1980). Clinicians should carefully analyze the vocabulary used in the instructions as well as in the test. Ambiguous terms also should be noted. Groshong (1980) found that language impaired children had more difficulty detecting ambiguous words in context than did their normal peers. In some instances, children with language and learning disabilities comprehend abstract language but they cannot express their ideas. Blalock (1977) and James (1972) found that these youngsters often understood the concepts involved in the tasks but that they could not give good verbal explanations.

In general, the researcher or diagnostician who selects and designs tests for learning disabled children should be aware of the multiple reasons for failure and/or for variability of performance. They should be equally aware of the variability that might be observed when assessing intelligence. Many of the processing disturbances described above will interfere with a child's performance on intellectual measures. It is not uncommon to see considerably scattered scores among tests or sub-tests. Often the children with a verbal disorder will score well on nonverbal measures. Similarly, children with visual nonverbal disorders may do well on auditory verbal tasks except on those tasks which involve picture interpretation. By analyzing test performance along some of the parameters described above, it is possible to ascertain more about the cognition and processing disorders in children who have learning difficulties.

References

Birch, H. and Belmont, L. 1964. Auditory-visual integration in normal and retarded readers. *Amer. J. Orthopsychiat.* 34:851-61.

Blalock, J. 1977. A study of conceptualization and related abilities in learning disabled and normal preschool children. Unpublished doctoral dissertation, Northwestern University.

Bryant, P. 1968. Comments on the design of developmental studies of cross-modal matching and cross-modal transfer. *Cortex* 4:127-37.

Eisenson, J. 1972. *Aphasia in children.* New York: Harper and Row.

Ettlinger, G. 1967. Analysis of cross-modal effects and their relationship to language. In *Brain mechanisms underlying speech and language*, eds. C. Millikan and F. Darley. New York: Grune and Stratton.

Groshong, C. 1980. Ambiguity detection and the use of verbal context for disambiguation by language disabled and normal learning children. Unpublished doctoral dissertation, Northwestern University.

Hallahan, D. and Kauffman, J. 1976. *Introduction to learning disabilities.* Englewood Cliffs, NJ: Prentice-Hall, Inc.

Hebb, D. 1963. The semi-autonomous process; its nature and nurture. *Amer. Psychologist* 18:16.

James, K. 1972. A study of the conceptual structure of measurement of length in normal and learning disabled children. Unpublished doctoral dissertation, Northwestern University.

Johnson, D. 1977. Psycho-educational evaluation of children with learning disabilities: study of auditory processes. In *Learning disabilities and related disorders*, ed. G. Millichap. Chicago: Year Book Medical Publishers.

Johnson, D. 1979. Process deficits in learning disabled children and implications for reading. In *Theory and practice of early reading*, eds. L. Resnick and P. Weaver. Hillsdale, NJ: Lawrence Erlbaum Associates.

Johnson, D. and Mykelbust, H. 1967. *Learing disabilities: educational principles and practices.* New York: Grune and Stratton.

Kagan, J. 1965. Impulsive and reflective children: significance of conceptual tempo. In *Learning and the educational process*, ed. J. Krumbolz. Skokie, IL: Rand McNally.

Keogh, B. and Donlon, G. 1972. Field dependance, impulsivity and learning disabilities. *J. Learn. Disabil.* 5:331-36.

Myklebust, H. 1954. *Auditory disorders in children.* New York: Grune and Stratton.

Myklebust, H. 1960. *Psychology of deafness.* New York: Gune and Stratton.

Orton, S. 1937. *Reading, writing and speech problems in children.* New York: Norton.

Pistono, K. 1980. Certain aspects of problem solving abilities of learning disabled and normal 6 to 7-year-old boys as reflected in external cue incorporation on a memory task. Unpublished doctoral dissertation, Northwestern University.

Strauss, A. and Lehtinen, L. 1947. *Psychopathology of the brain-injured child.* New York: Grune & Stratton.

Vellutino, F. 1977. Alternative conceptualizations of dyslexia: evidence in support of a verbal-deficit hypothesis. *Harvard Ed. Rev.* 47:334-54.

Wepman, J. 1958. *Auditory discrimination test.* Chicago: Language Research Associates.

Zaporozhets, A. and Elkonin, D. 1971. *The psychology of preschool children.* Cambridge, MA: The MIT Press.

6

A Pediatrician's View of Central Auditory Disorders: Bridging the Gap Between Diagnosis and Treatment

Sylvia O. Richardson, M.D.

To speak of "Bridging the Gap" between diagnosis and treatment implies that the diagnosis has been made and the treatment can be planned. Hopefully both are correct. To bridge the gap one must provide a structure to get from one side to the other. It is doubtful that a pediatrician can be very helpful in providing this connection for children who have central auditory dysfunction since he usually has only one foot on the one side (diagnosis) and none on the other (treatment).

The pediatrician rarely makes a diagnosis of central auditory dysfunction. The concern of the pediatrician is not "disease of children." It is rather "children with diseases." This is no academic distinction. The latter implies an interest in the influence of growth and development upon disease processes. The physician's concern, then, is the child with a language problem. Central auditory dysfunction is the concern of the Speech-Language Patholgist and Audiologist, as it should be.

The pediatrician would ask: What does the child with central auditory dysfunction look like? What are the signs and symptoms of his condition? Where in the central nervous system is this dysfunction? How would one treat it? Is this a permanent dysfunction or will it change as the child grows? Will other difficulties develop during the stressful change from dependence to maturity? Is this language problem an expression of a maturational lag, a developmental deviation, or, in fact, a disability? And of major importance, of course, what is the child's age and what are the conditions of his life?

The pre-schooler with a central auditory disorder will demonstrate different symptoms from a school age child. In both cases the presenting problem probably will include some kind of a language disorder involving listening and speaking, while the school age child may also have problems with reading and/or writing. There may also be related behaviors which are more difficult to interpret, such as attentional problems or uncontrolled activity.

Frequently, the child's presenting problem may not involve language per se, but he may be brought to the physician because of "hyperactivity," the popular term used to describe the child with a primary attention deficit. An attention deficit may be associated with excessive activity, or ina-

85

bility to monitor his activity; impulsivity, or an inability to "look before he leaps"; distractibility, or the inability to ignore extraneous stimuli; attention absences, or the inability to concentrate; purposeless motoric overactivity or fidgetiness; perseveration rather than persistence.

It is important to recognize that a child may demonstrate attention-activity problems which are secondary to language disorders and/or memory deficiencies. Indeed, attentional deficits or activity problems also may be due to situational stress of psycho-social origins, but the better label in this case would be hyper-reactivity (Richardson and Smith, 1979). My intention here is to highlight the importance of considering the possibility of a primary language disorder when the parent's or teacher's chief complaint about a child is an attention-activity disorder. The child who is unable to understand or process the language he hears is bound to vent his anxiety and confusion in some kind of disruptive behavior.

The need for a multi-disciplinary evaluation in order to accurately diagnose the problem cannot be over emphasized.

If the pediatrician is wise he will become acquainted with the speech, language, and hearing professionals in his community, appraise his own abilities candidly and discover his own biases. At least he should be able to cooperate with other respected professionals. At best he can participate actively in the multidisciplinary evaluation. His position allows him to help or to hinder other efforts, but unless he is willing to prepare himself more thoroughly than the others, he should cooperate with the diagnostic team rather than direct it.

Intelligent parents, faced by the literature and advice which pours in upon them, need someone who can interpret for them. Sometimes they may be unable to get rid of the feeling that their difficulty cannot be discussed with the teacher, without involving the appearance of criticism or special pleading. They may be unwilling to expose themselves to a psychologist whose language and intent they don't always understand. The obvious person to call is the pediatrician. Only if the child's doctor shows lack of interest or great lack of skill will the parents fail to listen to his advice. If the pediatrician has previously helped the parents adjust to their child's illnesses, and if the doctor has helped them understand other difficulties before the child began school, they will listen to his suggestions and eagerly accept his referral to other professionals. It is essential, then, that the speech-language pathologist and the audiologist present their results to the pediatrician simply and clearly in words that describe the child's learning and language behavior rather than in formal linguistic terminology.

The parents often will rely on their child's doctor to help them handle the youngster at home. The language specialist or audiologist would be the more appropriate person to provide parental guidance but the pediatrician often has more clout. Therefore, in addition to explaining the diagnostic results and remedial procedures, the specialist must explain to the physician how the parents might guide the child at home and how they could establish a good language environment.

Current discussion of auditory processing problems usually gets into phonemic analysis, or the minutiae of linguistic decoding. However, there is increasing recognition that skills such as auditory discrimination, sequential memory, temporal-sequential organization and the like need to be interpreted within the context of what we know about the semantic aspects of language. Do we look so closely at the threads of the material that we fail to see the pattern? Do we tend to isolate details until they lose meaning out of context? Can we really consider central auditory dysfunction as an entity separate from expressive language, for example?

If scanning is an aid to vision, articulation is an aid to hearing. When we try to remember a tune, we hum it. The decisive factor in the evolution of human speech was not the development of the ear, but the development of the vocal organs and the speech area in the motor cortex. The multiple feed-backs of auditory-vocal coordination exceed even those of oculo-motor cooperation. The child learns words by articulating them; adults learning a foreign language follow a similar procedure. Reading is more often accompanied by sub-vocal articulation than by images in the ear (unless you know intimately the author of the material you are reading). The analysis of speech sounds by matching them against the innervation-patterns of the vocal tracts is a much simpler procedure than the acoustic analysis of the ambiguous sound spectra. No matter how complex or variable the vowel's wave form may be, its identity as a language unit depends on its two formants, which in turn depend only on the resonance effect produced by the alterations of shape of two vocal cavities, mouth and pharynx. Fifty years ago Paget (1930) proposed that "in recognizing speech sounds the human ear is ...listening...to indications, due to resonance, of the position and gestures of the organs of articulation." Much more recently, researchers in the Haskins Laboratories came to the same conclusion, that "speech is perceived by reference to articulation — that is, that the articulatory movements and their sensory (proprioceptive) effects mediate between the acoustic stimulus and the event we call perception" (Ladefoged 1959).

Perception is something the organism does, not something which happens to the organism. Responses enter at every level of the hierarchy into the processing of stimuli, and motor activities intervene to analyze the input long before it has achieved its full status as a "stimulus"—before it has, for instance, become a meaningful word capable of stimulating the central process which is going to mediate the response.

We are beginning to re-examine some of our assumptions about the assessment of children's sensory acuity, perceptual functions, and information processing operations. We may find that understanding the ways in which children synthesize their sensory-perceptual-cognitive experiences during their environmental adaptation is more significant for their lives than the exact measurement of sensory thresholds or auditory perceptual functions, no matter how refined those measurements may be.

A major requisite for successful language development in children is the ability to listen effectively to speech. How does one measure the efficiency with which the child listens? Friedlander and Cohen de Lana (1973) reported an excellent study which I believe merits review. They were interested in selective listening and sought to evaluate children's competence for integrative listening to extended sequences of the stream of speech. The purpose of this study was to apply a precise, systematic data-gathering technique to assess one important aspect of receptive language functioning in normal children in regular primary grades. They chose to study the ability to select between speech that is clear and highly intelligible and speech that is "degraded" by interfering sounds (multivoice "cocktail-party chatter") to various degrees of unintelligibility. A two channel audiovisual playback system called Playtest was used.

The study was conducted in a public school setting in an affluent Connecticut community with excellent diagnostic services and special education facilities. All 44 of the 5 to 8 year old children in the study were in regular ungraded classes. None was regarded as having any degree of learning disability or other educational handicaps that might justify special placement, but they were distributed across a spectrum from high to low achievement.

The task called for the children to move the lever on a switch to one side to turn on a pre-recorded program of television cartoons of the Muppets with a clear, upgraded audio soundtrack. If they moved the switch to the other side, they turned on the same video program but the sound track was mildly, moderately, or severely degraded with voice interference. Because the researchers hypothesized an association between selective listening and progress in reading skills, estimates of the children's reading progress were made by classroom teachers and the school principal on the basis of standard test scores and their knowledge of the children's class performance. These estimates were made and recorded before the teachers and the principal had any knowledge of the research results.

Of the 44 children tested, 33 consistently attained or surpassed the 65% selective listening criterion in favor of the upgraded sound track, clearly rejecting the degraded dialogue. Eleven children consistently failed to attain the 65% selective listening criterion and remained at or near the 50/50 range of random, non-selective listening responses. In other words, the non-selective listeners each spent almost half of at least 9, 6-minute sessions (54 minutes!) watching highly verbal cartoons which were almost entirely incomprehensible. Yet the perfectly clear sound track was freely available simply by moving the switch to the opposite position on the switch box. The time on task for both groups was almost identical at the high level of 92%. Evidently both groups showed approximately the same interest in the cartoons but the non-selective listeners had a high tolerance for "linguistic garbage."

Significantly, when the reading progress reports were available, all 33 selective listeners were judged to be competent readers, while all eleven non-selective listeners were independently rated as having reading difficulties. The study was replicated with 66 other children and the results were almost identical (Rileigh 1973).

A similar study was carried out with a group of normal pre-schoolers and emotionally disturbed pre-schoolers who had expressive language disorders (Friedlander, Wetstone, and McPeek 1974). Again the normal children rejected the degraded channels with some decisiveness; the moderately disturbed children rejected the less comprehensible sound tracks to a moderate degree; the severely involved children did not reject the degraded sound track at all, listening to the incomprehensible dialogue and the comprehensible dialogue with about equal acceptance. The authors felt that whatever problems the children had with expressive language, they also had serious problems in receptive language. If they would listen so eagerly and acceptingly to meaningless babble, there was no reason to assume that ordinary, sequential, meaningful speech would have any special meaning for them. They could not be expected to understand speech directed toward them any more than they could be expected to speak clearly to others. These findings had considerable effect on the children's treatment. Therapists and teachers were alerted to their problems in language comprehension which had not been fully appreciated because of the more obvious expressive language disorders.

We have been aware of different learning styles ever since Charcot categorized us as visile, audile, or motile types of learners. It has also been shown that those who learn best by ear, the listeners, tend to be reinforced when they verbalize the material to be learned. The advantages of verbalization become obvious in the old experiment by Woodworth (1938) in which 40 subjects were seated in front of a table with a grooved maze on it. The maze was of the same type as in rat experiments, with various cul-de-sacs; the subject had to feel his way through it with a stylus in his hand because the maze was covered with a screen. The number of trials required until the maze was completely learned varied between 16 and 196! At the end of the experiment each subject had to report whether he had memorized the maze by the feel of it (by motor-kinesthetic imagery), by making a visual map, or by verbal formula—e.g., "first left, third right, fourth right," etc.

Out of 60 subjects, 17 adopted the motor method. These needed an average of 124 trials, ranging from 71 to 195, to learn the maze. Eighteen adopted the visual method averaging 68 trials ranging from 41 to 104. Twenty-five adopted the verbal formula averaging 32 trials, ranging from 16 to 62. In round figures, the visualizers learned twice as fast and the verbalizers learned four times as fast as the motor learners. The subjects were normal adults. Each stuck to the preferred learning style no matter how long it took. There certainly should be some implications here for teachers in the regular classroom as well as in special education. Individual differences are built-in and do not necessarily indicate defect nor dysfunction. Teaching methods must be appropriate to be effective.

As there are differences in style, or preferred modality if you like, in learning and language, there are also anatomical differences in normal brains. As Dr. Ferry pointed out during this meeting, Geschwind has investigated the gross anatomical differences between the two hemispheres readily visible to the naked eye. He and Levitsky (1968) sectioned 100 brains through the sylvian fossa in order to look at the upper surface of the temporal lobe on the two sides. The area they looked at was the region lying behind Heschl's gyrus and the back end of the sylvian fossa. This area is called the planum temporale.

In the 100 brains examined, they found that the left side was larger in 65, the right larger in 11, with approximate equality in 14. This difference was significant at better than the .001 level. Although the left side was often dramatically larger than the right, the reverse was rarely true. There is no asymmetry like this known in any other animal of the mammalian series. Interestingly enough, the area which is larger on the left turns out to be part of Wernicke's area, probably the most important of the speech regions of the hemisphere, and predominantly auditory in function.

Wada (1969) repeated the study and confirmed Geschwind's results with similar statistics. Wada, Clarke, and Hamm have also studied the brains of newborn infants and fetuses and found that the differences described in adults were present to the same degree at birth. Thus these differences are not the result of life experiences, maturation or learning, but are present even in utero. (Dr. Ferry earlier referred to fixed structural deficits that no amount of treatment will reverse.)

Hier et al. (1978) have found the same brain asymmetry in computed tomographic brain studies. They and others have found that this asymmetry was reversed in 9% of normal right handed individuals and in 17% of normal left handed individuals whom they examined. The tomographic studies showed reverse cerebral asymmetry in 10 of their 24 dyslexic subjects. All 10 had lower verbal IQ's than performance IQ's, and 4 had a history of delayed speech acquisition. Hier et al. hypothesized that individuals with reversed brain asymmetry had a five times greater risk of having specific language disability (dyslexia).

I wonder increasingly if we are correct in treating all of the specific learning deficits as abnormalities. There are so many normal variations of the human species. Most of us have some special learning disabilities and it is merely a cultural accident that these disabilities do not get us into trouble. For example, some individuals can't carry a tune despite valiant attempts to learn, while others have exceptional musical talent without ever having a lesson. Some children are fine artists and others, like myself, can't draw an acceptable stick figure. Some individuals are voracious readers but poor speakers and some excellent speakers have difficulty putting their thoughts on paper. Some children are natural athletes and others are forever "klutzy." Such difficulties are widespread throughout the human race, yet the unmusical or unartistic or physically inept are not labeled as having "minimal brain dysfunction." In fact, these characteristics are a frequent source of friendly teasing in the adult.

We happen to live in a society which places extremely high value on verbal and reading skills yet we have all known dyslexic children who are excellent artists, with superior visual perception and/or visual motor skills. Such a child living in a illiterate society would have no difficulty; in fact, this child might be at the top of the class because of visual-perceptual talent. In such a society, many of us who function well here might be considered to have "minimal brain dysfunction." As Geschwind and Levitsky (1968) stated, "Once we have learned to examine the normal brain grossly, we may have a powerful means for finding the source for those remarkable variations in perceptual and learning capacities in different areas which exist in *normal* children" (italics mine).

We cannot overemphasize the importance of accurately assessing a child's auditory-perceptual abilities, in spite of the viewpoint expressed by Hammill and Larsen (1974) that measures of auditory perception seem of limited value in predicting reading ability. More recent evidence has shown that sentence processing occurs simultaneously at all available levels and that "information at each level can constrain and guide simultaneous processing at other levels" (Marslen-Wilson 1975).

The complexity of auditory language processing deficits is great. The challenge to analyze deficits is often such that we overlook the necessity to be as careful in our assessment of a child's *assets* as well. I believe that we must be able to delineate with equal clarity a child's abilities and his disabilities in language processing and use (Richardson 1977). Unless we can do this, I am not sure that we can truly differentiate between individual difference, mild deviaton and disability. The course of treatment and the course of the child's life lies in the hands of the diagnostic team. The pediatrician should be a member of that team. His first and unavoidable medical responsibility is the duty of being correct in the medical diagnosis. Of particular importance, however, by virtue of his specialty, the pediatrician is always mindful of the many normal variations of the maturing, developing members of the human family.

References

Friedlander, B.Z. and Cohen de Lana, H. 1973. Receptive language anomaly and language/ reading dysfunction in "normal" primary grade-school children. *Psychology in the schools* 10:12-18.

Friedlander, B.Z., Wetstone, H.S., and McPeek, D.L. 1974. Systematic assessment of selective language listening deficit in emotionally disturbed pre-school children. *J. Child Psychol. Psychiat.* 15:1-12.

Geschwind, N. and Levitsky, W. 1968. Human brain: left-right asymmetries in temporal speech region. *Science* 161:186-87.

Hammil, D.O. and Larsen, S.C. 1974. The relationship of selected auditory perceptual skills and reading ability. *J. of Learn. Disabil.* 7:40-6.

Hier, D.B., LeMay, M., et al. 1978. Developmental dyslexia: evidence for a subgroup with a reversal of cerebral asymmetry. Arch. Neurol. 35:90-2.

Ladefoged, P. 1959. Mechanisation of thought processes. London: H.M. Stationery Office.

Marslen-Wilson, W.D. 1975. Sentence perception as an interactive parallel process. Science 189:226-28.

Paget, Sir Richard, BT. 1930. Human speech, London: K. Paul.

Richardson, S.O. 1977. Communicating results of central auditory tests with other professionals. In Central auditory dysfunction, ed. R.W. Keith. New York: Grune and Stratton.

Richardson, S.O. and Smith, R. 1979. Learning disabilities. In Family practice, 2d ed., eds. R.E. Rakel and H.G. Conn. Philadelphia: W.B. Saunders.

Rileigh, K.K. 1973. Children's selective listening to stories. Psycholog. Repts. 33:255-66.

Wada, J.A. 1969. Presentation at Ninth International Congress of Neurology, New York.

Wada, J.A., Clarke, R., and Hamm, A. 1975. Cerebral hemispheric asymmetry in humans: cortical speech zones in 100 adult and 100 infant brains. Arch. Neurol. 34:239-46.

Woodworth, R.S. 1938. Experimental psychology. New York: Holt Reinhardt.

Questions and Answers

Q: How do you propose a speech pathologist approach physicians and get them to listen? Most physicians appear not to have the time or the desire to listen and learn about our field.

A: You will find that physicians are changing, especially pediatricians, because of in-service training that is going on all over the country. So, they not only will be more interested in the field, they will need to talk to you and they will be more aware of their need in that regard.

A physician will talk to you about a patient whom you both have seen, and the quickest way I know to get him to talk to you is to phone him. Tell him that you would like to talk to him about a particular child. It helps a great deal when you phone the physician to leave word with the secretary first that "This is Dr. Jones and I would like to talk to Dr. Smith about his patient John Doe." At least give the pediatrician a chance to look at the patient's record. I think you will find that physicians will be easier and easier to communicate with and are really not hard to communicate with as long as you are very specific and concise.

Q: In the last analysis, aside from self-esteem and other such related psychological affective factors, does it matter if dyslexic children have other superior talents. The culture they live in demands reading skills. Aren't we begging the question?

A: It matters a great deal what the child's assets are as well as his disabilities. Dyslexic children can be taught to read. They are being taught to read every day, so we are not begging any questions, but their superiority in other skills is very important to their lives. There are large numbers of successful engineers, surgeons, artists, sculptors who are dyslexic. They have learned to read, but in the last analysis, in their lives they got their recognition for their skills, not for their reading abilities.

Q: In Woodworth's experiment, were the people who stuck to their own way of doing things in the maze aware of the fact that there were other ways of approaching it? If they were made aware of various ways of solving the problem, would they have changed? Also, can children or adults learn new style?

A: I don't think Dr. Woodworth asked any of his subjects if they were aware of other ways to go about it. Remember, these were adults. We pretty much stabilize as adults. Even though we know that there are other ways of doing things, we usually stick to the way we do things because it is easier for us. Children can be taught different strategies for learning. If you find that the child displays more strength in visual skills or in tactile kinesthetic skills, then you can help him choose those kinds of strategies in his learning. You can teach those strategies. You can teach adults, too, and it is up to them if they want to re-learn or not.

7

Saying More Than We Know: Is Auditory Processing Disorder a Meaningful Concept?

Norma S. Rees, Ph.D.

In an earlier paper (Rees 1973) I described auditory processing explanations for failures of articulation, language development, or reading acquisitions as "procrustean" because of Procrustes, the king of antiquity who put his captives in an iron bed and made them fit by stretching them if too short and chopping off their legs if too tall. Auditory processing disturbances have become the iron bed into which all sorts of language and learning deficits are made to fit. The popularity of this explanation persists despite significant criticism (Bloom and Lahey 1978) and despite lack of evidence that remedial programs based on auditory processing approaches produce useful results for the children so classified (Hammill and Larsen 1974). The purpose of this paper is to explore pertinent theory, research findings, and clinical practices to reveal some serious problems with current versions of the auditory processing explanation.

Some introductory observations may set the stage. The auditory processing explanation has been embraced in two quite different ways by discrete groups of workers. On the one hand, workers primarily concerned with remediating children having speech, language, or learning difficulties, among them speech-language pathologists, have adopted the notion that complex skills can be analyzed into simple or basic component skills for the purposes of assessment and intervention. Complex language behavior, in this view, is composed of a finite number of subskills that can be reduced even further to fundamental perceptual-motor abilities. This view characterizes many of the typical "psycholinguistic" training programs which, according to Hammill and Larsen (1974), are "based on the assumption that discrete elements of language behavior are identifiable and measurable and that if defective they can be remediated."[1] The basic skills or discrete abilities are presumed to include auditory discrimination, auditory sequencing, and auditory memory. This approach concentrates on finding basic weaknesses that can be attacked directly in training and gives little attention to root causes other than a general nod in the direction of neurological variances as the ultimate explanation.

1. From the review of 38 studies which attempted to train children in specific "psycholinguistic" skills, Hammill and Larsen (1974) concluded that the specific abilities approach is not particularly successful in improving these same specific abilities and, moreover, even if successful has little effect on the goal of improving the child's ability to use language in communication.

In contrast, workers primarily concerned with diagnosis along medical model lines, among them clinical audiologists, have started from a site-of-lesion orientation and produced the "central auditory processing" focus as accounting for a variety of languge and learning failures. These workers have concentrated on test development and have less to say about remedial approaches.

That the available clinical approaches are innocent of anything like a coherent, unified theory is easy to demonstrate by a glance at the wide range of tasks that may be used to determine a child's "auditory processing skills." At one extreme are tasks requiring same-different judgments about speech sounds, at the other extreme tests of the school-aged child's ability to make inferences from a paragraph read aloud by the teacher, while between the two extremes are items like digit span, sequencing of words in a sentence, identification of environmental noises, speech discrimination against a background of noise, other tests of recognition of degraded speech material, and sentence comprehension.

The following sampling from the booklet *A Guide to Tests of Auditory Processing Abilities for Young Children* (Plummer, n.d.) illustrates further the variety of skills presumably included in auditory processing: 1) Rosner and Simon's Auditory Analysis Test, K-6. The examiner says to the child, "Say *cowboy*. Now say it again without the boy." 2) The Composite Auditory Perceptual Test by Witkin and Butler, including but not limited to selective listening, competing messages, speech sound sequencing, consonant discrimination, auditory closure, recognition of the number of syllables in a word, discrimination of linguistic forms (such as *not, actor agent, neither*-nor), and discrimination of verb tenses. 3) The Goldman-Fristoe-Woodcock tests of auditory discrimination for speech sounds, in quiet and in noise. 4) Auditory subtests of the *Illinois Test of Psycholinguistic Abilities*, including digit span and "auditory reception," or the child's "ability to derive meaning from verbally presented questions" and to respond accurately with yes/no. (Example: *Do bananas telephone?*) 5) Elizabeth Carrow's Screening Test for Auditory Comprehension of Language, which has the purpose of discovering if the child needs a "complete auditory comprehension test."

While the foregoing examples are taken from a listing of tests used by remediators, the presumed auditory processing skills overlap considerably with the "central auditory abilities" presumed to have diagnostic significance for audiologists (adapted from Keith 1980):

- Localization (locating the source of sound);
- Behavioral synthesis (integrating incomplete stimuli presented simultaneously or alternately to opposite ear);
- Figure-ground (identifying a signal against a background of competing sounds);
- Binaural separation (attending to stimuli presented to one ear while ignoring stimuli presented to the opposite ear);

- Memory (recalling auditory stimuli, both in terms of number and sequence);
- Blending (reconstructing words from separated phonemes);
- Discrimination (judging whether two acoustic stimuli are the same or different);
- Closure (reconstructing the whole word or message when parts are omitted);
- Attention (listening over a reasonable period of time);
- Cognition (establishing a correspondence between a sound and its meaning).

The vast range of complexity and varied nature of the tasks and presumed abilities listed in the foregoing review are obvious. About the only common denominator is that in each case the subject must operate on stimuli presented via the ear; any other similarity among instances is largely metaphoric. The inescapable conclusion is that the term "auditory processing," in referring to these and other tasks, represents a non-existent simplicity and unity. One may as well assert that a test wherein an examiner asks a child what hand he writes with is an auditory processing test because the question is presented via the ear; of course, that item is generally associated with a test of laterality.

The absence of coherent underlying theory springs into focus when the wide-ranging examples are reviewed. To put it more strongly, the auditory processing approach lacks a clear explanatory model to account for the role the abilities assessed by these tasks play in acquiring and manipulating language and in using language for academic learning. Just what does a child's auditory memory span for digits have to do with his ability to learn and use language? What is the relation between ability to utilize rapidly-changing acoustic spectra in speech discrimination tasks and language learning in general? What level of ability to recognize speech presented in alternating fashion to the two ears does a child need in order to learn in the classroom, and why? We have no answer to these questions, which is another way of saying that a satisfying explanatory model relating these presumed requisite abilities to language acquisition and academic learning has neither been proposed nor tested.

The remainder of this paper is devoted to examining some of the assumptions and logical implications surrounding current notions about factors in auditory processing to determine what, if anything, these factors might have to do with language learning, language disorders, and learning disability.

I. Auditory Sequencing

Our literature is full of attempts to relate a wide variety of langage and learning disorders to a fundamental problem with sequencing auditory stimuli. The explanation is generally a version of the well-known impairment of temporal ordering of auditory stimuli in brain-damaged subjects (Efron 1963; Lowe and Campbell 1965), proposing that because spoken utterances are events occurring in a time dimension, the problem in resolving the order of the units of spoken utterances is the basis of language and learning disorders (Aten 1972). Difficulty with auditory sequencing is supposed to interfere with the child's ability to perform a variety of tasks, including speaking in complete sentences, understanding complex directions, ordering pictures to form a story, reading comprehension, spelling, and reordering scrambled sentences.

Two major problems limit the persuasiveness of the auditory sequencing explanation:

1. Auditory Sequencing of What?

To speak of sequencing is to imply units to be sequenced. What are these units? Will any units do? Can we generalize from one type of unit to another? For example, does the finding that a child has difficulty repeating a tapping pattern mean that he will have difficulty ordering the parts of a sentence? Or that he will have difficulty comprehending connected discourse?

The search for units reflects an approach to the study of language that seems rather old-fashioned in the light of current research. In Jenkins' fine article "Remember that old theory of memory? Well, forget it!" (Jenkins 1977), the author describes the "presuppositions" that dominated his thinking in the 1950s as follows:

"1. *Units.* I believed that words were the fundamental units of language. To me this was natural and obvious.
2. *Relations.* I believed that there was one kind of relation between words, associative linkage. Words became linked to each other through use together or in the same 'frames.'
3. *Structures.* I believed that mental structures (if there really were any) were assemblies of links, essentially *chains* of the fundamental units in their fundamental relation....
4. *Complex behaviors.* I believed that complex behaviors were built of simple subassemblies and that things got more complicated but not different 'in kind'....
5. *Mechanistic explanation.* I believed that explanation ultimately rested on a descripton of the machinery that produced the behavior" (pp. 785-786).

Jenkins proceeds to show that this outmoded, associationist approach must be replaced by a more integrated, dynamic one if productive research on memory is to take place.

The need for units is an aspect of associationism, an approach that tried to break down complex behavior, such as language behavior, into its components and subcomponents to reach the primes, the indivisibles, the basic building blocks beyond which analysis cannot go. This reductionist approach leads us to want to believe that perception is simpler than and pre-requisite for cognition, although since by now we also know that cognitive structures affect perceptual organization, the neat one-way street has given way to the dynamic interactionist model mentioned by Jenkins (1977). The auditory processing explanation, however, continues to assume that per-ception is somehow prior to and prerequisite for cognition and compre-hension in a sort of building-block fashion. That kind of reasoning, in the next step, leads us on the chase for the true unit of auditory perception, which is something like questing for the Holy Grail. (The Holy Grail was actually found by Sir Galahad, who was the legitimate son of Sir Lancelot and Elaine. Now Sir Lancelot had gotten tricked into marrying Elaine, which was really quite a respectable arrangement for those times, but he quickly left her and kept carrying on with Guenevere, who was not only his queen but the wife of his best friend, King Arthur. Sir Lancelot was therefore not truly a worthy knight and could hardly be expected to be graced with the discovery of holy relics; Sir Galahad, on the other hand, was the knight whose "heart was pure," which means he was a virgin, and so he was vouchsafed the Holy Grail. If the story provides a useful analogy, we can understand why speech scientists have had no success in isolating the true unit of speech perception.)

The reductionist assumption that auditory perception is simpler than and/or prior to processing of spoken language at the level of comprehen-sion of course does not hold up under close scrutiny (Rees 1973). It is none-theless instructive to review the results of the search for the perceptual unit in sentence processing. One approach in experimental attempts has been to examine the phoneme as a possible candidate. Inasmuch as the pho-neme is known to be an abstraction rather than a clearly segmentable unit of the acoustic signal of spoken utterances, what these experiments look for is evidence of the "psychological reality" of that abstraction as a unit of perception. A particularly interesting experiment was reported by Savin and Bever (1970), who gave subjects lists of spoken nonsense syllables like those in (1), presented at the rate of 600 msec/syllable:

(1) /Ɵowj/ /tuwp/ /sarg/ /tiyf/ /friyn/

The subjects were instructed to press a button as soon as they heard a syl-lable beginning with /s/. This phoneme was selected because its acoustic properties are relatively independent of the context created by the follow-ing vowel. In the phoneme-monitoring condition, the subjects were given no further instructions. On a second list, however, the subjects were told what syllable to listen for: "The target is /sarg/." This was the syllable-mon-itoring condition. The investigators recorded and compared reaction times (RTs) for the phoneme-monitoring and the syllable-monitoring conditions.

Savin and Bever's results showed that the phoneme-monitoring RTs were significantly larger than the syllable-monitoring RTs (354 msec vs. 311 msec). Apparently the subjects utilized information about the syllable, or at least the consonant-vowel combination, in order to reach a decision about the initial consonant. "We take our results to show that phonemes are perceived only by an analysis of already perceived syllables (or at least already perceived consonant-vowel pairs)." Phonemes, then, may have psychological reality but do not qualify as primary perceptual units in processing spoken syllables.

Foss and Swinney (1973) pursued the Savin and Bever approach to test their hypothesis that the syllable is not necessarily a less abstract (or more "real") construct than is the phoneme. They showed that subjects' RTs for two-syllable words were significantly shorter than their RTs for the first syllables of these words, whether or not that syllable was itself a meaningful word (candy). Perhaps with tongue in cheek, they state: "...we must now conclude that single syllables are not units of perception, but rather that this honor is reserved for the word."

Foss and Swinney (1973) also point out that Bever elsewhere reports an experiment by Bever, Savin, and Hurtig, where listeners responded to three-word sentences like *monks ring chimes* and *cows give milk* in an initial-word-monitoring task or a three-word-sentence-monitoring task, and quote Bever: "Our results so far show that subjects respond consistently faster when they know the entire sentence target than the initial word target." They conclude that "we must now reject the word as a basic unit of speech perception and accept the phrase or clause as basic."

We have arrived at sentences without achieving an answer to the question about perceptual units. Yet even if we had the answer, it would not be enough. Johnson-Laird (1970) points out that even "if it were possible to give a comprehensive account of the way spoken sounds are identified as words ... the principal problem would be to explain how the meanings of words are combined to form the meanings of sentences." In 1962 George Miller wrote about sentence comprehension in terms of the hearer's analysis of the sentence into its syntactic constituents, and argued for the psychological reality of syntactic categories: "We cannot understand a sentence until we are able to assign a constituent structure to it." In a landmark study, Miller and Isard (1963) constructed grammatical, anomalous, and ungrammatical sentences (Gadgets simplify work around the house; *Trains steal elephants around the highways*; scrambled versions of these) for subjects to hear and repeat. Listening in quiet and in noise, subjects repeated least well with ungrammatical, better with anomalous, and of course best with grammatical sentences. The results indicated that sentence context facilitates perceptual decision not only because it reduces the variety of competing alternatives, but enables the hearer to organize the flow of sound into decision units larger than individual words — "more nearly the size and shape of a syntactic constituent" (Miller and Isard 1963).

To cope with ambiguous sentences such as

(2) The policeman's arrest was illegal. (Johnson-Laird 1970),

it appears that analysis of surface structure is insufficient and that underlying structure must somehow also be retrieved. That the sentence's underlying structure is in some sense "perceived" receives support from the work of Bever, Lackner, and Kirk (1969). These investigators concluded from the results of various experiments employing the "clicks" technique developed by Ladefoged and Broadbent (1960) that "immediate segmentation of sentences is responsive to underlying structure sentences." Their results showed that listeners subjectively locate superimposed clicks at the boundaries reflecting underlying sentences, displacing these clicks from their actual location elsewhere in the recorded sentence. For example, listeners reported hearing the clicks between the second and third words in sentence (3), but not in sentence (4):

(3) They watched the light turn green.

(4) They watched the light green car.

Bever et al. reached this general picture of speech processing: "As we hear a sentence, we organize it in terms of underlying structure sentences, with subjects, verbs, objects, and modifiers. In this process we ignore structural features which are not immediately useful to the discovery of the sentence's potential underlying structure.... The underlying structure segmentation of sentences and organization within sentences is projected immediately and directly from the structural potentialities of the words in a sequence" (p. 232). Although Bever, Lackner, and Kirk's (1969) strong claims for the perceptual primacy of underlying structure sentences were not fully supported by subsequent research (see Chapin, Smith, and Abrahamson 1972; Lehiste 1972), their findings are nonetheless pertinent for this review.

The search for the unit of perception in processing spoken utterances has led from the phoneme through the syllable, the word, the clause, the sentence, and ended with the underlying sentence. The above brief review fails to offer any guidance about which type of unit is a better candidate than the others for the true or basic perceptual unit. Foss and Swinney (1973) conclude that "it does not seem feasible to divide the units of perception into those that are abstract and those that are 'real.' All levels of analysis, from phonetic to semantic, result in entities that are 'abstract' in the sense that they are not simply given in the acoustic signal." At the close of a detailed review of research findings on units of speech perception, Lehiste (1972) concludes that there is evidence for units at all levels from the subphonemic to the syntactic, and that processing takes place at the various levels with "extensive interaction" among them. The answer to the question about the true unit of perception is, therefore, in one sense "none of the above" and in another sense "all of the above," and under either interpretation the assumptions of the auditory sequencing explanation are inadequate to deal with the complexities of the matter.

Because the auditory sequencing explanation ultimately requries a decision about what units are sequenced, it also runs into difficulty with

100

the differing nature of the various types of units. For example, Lehiste (1972) distinguishes among 1) nonspeech signals, 2) speech signals, and 3) higher-order units like phonemes, morphemes, and syntactic structures, relating these units to auditory processing, phonetic processing, and linguistic processing, respectively. Similarly, Foss and Swinney (1973) hypothesize a crucial distinction between perceiving and identifying units of speech processing, pointing out that the reaction time experiments may in fact have revealed the ease with which units are identified rather than the order in which they are perceived. Identification implies conscious awareness, and Foss and Swinney suggest that units such as phonemes and syllables are ordinarily inaccessible to consciousness while phrases and clauses are more available to identification on the basis of conscious awareness. The processes of fractionating larger units into phonemes and syllables, perhaps even into words, is probably learned and therefore not readily available to children on the basis of their linguistic intuitions. According to Foss and Swinney, for a unit to enter awareness requires that it lead to a change in stored (long-term) memory. In the case of phonetic or phonological analysis, no change in long-term memory is implicated, while the output of processing phrases, clauses, and sentences is new meaning which alters the contents of long-term memory. Units that produce long-term memory changes, then, are easily identified in sentence-processing tasks, while units below the level of conscious awareness are not. This account is, of course, compatible with the general finding that the meanings of sentences, not their syntactic forms, are stored in long term memory. As put by Johnson-Laird (1970), "all forms of syntactic structure are normally lost to memory within a few seconds," implying that the function of linguistic structure is to serve as an avenue to meaning rather than to retain meaning. The proposal is likewise compatible with the given-new construct (Clark and Haviland 1977) which asserts that listeners segment new information from spoken utterances and integrate it with old or given information to form new, modified meanings for the memory store. In short, the proposed perceptual units vary greatly among themselves in size and complexity as well as in their status and role with respect to recognition, identification, and the retrieval of meaning in the larger picture of language processing. Auditory sequencing ability (or disability) is difficult to relate to this complexity in any meaningful way.

In summary, if auditory sequencing is to be accepted as a basic skill to be identified, measured, and remediated, a first question is, sequencing of what? Inasmuch as it appears that no one unit is a better candidate than any other unit, we can only conclude that if sequencing means anything at all it must take into account the simultaneous sequencing of all various and pertinent units in their patterns or interrelated organization at the various levels of complexity and in their differing natures with respect to language processing. Teaching a child to imitate a non-verbal tapping or clapping rhythm, or a string of words, or a sequence of letters, seems in the light of this review to have very little connection with the complex skill he needs to acquire.

2. What Is the Relationship Between Auditory Sequencing Ability and Comprehension of Spoken Language?

We seem to operate as if the meaning of a sentence is inherent in the order of its constituents. Certainly word order is one of the ways that internal relations, both syntactic and semantic, are signaled in linguistic constructions, so that

(5) John kissed Mary.

is entirely unambiguous with regard to who did what to whom in spite of the lack of inflectional endings to differentiate the cases of the two nouns. But we also know that word order is not the only means for achieving this purpose, and that in the case of

(6) Mary was kissed by John.

the order of the two nouns relative to the verb is reversed, but the matter of who did what to whom is not altered. Perhaps there is a general tendency to believe in an inherently "right" order of words that is "right" because it somehow reflects reality. An illustration of this prejudice may be found in Chomsky's (1965) charming reference to Diderot, who stated in 1751 that "French is unique among languages in the degree to which the order of words corresponds to the natural order of thoughts and ideas," French therefore being the most suitable language for the sciences.

Clinicians and teachers sometimes defend their emphasis on auditory sequencing on the grounds that children must learn to pay attention to the order in sentences if they are to be able to follow two-part instructions like

(7) Sit down and open your book.

While agreeing that children should be able to perform such tasks, we question whether auditory sequencing or "temporal ordering" will be in accord with the pertinent facts about sentence comprehension. Two interesting studies that deal with word order will illustrate the point.

De Villiers and de Villiers (1973) showed that children around the two-word utterance stage of language development, when asked to act out sentences like

(8) Make the cow kiss the horse.

sometimes did it right and sometimes made the horse kiss the cow, but sometimes the child kissed the cow or the horse or both. For the least linguistically developed children the three types of response appeared almost equally often. They concluded that children at this stage do not use word order as a clue to meaning. In a related study, moreover, they asked the children at this early stage of language development to make judgments about imperatives like *build a house* vs. *house a build* and to correct the wrong ones (de Villiers and de Villiers 1972). The least linguistically developed children couldn't do much with this task; but an interesting sidelight was that when they heard as sentence like *eth your brush*, they acted out teeth brushing. That finding tells us that while word order may be a clue to meaning, a better clue, at least at this early stage, is the interrelations among the meanings of the words in the sentence.

The work on comprehension of *before* and *after* by Clark (1971) is a second illustration. Clark showed that young children use an order-of-mention strategy when acting out sentences like

(9) The boy patted the dog and jumped over the fence.

That works out very well until you get to sentences like

(10) Before the boy patted the dog he jumped over the fence.

where the order-of-mention strategy does not apply and younger chldren get it wrong.

It is plain from these two examples that paying close attention to the sequencing of words in a sentence is insufficient to insure that the child can understand a sentence or observe the required order of events the sentence encodes and thus carry out instructions correctly. Meaning in language is not a simple function jof the temporal ordering of words in sentences.

Perhaps the most extreme example of using temporal ordering or sequencing ability to explain comprehension appeared in a study on the use of the Token Test in children, normal adults, and aphasic adults (Wertz et al. 1973). The authors found, generally, that four-year-old children did about as well as the aphasics, while both of these groups performed more poorly than normal adults. They also noted that certain items were more often missed than others. The test stimuli are colored chips in circle and rectangle shapes, six different colors in all. Part V of the Token Test requires the subject to follow directions like

(11) Touch the blue circle and the red rectangle.
        Put the green rectangle beside the red circle.

They discovered that the following items were missed most often:

(12) Put the white circle before the blue rectangle.
        When I touch the green circle, you take the white rectangle.
        Touch the rectangles slowly and the circles quickly.
        After picking up the green rectangle, touch the white circle.
        Before touching the yellow circle, pick up the red rectangle.

103

Their explanation for this finding is: "All of these items include a temporal element — 'when, slowly - quickly, after, before'. Difficulty with temporal ordering is well documented in brain injured adults..." (p. 8).

This conclusion, unfortunately, rests on an unwarranted inference. From data showing that some brain damaged adults have difficulty telling which of two pure tones come first unless they are separated in time for about a second, some authors have concluded that the reason aphasic adults (and also aphasic children) have language comprehension problems is that they have trouble resolving the order of words in the sentences they hear; this point was covered earlier in this paper, and attention called to the weakness of reasoning. In Wertz et al. (1973), the authors assume that aphasic adults not only have difficulty with temporal ordering of words, but, more surprisingly, that they have difficulty understanding words that *refer to* temporal ordering concepts. That conclusion can only be regarded as metaphorical.

To summarize this section, neither the analysis of units nor the considerations of how sequencing relates to sentence comprehension offers support for a theory of auditory sequencing as a basic skill needed for language development and learning, nor for a specific disability in auditory sequencing as an explanation for language and learning failures.

II. Auditory Synthesis and Auditory Closure

Auditory synthesis (or auditory fusion) is exemplified by the sound-blending subtest of the Illinois Test of Psycholinguistic Abilities wherein the child must put together a string of separate phonemes (/k -æ-t/) to produce a word (cat). Aten (1972) classifies this test as a test of auditory memory because "the phonemes must be retained in serial order, then fused to form a familiar word" (p. 114). Auditory closure, exemplified by the ITPA subtest of the same name, is the skill required for the child to be able to complete a word with a segment missing (banan _____). Wood (1972) defines auditory closure as the "ability to respond accurately to auditory signals which are interrupted or have part of the message missing," and she states that it is a skill important to speech and language development.

Aten (1972) and Wood (1972) seem to have put the matter in reverse. Auditory synthesis and auditory closure, far from being basic perceptual skills needed for language learning, are in fact metalinguistic skills that presuppose a good deal of linguistic sophistication. The metalinguistic function is that function wherein language itself becomes an object of knowledge. To deal with words the way the above tasks require, the listener must be capable of what Mattingly (1972) has termed "linguistic awareness" (also see Foss and Swinney 1973). The particular skill required is that of consciously regarding words as if they are comprised of discrete phonemic units, in place of the ordinarily unconscious linguistic operation on the acoustic signal of connected speech.

Mattingly (1972, 1978) and others have hypothesized that this skill is called upon in learning to read, but is not needed for learning to speak and understand a first language. In fact, to function as speaker or listener, the language user needs to know very little about the rules of his language on a conscious basis, while for learning to read the situation is quite otherwise. Mattingly (1978) speculates that children vary among themselves with respect to level of linguistic awareness for phonology and other rules of the grammar they will need for learning to read, but he leaves room for the reading teacher's involvement in creating linguistic awareness. The skills required to perform the above-mentioned tasks of auditory synthesis and auditory closure, therefore, are not basic to language learning but are abstract skills better described as metalinguistic than auditory or even linguistic.

Unexpected support for this conclusion comes from the findings reported by Witkin et al. (1973) in a study of the parameters of auditory processing. Of the many findings reported, two particularly interesting ones were that oral reading ability in second-grade children was more closely related to auditory closure and auditory synthesis than to speech sound discrimination, while auditory closure and synthesis did not cluster with expressive and receptive language ability in the results of factor analysis. This limited evidence is compatible with the position taken above, that auditory synthesis and auditory closure are metalinguistic skills that predict success in learning to read but are not prerequisite for language development. There is in fact little justification for including these skills on any list of hypothetical "auditory" abilities.

III. Auditory Discrimination for Speech Sounds

Three assumptions underlie the widespread practice of measuring and training speech sound discrimination in children exhibiting a wide range of articulation, language, and learning disabilities:

1. That speech sound discrimination is an "auditory" skill no different in kind from acoustic perception in general;
2. That a specific level of speech-sound discrimination ability is required for the development of higher-order linguistic skills; and
3. That a deficiency in speech sound discrimination is the least common denominator responsible for various kinds of communication and learning problems in childhood.

It is not difficult to show that these assumptions may be incorrect or at least unwarranted. To begin with, it is by now well recognized that the listener's knowledge of his language is a component in a comprehensive model of speech perception. Speech sound perception is the outcome of what Liberman et al. (1967) call "perception in the speech mode."

Studdert-Kennedy (1976) summarizes the special nature of this kind of perception, stating that "speech perception differs from general audi-

105

tory perception in both stimulus and percept. First, the sounds of speech constitute a distinctive class, drawn from the set of sounds that can be produced by the human vocal mechanism. Speech does not lie at one end of an auditory (psychological) continuum which we can approach by closer and closer acoustic (physical) approximation. The sounds of speech are distinctive. A signal is heard as either speech or nonspeech, and once heard as speech, elicits characteristic perceptual functions." He goes on to say that "the second peculiarity of speech perception ... is in perceptual response," that the identification of the speech and sound stimulus can be only that speech sound and nothing else; he calls it the "inevitable percept" that is the "central problem for the student of speech perception to define."

To illustrate the special properties of speech perception consider the so-called parallel processing of CVC syllables. The spoken word *bag* may be divided into three successive phonemes, but in actual production the utterance is a continuous signal in which information about more than one segment is carried by part of that signal. The specific acoustic characteristics of the /b/ in *bag* are in part determined by and carried over to the following vowel, while the specific acoustic characteristics of the final /g/ are determined in part by the characteristics of the preceding vowel and in turn affect that vowel. The /æ/, in turn, affects and is affected by both initial and final consonants (Liberman 1970). Parallel processing makes it possible to handle the speech signal faster than the order of successive phonemes could be resolved, but also makes it difficult to draw discrete boundaries between phonemes (Lehiste 1972). The phenomenon of parallel processing renders impossible any explanation of auditory perception of speech that depends on the discrimination and sequencing of individual phonemes. Such theories are in conflict with the plain facts about speech perception.

We must conclude that there is something about speech perception that ordinary models of processing acoustic stimuli do not account for. Processing the speech sounds of the spoken language is a linguistic skill, not a general auditory skill. But speech perception is only a part of a far more complex set of operations. Processing spoken utterances includes operations that are auditory, phonetic, phonological, lexical, syntactic, and semantic. As Studdert-Kennedy (1976) describes it, at the phonetic level the processing results in "a set of properties not inherent in the signal. They derive from the auditory display of processes that must be peculiar to humans, since they can only be defined by reference to human vocal mechanism."

According to Studdert-Kennedy (1976), at the next level, the phonological, "processes peculiar to the listener's language are engaged. Here, the listener merges phonetic variatons that have no function in his language, treating, for example, both the initial segment of (pʰ ɪ t) and the second segment of (spɪ t) as instances of /p/.... In short, this is the level at which phonetic variability is transformed into phonological system." In other words, at this level the listener makes decisions about what variable instances count as instances of the same linguistic category, the phoneme. (It is worth repeating that the phoneme is an abstract linguistic category with known "psychological reality," but that it does not exist as an entity in the acoustic spectrum). Studdert-Kennedy (1976) points out that "listeners hear speech in terms of the categories of their native language," meaning, of course, that speech perception is an acquired linguistic skill, or to put it another way, that the listener learns speech perception as he learns his language. Speech sound perception cannot therefore be a skill prerequisite to acquiring language; it is logical to put it the other way round, to conclude that speech perception skills are the *result* of having learned one's language. In clinical application, therefore, if a child may be unambiguously shown to have a speech sound perception deficit, we might conclude that we have found a child with a language learning problem, but not that we have found the *source* of his language learning problem. To put it otherwise, to ask a child to distinguish between two syllables that differ in a single sound segment is to ask him to make a linguistic, not merely an auditory, judgment. To get it right the listener must know not only what differences to note but also what differences to ignore.

The story, however, continues well beyond the phonological level. "The upper levels of lexical, syntactic, and semantic processing complete the normal process of speech perception." (Studdert-Kennedy 1976). There is considerable evidence that listeners use information from these more abstract levels to resolve uncertainties about what speech sound segments they are hearing. For example, it is well known that it is easier to recognize individual words in a sentence than in an unrelated list (see the earlier reference to Miller and Isard 1963).

While awaiting a fuller understanding of the nature of speech perception and of the interactive role of speech perception in acquiring and using language for communication, we can be quite certain at least that 1) speech discrimination skills as measured by some of our clinical tests cannot be regarded as prerequisite to the development of language; that 2) measuring speech discrimination through these tests is unlikely to give us any useful insight into the source of the child's presenting difficulty; and that 3) working to improve the child's speech discrimination as a discrete skill is most unlikely to give him anything useful, as the Hammill and Larsen (1974) review indicated.

Meanwhile, however, many clinicians remain convinced that speech discrimination problems are really at the heart of things for many of the children they work with. A clinician reported that a ten-year-old learning-disabled child "obviously" had a speech discrimination problem that caused his learning difficulties, as indicated by the following evidence: She was having a conversation with the boy about a story in the morning newspaper, saying to him, "I read in the paper about a man who got shot." He responded, "That's silly, you can't get a shock from paper." Her interpretation was that he did not hear the difference between *shot* and *shock*, accounting for his failure to understand the sentence. But that explanation is most unsatisfactory in the context of the sentence's complexity containing, as it does, besides the Noun-Verb in the main clause, two prepositional phrases followed by a relative clause, known to be especially difficult to process syntactically. To be sure, one would expect a normal ten-year-old to have mastered all that, but this child is not learning normally. The question is how best to describe his problems. To ascribe them to a deficit in distinguishing minimal pairs like shot/shock, especially at the end of a sentence when the final stop consonant is likely to have low acoustic power, to be imploded, or even to be replaced by a glottal stop in ordinary discourse, seems totally indefensible. Processing sentences to extract meaning is more complex than speech sound discrimination, and k/t confusion is an inadequate explanation for this ten-year-old's lack of comprehension.

A special aspect of auditory discrimination, one that overlaps considerably with auditory sequencing and temporal ordering notions, has been explored in detail by Tallal (1978). In her experiments, Tallal presented pairs of nonspeech and speech sound stimuli to "dysphasic" children between 6.8 and 9.3 years. The non-speech stimuli were complex steady-state tones of differing fundamental frequency, and the subjects were trained to indicate whether the tones were the same or different and to press the appropriate response panels in the correct order. The experimental subjects' performance was significantly affected by the length of the interstimulus interval. Further, she found that although normal children between 4.6 and 8.6 improved with age in their ability to respond to these auditory stimuli at shorter interstimulus intervals, the dysphasic children did worse than even the younger normal children at interstimulus intervals below 305 msec, while their performance at higher interstimulus intervals was normal. (The relation of this approach to the work of Efron [1963] is noteworthy, once again.)

Tallal concluded from these findings that dysphasic children have difficulty with auditory discrimination as well as with auditory perceptual ordering of complex tones presented in rapid sequence. A subsequent experiment showed that the duration of the stimulus tones also significantly affected dysphasics' performance; longer tone durations produced fewer errors. Tallal suggests that "for developmental dysphasics, the time available for acoustic processing is critical to performances. Accordingly, previously reported impairment of auditory sequencing and memory in dysphasics may well be attributable, at least in part, to a more primary ability to discriminate between stimulus elements presented at rapid rates" (1978, pp. 40-41). Tallal did not find comparable results for visual perception. Regarding speech sound stimuli, synthesized vowels and stop-consonant-vowel pairs were presented in a similar experimental procedure. The dysphasics' performance on steady-state vowels was similar to that for nonverbal stimuli but was significantly poorer for stop-consonant-vowel pairs (ba and da). Tallal asserts that the brief transitional component of the consonant-vowel sequence makes such combinations difficult for dysphasic children to process.

Evidence from these experiments leaves little doubt that Tallal's subject population had difficulty with the auditory processing tasks involving judgments about auditory stimuli presented in rapid succession or characterized by rapid acoustic transitions. Her interpretation of the findings, however, is far stronger: "The language impairment of these children appears to reflect their primary inability to analyze the rapid stream of acoustic information that characterizes speech and is essential to normal speech perception and language development" (p. 56).

Just what kind of and how severe a language deficit should this kind of difficulty cause? Should it affect production only, or comprehension as well? Unfortunately nothing in Tallal's reports answers these questions. She does not state what her subjects could or could not do in terms of language skills. That speech perception skill as narrowly defined by Tallal's experiments is specifically required for normal language development is open to question. Even if it could be shown that Tallal's subjects had articulatory problems that corresponded to their stop-consonant-vowel confusions, it is not clear how these difficulties could affect other aspects of language development that were defective in children labelled "dysphasic." Moreover, if the children could perform adequately when allowed sufficient processing time, it seems that they had learned the linguistic distinctions between the consonants in the stimulus pairs; therefore, they must have had whatever auditory processing skills are required for phoneme learning. Leonard (1979) concludes from his review of Tallal's work that the presence of an auditory processing deficit in language disordered children is insufficient evidence from which to argue causality; and he makes the cogent point that "despite the fact that normal children improve across time in their performance on auditory processing tasks, there has been no serious attempt to explain normal language development on the basis of developing auditory skills."

A related study that sheds some light on the data as well as on their possible interpretation was reported by Liles et al. (1978). These investigators found that five language disordered children below the age of 5 years made fewer errors in a sentence comprehension task with sentences of the type *Put the man's face on the red vest* and *Put the small blue ball in the clown's hand* when a 3-sec pause was inserted before the prepositional phrase. This effect was not found for older language disordered children or with conjoined sentences like *Put on the clown's face and the red ball*, where the pause was inserted before the conjunction. Unfortunately, the authors do not provide data on normal children, so we do not know whether the effect is a developmental one only. But once again there is evidence that additional processing time helps these children perform correctly. As was the case with the Tallal data, it appears that these children have learned the language in the sense that they can perform correctly under optimal conditions; so it must be concluded that they have the minimal abilities necessary for language acquisition. If they had not, they could not demonstrate accurate comprehension under any condition.

A version of the approach promoted by Tallal was applied to clinical practice by Harris (1977). This author presents a case report of a five-year-old girl who underwent 16 months of treatment for a language disorder (unfortunately Harris does not say whether the subject was five years old at the start or at the termination of treatment). The child was "suspected of having difficulties processing auditory signals similar to that described by Tallal." She spoke in telegraphic and often unintelligible sentences up to five words in length and demonstrated receptive vocabulary, comprehension, and auditory memory span below age level. Interestingly, after three months of "language stimulation" her receptive vocabulary and language comprehension rose to near normal levels. Subsequently she was treated in a "phoneme discrimination program," after which her speech was completely intelligible, her grammatical structure was appropriate, her ceiling length of utterance increased to 16, and her vocabulary and comprehension rose above age level. However, her "verbal retention span" remained below age level! This report provides the basis for some interesting speculations. Is it reasonable that with an auditory processing deficit so severe as to cause such a wide range of spoken language and comprehension delay the subject could so quickly come up to age level in acquiring vocabulary and comprehension skills? If at some point she had normal vocabulary and comprehension skills, is it logical to attribute her continued deficit in production to defective auditory procesing? Can one even account for her broad productive speech and language deficit on the basis of speech sound discrimination difficulty? The explanation does not seem to fit the facts.

IV. Auditory Memory

Measuring and training auditory memory span in children with language and learning disabilities is a clinical activity based on the assumption that a child needs a given size of memory span in order to — do what? The usual answers include functions like these: to synthesize unconnected phonemes into words; to comprehend sentences consisting of that number of words; to be able to follow directions; to be able to answer questions correctly. An initial problem with this notion is therefore the unanswered question, memory for what? What is the proper unit to measure memory span? Usually digits or words are used in tests of auditory memory span, but it has already been shown that there is little reason to conclude that the word is a natural or basic unit in perception of spoken utterances. There are, however, a number of difficult questions with respect to memory itself.

1. What Memory is Under Consideration?

In cognitive psychology, or what has come to be called information processing, it is generally recognized that there are "At least three distinctly different types of memory: a *sensory information storage*, a *short-*

term memory, and a *long-term memory*" (Lindsay and Norman 1972). The sensory information storage system is of short duration, between one-tenth to one-half of a second, and "maintains a rather accurate and complete picture of the world as it is received by the sensory system" (Lindsay and Norman 1972). We might say that the sensory information storage contains sounds as actually heard, but only very briefly. The short-term memory system also has a limited capacity, but for a different form of material: "Here the information retained is not a complete image of the events that have taken place at the sensory level. Rather, short-term memory seems to retain the immediate *interpretation* of those events. If a sentence has been spoken, you do not so much hear the sounds that made up the sentence as you remember the words." If the units in question are words in a list, "Only about the last five or six items that have been presented can be retained" (Lindsay and Norman 1972), but this amount of material can be maintained in short-term memory indefinitely by rehearsal. Long-term memory, in contrast, appears to be of infinite capacity. Long-term memory must contain everything that is retained over time because, otherwise, due to the limited capacity of STM, new items would push out the old and they would get lost. Even the rules of language reside in long-term memory, while the problem of how information is retrieved from long-term memory is the most difficult one in the study of memory.

Even so brief a review of the memory systems reveals that there is nothing simple or unitary about memory. Measuring and training auditory memory span therefore seems at the very least to be based on a rather astounding oversimplification.

2. What Determines How Many Items/ How Much One Can Remember?

Considerable interaction exists between the organization of information and its recall or retrieval. Two examples will illustrate the point.

a. If you present a subject with a list of words, either by eye or ear, he will, if he can, organize the list into groups the members of which in some way, probably semantically, relate to one another. These groups will tend to be produced together if the subject is asked to repeat or identify the words he has heard or seen. So, if the list contains words like *car, bicycle, wagon, locomotive,* assuming that these have been randomly dispersed throughout a list of 10 words, the subject is likely to exhibit clustering, that is, to produce these words as a group although they were not presented that way and he was not asked to "find the words that go together" or to "find the words that have to do with transportation." Furthermore, this type of strategy aids recall; more words are remembered if the list can be organized into clusters.

b. Other types of organization of material aid retrieval from long-term memory. If you use the mnemonic device HOMES, you will find it easier to recall the names of the Great Lakes: Huron, Ontario, Michigan, Erie, Superior.[2] Organization of material can therefore be a kind of "searching strategy" to access material in LTM.

A good discussion of this effect on children's language growth is by Olson (1973). Having referred to George Miller's well-known paper on the magical number seven plus or minus two, wherein it is observed that we can hold only about five to seven units in immediate memory (STM), Olson points out that "there is flexibility as to what the ... units in immediate memory can be. If we encode our information cleverly we can store five to seven units of incredible richness while still constrained by the same overall restrictions on capacity. This means that the practical effect of a severely limited immediate-memory span can be alleviated if we can recode the material into informationally richer units. Instead of storing elementary units of information we can store the components of an organized retrieval scheme." When my son Raymond at age four persisted in saying "when it gets morning" in favor of "tomorrow," he could have been unable to "chunk" the units into one richer one, but the curious result is that he had to produce a longer utterance to do it his way. Olson (1973) suggests a similar explanation: "My hypothesis is that ... nominal quantitative changes in the amount of externally defined information that can be handled have to do with the nature of the child's internal representations." The limit comes from the child's ability to organize the input to language, not from the internal representations which are the linguistic meanings translated into words and sentences. Olson follows Bruner's proposal that "the dominant form of internal representation in the child progresses from the enactive to the iconic to the symbolic...." Olson concludes that the reason why memory span and utterance length seem to increase together is that they measure the same thing, namely, the increasing ability to handle verbal information. One is not a cause of the other.

3. What Is the Interaction Between Language and Memory?

The foregoing examples make it clear that while memory is needed for language, it is also the case that language affects memory for linguistic material. For example, it is known that sentences that can be comprehended can be recalled accurately even when they are longer than the limits of memory for digits. As already noted, imposing a structure on an assortment of items makes it easier to recall the items. In this case the structure is provided by the hierarchical, syntactic organization of a sentence. Sentences are not like strings of digits because the former, unlike the latter, have an internal organization. When a sentence is comprehended, its internal organization must have been available to the listener, explaining why comprehension aids recall.

Moreover, knowledge of the structural properties of grammatical sentences is among the "rules of language" that are stored in long-term memory, while digit-span measures only the capacity of short-term memory. The ability of a listener to impose grammatical structure on a heard sentence

2. Courtesy of Louis Gerstman.

must therefore require interaction between STM and LTM; to put it differently, information about a sentence's internal structure must be retrieved from LTM to play a role in sentence processing. Measuring a child's auditory memory span for digits or unrelated words is unlikely, therefore, to tell us much of what we want to know about his ability to understand sentences, while increasing his auditory memory span would seem unlikely to have much effect on increasing his language comprehension ability.

Even with grammatical sentences ease of comprehending sentence processing is not a simple function of length. A dramatic illustration revealing that some shorter sentences are harder to process than some longer ones is the following pair of sentences that are paraphrases of one another:

(13) The boy the girl the man watched left slept.
(14) The man watched the girl, and the girl left the boy, and the boy slept.

4. What Happens to a Sentence When It Is Stored in Memory?

It is intriguing to note that when a heard and comprehended sentence moves into LTM, its original structure may be lost entirely and only the meaning retained (Johnson-Laird 1970). Even the original lexical items may be discarded. A sentence recalled from LTM is likely to be a paraphrase of the original sentence, which explains why some people are such rotten joke-tellers. If the joke revolves around a particular word or turn-of-phrase, but only the meaning is recalled in paraphrase form, the joke will fail.

What has sometimes been called "memory-for-gist" speaks to the great complexity of the memory system itself and to the complexity and subtlety of the interaction between language and memory. Bransford, Barclay, and Franks (1972) in an important study illustrated this phenomenon by presenting subjects with the following pair of sentences:

(15) Three turtles rested beside a log and a fish swam beneath them.
(16) Three turtles rested on a floating log and a fish swam beneath them.

Later they asked the subjects whether they had previously heard these (actually) novel sentences:

(17) Three turtles rested on a floating log and a fish swam beneath it.
(18) Three turtles rested beside a floating log and a fish swam beneath it.

The subjects tended to report that they had heard (17) but not (18) (although in fact they had heard neither one). It seems, then, that not only is meaning rather than form retained, but also that the meaning itself undergoes changes over time as it is integrated with other information in long term memory.

It is unrewarding, therefore, to search for the boundary between memory processes and linguistic processes. In the face of this complexity, the auditory memory span notion appears simplistic and unproductive.

V. Central Auditory Processing Function

In the past decade a number of measures have been devised to assess the integrity of the central auditory processing mechanism. The tests I refer to here are the behavioral rather than the physiological tests; together they represent procedures that, by a series of correlational studies, had been shown to relate poorer-than-normal performance in adults to anatomical lesions of the central auditory mechanism (Berlin and Lowe 1972). By extension it was presumed that children who perform below age level on similar tasks could be considered to be suffering from central auditory dysfunction. This label is therefore both a descriptive and a diagnostic one. According to Keith (1980), "a potentially serious and complex problem arises when central hearing tests are used on the one hand to identify lesions of the central auditory pathways, and on the other hand to identify auditory perceptual difficulties in young children with learning disabilities."

Most of these tests present words or sentences that have been treated in numerous ingenious ways so as to reduce redundancy and otherwise render listening more difficult. They include measures of recognition of sentences that have been altered by such devices as low-pass filtering, time-compression, interruption, alternation between the two ears, and presentation of competing noise in the same or opposite ear (Willeford 1978). In another type of sentence test the content of the speech signal is manipulated to represent controlled degrees of normalness by applying decreasing orders of approximation (Jerger, Speaks, and Trammel 1969). Dichotic speech tests, in which differing stimuli are presented to each ear simultaneously, may consist of words rather than sentences: among these are tests using stop-consonant vowel pairs (Berlin and McNeil 1976) and staggered spondee words (Brunt 1972). A test using nonspeech stimuli for similar purpose is the one developed by Pinheiro (1977).

The basis for using degraded speech material to assess the integrity of the auditory neurological mechanism is offered by Keith 1980. Both spoken language and neuroanatomical pathways are ordinarily characterized by high degrees of redundancy. When the spoken signal has normal redundancy, even a defective neurological mechanism, i.e., one lacking normal redundancy, can handle it. Therefore, non-normal mechanisms may give normal results to tests utilizing normal speech signals. In contrast, degraded speech stimuli, normal redundancies lacking, are more difficult for non-normal mechanisms to handle and therefore provide diagnostic information. The "subtlety principle" provides that at central sites "the presence of a lesion can only be demonstrated by means of considerably more subtle auditory tasks, such as sensitized speech tests."

Many of these tests have been used or adapted for children (Keith 1980; Willeford and Billger 1978). The recent designation of learning disability as a handicapping condition for educational purposes gave considerable impetus to the expansion of central auditory testing in the clinic. Among audiologists the tests originally developed for site-of-lesion identification have become commonly applied to children, although the relationship of the skills so measured to language development and disorders is not clear (Willeford 1977; Keith 1980).

An interesting example is the work on time-compressed speech with children having "auditory perceptual problems" identified primarily through low scores on the auditory subtests of the ITPA (Manning, Johnston, and Beasley 1977). Their general findings were that eight-year-old children so identified performed more poorly than normal eight-year-olds at 0% time compression and at 60% time compression, but as well as normal chilren at 30% time compression. How may these puzzling findings be explained? The authors state, "Perhaps children with auditory perceptual problems experience an excessively rapid decay of information from their short-term memory systems. In turn, presentation of stimuli at a moderately increased rate (for example, 30% time compression), while not excessively distorting the acoustic characteristics of the speech signal, may result in a neutralizing effect for the rapid decay of the stimuli from the short-term memory system." The logic here is mystifying because the 30% condition did not improve performance; the authors seem to assume that *something* about 30% time compression negatively affects performance for all listeners, while for children with auditory perceptual disorders something *else* about 30% time compression has a positive effect that cancels the negative effect. The highly speculative character of this interpretation is worth noting. Even more interesting is the implied contradiction of the usual assertion that auditory perceptual problems are characterized by difficulty with rapid temporal processing. Manning, Johnston, and Beasley (1977) proceed to speculate that children with "certain types" of perceptual problems will do worse at slower than optimum (whatever that is) processing rates because of inattentiveness or distractibility. In short, we are told by some authors (Manning, Johnston, and Beasley) that children with auditory perceptual problems process more successfully at greater than normal rates (although why they suddenly do much worse at 60% time compression is not explained), and by others (Tallal 1978; Liles et al. 1978) that these same children cannot process rapidly changing stimuli. Moreover, Manning, Johnston, and Beasley's speculations seem far removed from the initial findings reported by Bocca and Calearo (1963) that decreased speech discrimination in the time-compressed condition is related to temporal lobe lesions.

115

Assuming Manning, Johnston, and Beasley's (1977) findings to be typical of children who do poorly on the ITPA auditory subtests, one may nonetheless wonder what these findings imply for children with communication or learning difficulties. Interestingly, Ormson and Williams (1975) found no difference in performance on time-compressed speech discrimination when they compared normal first and second graders with those exhibiting articulation and/or reading disorders. Williams, Medsker, and Vaughan (1977) found that while a dichotic speech test yielded somewhat poorer scores than normal for learning disabled adolescents, these same children did as well as normals on the SSW and *better* than normals on the time compressed stimuli at 60% compression. In short, the findings on time-compressed speech are at best equivocal and at worst devoid of any clear rationale for use with learning disabled children.

In the case of dichotic speech, Tobey et al. (1979) reported that nine-year-old children with "previously demonstrated" auditory processing disorders (they do not say how demonstrated) performed more poorly than normal controls on dichotic listening tasks, and they were particularly distinguished from the normals by failing to benefit from as much as 150 msec. separation of stimulus onsets. They conclude that "learning disabled children with auditory processing disorders may have a reduced temporal efficiency in processing rapidly varying acoustic patterns associated with stop-consonants that is observable when speech perceptual mechanisms are stressed through dichotic competition." Regrettably, they do not give the evidence for learning disability, although they mention that the children were given relevant tests. In any case the correspondence with Tallal's (1978) work is notable, although how this type of deficit interferes with learning is not given by Tobey et al. (1979).

As Keith (1980) summarizes this difficulty, "how the test results related to functional behavior is not clear.... In addition, site of lesion information is probably of little value in determining remediation programs." The latter point is especially relevant to the findings on the Pitch Patterns test (Pinheiro 1977), wherein the child listens to a three-tone pattern varying between two pitch levels and points to a tall and a short block in the same order. Pinheiro concludes that poor performance on this test reflects dysfunction in interhemispheric interaction, or deep in the left hemisphere. Since her subjects were dyslexic rather than language disordered, we may conclude that whatever neurological abnormality the test uncovers, it does not interfere with learning spoken language. Precisely how the task or the neurological integration it purportedly reflects relate to learning to read is not clear, and no relevant comments regarding remediation are offered. One may point out, however, that it is misleading to call this a central auditory processing test at all. Pinheiro notes that these children often could hum the melodies, so they seemed to be processing the auditory sequences well enough. They performed poorly when asked to translate the heard sequence into a visual representation, a task that she believes requires encoding. In that sense the task is analogous to the old verbal me-

116

diation tasks, which have long been associated with poorer performance in younger children and other special groups. It only adds to the confusion to call this auditory processing.

That learning disabled children tend to perform more poorly than normal chilren on the various central auditory tests is by now well known, although the findings are by no means unequivocal (Keith 1980). Although poor performance is taken to have both diagnostic significance and remedial implications, there is no agreement about whether deficits in auditory perception as measured by these tests actually produce language and/or learning disorders or are behavioral correlates of these and other disabilities. Kleffner (1975) makes the point that in the case of children with normal hearing acuity who have poor language development, "there is virtually no test which presumes to identify problems in aspects of memory, cognition, integrative behavior, perception, or sensory processing on which these children will fail to yield positive findings" (p. 66). The same comment could be made about learning-disabled children.

For that matter, it seems likely that the tests developed to assess central auditory function are difficult not only for learning disabled but for other special groups as well. Toscher and Rupp (1978) found that teen-age and adult stutterers did more poorly on the Synthetic Sentence Identification (SSI) test, mentioned earlier, than did a normal control group. While Toscher and Rupp are willing to conclude that stutterers may have a central auditory deficit, it becomes painfully clear that the reasoning is somewhat circular and that we are in danger of ascribing just about anything to central auditory dysfunction. To illustrate, we are on the verge of saying that if a child has trouble with reading but talks normally the cause is a central auditory dysfunction, while if the child speaks dysfluently but reads normally the cause is a central auditory dysfunction. Moreover, if the child has either a language disorder or a learning disability or both, findings of reduced auditory processing skills as measured by tests of central auditory functioning are supposed to be of diagnostic significance; yet if such a child has a learning disability but is normal with respect to speech and language development (including fluency), it is apparent that whatever the tests are measuring, they are not skills needed for learning to speak the language normally. Cases of learning disabled children with normal or superior language skills who do poorly on a battery of central auditory tests are reported by Willeford (1977). Johnson and Newman (1979), in another interesting example, report findings on an eight-year-old boy with chronic otitis media, significant results on tests of competing sentences, binaural fusion, and time-compressed speech, a "learning disabilty" manifested by difficulty attending to tasks in the presence of background noise, who nonetheless had "strong academic skills" and normal language ability! Johnson and Newman described four subjects in all, all of whom had histories of chronic otitis media, "positive central auditory findings," and "significant attentional deficits," while only two had language and academic problems. If low scores on tests of central auditory function can be found in children who speak and learn within normal limits, it is difficult to understand just what if any clincial or diagnostic significance may be attached to similar findings in children with language and learning disorders.

A reasonable conclusion is that the tests reviewed in this section are sophisticated audiological measures which tap abilities that normal language users have mastered and control quite well under most conditions. The tests, moreover, seem to identify certain difficulties in children, although in many cases the problem seems to be one of immaturity inasmuch as normal children perform poorly but improve as they get older (Keith 1980). The research results may be interpreted to mean that listeners differ in their ability to (1) engage the speech processor in cases of limited redundancy, like competing speech, and (2) deal linguistically with distorted or unexpected versions of the input. These test may, unlike the measures reviewed in the earlier sections of this paper, be getting at something more "auditory" than "linguistic," although thus far no one has developed an intelligible account of how these central auditory processing skills, or the lack of them, relate to language acquisition or academic learning.

In summary, the wealth of statements and studies about assessment of central auditory function in children with language disorders and learning disabilities fails to provide an acceptable explanatory model and suffers from internal inconsistencies with respect to experimental findings and logical argument. It is unfortunate that these measurements occupy so much clinical time and energy when the payoff is so small in terms of the meaningfulness of the findings and their implications for clinical management. This area is as yet in a state of experimental exploration.

References

Aten, J.L. 1972. Auditory memory and auditory sequencing. In *Proceedings of the Memphis State University's First Annual Symposium on Auditory Processing and Learning Disabilities*, ed. D.L. Rampp. Las Vegas.

Berlin, C. and McNeil, M. 1976. Dichotic listening. In *Contemporary issues in experimental phonetics*, ed. N. Lass. New York: Academic Press.

Berlin, C. and Lowe, S.S. 1972. Temporary and dichotic factors in central auditory testing. In *Handbook of clinical audiology*, ed. J. Katz. Baltimore: Williams and Wilkins.

Bever, T.G., Lackner, J.R., and Kirk, R. 1969. The underlying structures of sentences are the primary units of immediate speech processing. *Percept. and Psychophys.* 5:225-34.

Bloom, L. and Lahey, M. 1978. *Language development and language disorders*. New York: John Wiley and Sons.

Bocca, E. and Calearo, C. 1963. Central hearing processes. In *Modern developments in audiology*, ed. J. Jerger. New York: Academic Press.

Bransford, J.D., Barclay, J.R., and Franks, J.J. 1972. Sentence memory: a constructive versus interpretive approach. *Cognitive Psychol.* 3:193-209.

Brunt, M. 1972. The staggered spondaic word test. In *Handbook of clinical audiology*, ed. J. Katz. Baltimore: Williams and Wilkins.

Chapin, P.G., Smith, T.S., and Abrahamson, A.A. 1972. Two factors in perceptual segmentation of speech. *J. Verb. Learn. Verb. Beh.* 11:164-73.

Chomsky, N. 1965. *Aspects of the theory of syntax*. Cambridge, MA: MIT Press.

Clark, E.V. 1971. On the acquisition of the meaning of "before" and "after". *J. Verb Learn. Verb. Beh.* 10:266-75.

Clark, H.H. and Haviland, S.E. 1977. Comprehension and the given-new contract. In *Discourse production and comprehension*, ed. R.O. Freedle. Norwood, NJ: Ablex.

De Villiers, J.G. and de Villiers, P.A. 1973. Development of word order in comprehension. *J. Psycholing. Res.* 2:331-41.

De Villiers, P.A. and de Villiers, J.G. 1972. Early judgments of semantic and syntactic acceptability by children. *J. Psycholing. Res.* 1:299-310.

Efron, R. 1963. Temporal perception, aphasia, and deja vu. *Brain* 86:403-23.

Foss, D.J. and Swinney, D.A. 1973. On the psychological reality of the phoneme: perception, identification, and consciousness. *J. Verb. Learn. Verb. Beh.* 12:246-57.

Hammill, D.D. and Larsen, S.C. 1974. The effectiveness of psycholinguistic training. *Except. Child.* 40:5-14.

Harris, C. 1977. Auditory processing disability: sixteen months of treatment. Paper read at the American Speech and Hearing Association, Chicago.

Jenkins, J.J. 1977. Remember the old theory of memory? Well, forget it! In *Perceiving, acting and knowing*, eds. R. Shaw and J. Bransford. New York: John Wiley & Sons.

Jerger, J., Speaks, C., and Trammell, J.A. 1969. A new approach to speech audiometry. *J. Speech Hear. Dis.* 33:318-28.

Johnson, A.F. and Newman, C.W. 1979. Central auditory and language disorders associated with conductive hearing loss. Paper delivered at the American Speech-Language-Hearing Association, Atlanta, GA.

Johnson-Laird, P.N. 1970. The perception and memory of sentences. In *New horizons in linguistics*, ed. J. Lyons. Baltimore: Penguin Books.

Keith, R.W. 1980. Central hearing tests. In *Speech hearing and language*, eds. N.J. Lass, L.V. McReynolds, J.L. Northern, and D.E. Yoder. Philadelphia: W.B. Saunders Co.

Kleffner, F.R. 1975. The direct teaching approach for children with auditory processing and learning disabilities. *Acta Symbolica* 6:65-93.

Ladefoged, P. and Broadbent, D.E. 1960. Perception of sequence in auditory events. *Quart. J. Exp. Psychol.* 12:162-70.

Lehiste, I. 1972. The units of speech perception. In *Speech and cortical functioning*, ed. J.H. Gilbert. New York: Academic Press.

Leonard, L.B. 1979. Language impairment in children. *Merrill-Palmer Quart.* 25:205-32.

Liberman, A.M. 1970. The grammars of speech and language. *Cognitive Psychol.* 1:301-23.

Liberman, A.M., Cooper, F.S., Shankweiler, D.P. and Studdert-Kennedy, M. 1967. Perception of the speech code. *Psychol. Rev.* 74:431-61.

Lieberman, P. 1972. *Speech acoustics and perception*. New York. Bobbs-Merrill.

Liles, B.Z., Cooker, H.S., Kass, M., and Carey, B.J. 1978. The effects of pause time on auditory comprehension of language-disordered children. *J. Communicat. Dis.* 11:365-74.

Lindsay, P.H. and Norman, D.A. 1972. *Human information processing*. New York: Academic Press.

Lowe, A.D. and Campbell, R.A. 1965. Temporal discrimination in aphasoid and normal children. *J. Speech Hear. Res.* 18:313-14.

Manning, W.H., Johnston, K.L., and Beasley, D.S. 1977. The performance of children with auditory perceptual disorders on a time-compressed speech discrimination measure. *J. Speech Hear. Dis.* 42:77-84.

Mattingly, I.G. 1978. The psycholinguistic basis of linguistic awareness. Paper delivered at the National Reading Conference, St. Petersburg, FL.

Mattingly, I.G. 1972. Reading, the linguistic process, and linguistic awareness. In *Language by ear and by eye*, eds. J.F. Kavanagh and I.G. Mattingly. Cambridge, MIT Press.

Miller, G.A. 1962. Some psychological studies of grammar. *Amer. Psychologist* 17:748-62.

Miller, G.A. and Isard, S. 1963. Some perceptual consequences of linguistic rules. *J. Verb. Learn. Verb. Beh.* 2:217-28.

Olson, G.M. 1973. Developmental changes in memory and the acquisiton of language. In *Cognitive development and the acquisition of language*, ed. T.E. Moore. New York: Academic Press.

Ormson, K.D. and Williams, D.K. 1975. Central auditory function as assessed by time-compressed speech with elementary school age children having articulatory and reading problems. Paper read at the American Speech and Hearing Association, Washington, DC.

Pinheiro, M.L. 1977. Tests of central auditory function in children with learing disabilities. In *Central auditory dysfunction*, ed. R.W. Keith. New York: Grune and Stratton.

Plummer, B.A. *A guide to tests of auditory processing abilities for young children.* Part of a federally funded project *The Model for Auditory Processing Remediaton*, Fairfield, CA, no date.

Rees, N.S. 1973. Auditory processing factors in language disorders: the view from Procrustes' bed. *J. Speech and Hear. Dis.* 38:304-15.

Savin, H.B. and Bever, T.G. 1970. The nonperceptual reality of the phoneme. *J. Verb. Learn. Verb. Beh.* 9:295-302.

Studdert-Kennedy, M. 1976. Speech perception. In *Contemporary issues in experimental phonetics*, ed. N.J. Lass. New York: Academic Press.

Studdert-Kennedy, M. 1979. Speech perception. Invited address to the IXth International Congress of Phonetic Sciences, Copenhagen.

Tallal, P. 1978. An experimental investigation of the role of auditory temporal processing in normal and disordered language development. In *Language acquisition and language breakdown*, eds. A. Caramazza and E.B. Zurif. Baltimore: Johns Hopkins Press.

Tobey, E.A., Cullen, J.K. Jr., Rampp, D.L., and Fleisher-Gallagher, A.M. 1979. Effects of stimulus-onset asynchrony on the dichotic performance of children with auditory processing disorders. *J. Speech Hear. Res.* 22:197-211.

Toscher, M.M. and Rupp, R.R. 1978. A study of the central auditory process in stutterers using the synthetic sentence identification (SSI) test battery. *J. Speech Hear. Res.* 21:779-92.

Wertz, R.T., Waengler, H.H., Rosenbeck, J.C., and Lemme, P.L. 1973. Linguistic influence on auditory comprehension in children, normal adults, and aphasic adults. Paper read at the American Speech and Hearing Association, Detroit.

Willeford, J.A. 1978. Sentence tests of central auditory dysfunction. In *Handbook of clinical audiology*, 2d. ed., ed. J. Katz. Baltimore: Williams and Wilkins.

Willeford, J.A. 1977. Assessing central auditory behavior in children: a test battery approach. In *Central auditory dysfunction*, ed. R.W. Keith. New York: Grune and Stratton.

Willeford, J.A. and Billger, J.M. 1978. Auditory perception in children with learning disabilities. In *Handbook of clinical audiology*, 2d. ed., ed. J. Katz. Baltimore: Williams and Wilkins.

Williams, D.K., Medsker, S., and Vaughan, R. 1977. Oral language, oral reading, and central auditory function in learning disabled and normal adolescents. Paper read at the American Speech and Hearing Association, Chicago.

Witkin, B.R., Butler, K.G., Hedrick, D.L., Manning, C.C., and Whalen, T.E. 1973. Parameters of auditory processing: two factor analytic studies. Paper read at the American Speech and Hearing Association, Detroit.

Wood, N.E. 1972. Auditory closure and auditory discrimination in young children. In *Proceedings of the Memphis State University's First Annual Symposium on Auditory Processing and Learning Disabilities*, ed. D.L. Rampp. Las Vegas.

8

Perceptual and Motor Deficits in Language-Impaired Children

Rachel E. Stark, Ph.D. and Paula Tallal, Ph.D.

Introduction

Traditionally, speech and language disorders in children have been viewed as having a strong relationship with auditory processing deficits. Many treatment strategies employed by speech and language clinicians in their work with language disordered children are based upon the belief that this relationship is causal in nature. More recently, however, this belief has been challenged. Rees (1973), for example, has shown that some uncritical assumptions were made by its original proponents. Rees has also pointed out that problems of speech sound discrimination may be attributed to deficits in higher level processing abilities as well as to more basic auditory processing deficits, and that the nonverbal auditory processing deficits that have been demonstrated in some language disordered children need not have any significant relationship with their higher level verbal processing abilities.

The work of Tallal and Piercy (1974) appeared to answer some of these criticisms. These authors showed that difficulty in processing both speech-like and nonspeech-like auditory stimuli was present in a group of 12 severely language impaired children of 7 to 9 years significantly more often than in a matched control group of normal childen. The deficits were demonstrated only when the children were asked to identify, discriminate and sequence auditory stimuli incorporating brief or rapidly changing temporal events. They were not present if the duration of these events was increased. Brief steady-state stimuli in series and brief interstimulus intervals (that is, onsets and offsets that followed one another rapidly over time) produced this effect, as did stimuli incorporating rapid spectral changes. Such rapid changes are highly characteristic of the speech signal. Thus, difficulty in processing these events in the auditory speech stream could conceivably be detrimental to the acquisition of language. In subsequent studies, Tallal, Stark and Curtiss (1976) and Stark and Tallal (1979) showed that the speech perception deficits of these children were accompanied by severe speech production deficits. The production of sounds in context which demanded fine control and precise timing of speech gestures was particularly affected. It still remained to be shown, however, that auditory deficits of this kind were significantly correlated with language disorders in children.

A recent large-scale project (Stark and Tallal 1980) was devoted to examining the relationship between sensory and perceptual functioning and language skills in young children who had normal or delayed language development. This project was designed to investigate the performance of three different groups of language impaired children (language impaired, speech articulation impaired, and reading impaired) on sensory, perceptual, and cognitive tasks and to compare their performance with that of a matched group of normal children. In the present report, only the findings for the languge impaired and normal children will be considered. They will be discussed in relation to central auditory processing and other deficits in language impaired children.

In the large-scale project, the population of language impaired children was defined to exclude those who had more obvious, primary deficits of sensory impairment, those who were mentally retarded, and those who had motor speech deficits classed as dysarthria. Children with structural anomalies of the vocal tract or with serious emotional disturbances were also excluded. The aim was to design test procedures which would uncover other clinically important variables, that is, variables which had a direct relationship with the communication impairment manifested, and which could be manipulated through treatment. In addition, it was hypothesized that the degree of impairment in sensory, perceptual, and/or cognitive subskills to be tested by an experimental battery would show a clear relationship with degree of language deficit in the language impaired children, and should make it possible to describe this deficit more completely and possibly to suggest etiological factors.

The project was designed to detemine:

1. Whether or not the perceptual or motor deficiencies of language impaired children were significantly greater than those of normal children.
2. Whether perceptual problems, if present, were confined to a single modality or involved more than one modality and whether or not they included problems of cross modal integration.
3. The relationship between patterns of sensory, perceptual, and cognitive deficits, if present, and type and degree of communication impairment.

The results of the project in relation to the normal and language impaired children will be considered in this paper and the implications for language intervention will be discussed.

Procedures

Subjects

The subjects of the study were 5 to 8 1/2 years in age. None of the children studied were visually impaired, hearing impaired, dysarthric, or mentally retarded. All subjects had a non-verbal IQ score of at least 85. All were from middle class families. American English was the only language spoken in the home.

Those children who had neurological disorders, for example, cerebral palsy and/or dysarthria, were excluded. Those children whose hearing thresholds for pure tones at 250, 500, 1000, 2000, 4000, and 6000 Hz were 25 dB or greater, and whose speech reception threshold was greater than 25 dB (ANSI S3.6 - 1969) in the poorer ear, were excluded. Also, those children with a history of chronic middle ear pathology were excluded. Those children whose visual acuity was less than 14/20 for near vision and 20/30 for distant vision with the best correcting lens in the better eye, or who had oculomotor disturbances were excluded. Children who were color blind were included, but their color blindness was noted. Children with malformation of oral structure, e.g., dental malocclusion, cleft palate, were excluded.

1. Normal control subjects were required
   a) to have a level of language development commensurate with their performance mental age (MAP) and chronological age (CA), that is, their language skills had to be at a level no more than six months behind their MAP and their CA;
   b) to have a level of reading skill on standardized reading tests commensurate with their CA and full scale mental age (MAF), that is, their reading skills had to be at a level no more than six months behind their MAF and CA;
   c) to be without speech articulation errors other than those developmental misarticulations which might be expected on the basis of their chronological age.

2. Children with language impairment were required
   a) to have a "language age" at least one year below their MAP and CA. The "language age" was derived from a composite score representing both expressive and receptive language skills. In addition these subjects had to have a receptive language age at least six months behind performance mental age (MAP) and an expressive language age at least one year behind MAP;
   b) have a level of reading skill no more than six months below their "language age;"
   c) have a level of speech articulation skill no more than six months below their "expressive language age."

The process of selection is described in greater detail in Stark and Tallal (in press). There were 35 language impaired and 38 normal developing children in the study. For the language impaired, mean performance IQ was 100 (SD + 9.2) and for the normal children it was 103 (SD + 11.3). The socioeconomic status of the two groups was 3.9 (SD + 1.4) for the language impaired and 3.4 (SD + 1.6) for the normals. There were 27 boys and 8 girls in the language impaired group and 18 girls and 20 boys in the normal group.

Tests Administered

Four different testing procedures were used in this study. These included 1) standardized tests including speech motor tests; 2) experimental sensory and perceptual tests; 3) neurodevelopmental tests; 4) visual scanning tests.

Standardized tests. Standardized tests were used for subject selection. Some, for example, the hearing screening procedures, were included only as criteria for inclusion or exclusion. Others, for example, the WPPSI and WISC - R (Wechsler 1963; Wechsler 1974) intelligence scales and the standardized tests of speech and language functioning, were included as criterion measures for subject selection or as dependent variables. Some speech motor and oral motor tests were employed initially to differentiate oral and verbal apraxias in children with articulation impairments. Scores on these tests were regarded as independent variables. Examples were tests of Isolated and Sequenced Oral Volitional Movements (Yoss and Darley 1974) and tests of diadochokinetic rates of movement of the speech articulators (Fletcher 1972). An additional test of Rapid Word Production was included.

Experimental sensory and perceptual tests. Experimental sensory and perceptual tests (Tallal and Piercy 1973b, 1974) were constructed to examine, first, basic aspects of functioning within a given sensory modality; then skills believed to be built upon these more basic functions were explored systematically. Thus, the tests were designed to examine a hierarchical set of skills and to enable the investigators to discuss each one independently of the others.

Repetition test procedure

Each test item included a stimulus pair which might be auditory, visual, tactile or crossmodal in nature. These pairs were presented in binary sequences or series within a procedure named the Repetition Test Procedure. The child was required to press one of two panels in response to each of the elements of these stimulus pairs. Each test item included a number of subtests which were always given in the same order. These subtests were: 1) Detection — in which the child learned to push one button or the other in response to a given element; 2) Association — in which the elements were presented in a random series one at a time and the children pushed the button associated with the elements presented; 3) Sequencing — in which the elements were presented in random order two at a time and the children pushed the two buttons associated with the signals presented and in the sequence in which they were presented; and 4) Serial Memory — in which the elements were presented in random order 3 to 7 at a time and the children again followed these longer sequences in their button pushing responses. Special Sequencing Subtests, in which consonant-vowel transition rates or interstimulus intervals were varied, were presented for some test items as well as the standard Sequencing Subtest. Those with brief interstimulus intervals were referred to as Rate Processing Subtests. If the children failed the standard Sequencing Subtest, they were given a Same/ Different Discrimination Subtest to explore the reasons for failure at the sequencing level.

Tallal and Piercy (1973a, 1974b) have shown that some of the test items vary in difficulty. This difficulty was believed to be related to 1) the number of elements presented within a binary series; 2) the duration of the stimulus elements and/or the interstimulus interval within a subtest; and 3) the rate of change of important parameters within the stimulus elements.

It is important in a project of this magnitude not to subject the children to unnecessary failure. If the children did not reach a criterion level for performance on the Association Subtest where items were presented one at a time, it was highly unlikely that they would perform above chance level on the Sequencing Subtest where items were presented two at a time; therefore, they were not required to take this subtest. Similarly, if they did not succeed in reaching criterion on the Serial Memory Subtest with 3 elements, they were not given the Serial Memory Subtest with 4 elements because they were unlikely to succeed at the 4-element level.

Stimulus pairs

Complex tones, vowels, CV and CVC syllables, words, lights of different hues, nonsense shapes, letters, and tone and light combinations were all presented within this experimental paradigm. In addition, three dimensional forms were presented to the mouth and to the hand in stereognostic test items. In some additional subtests the response to these forms was made by selecting the target form from a set of three presented visually, so that the test was again crossmodal. Manual and oral stereognostic tests were also administered by means of a Go-No go Procedure in which one response panel only was used. The child responded by pressing that panel each time a target stimulus was presented.

Neurodevelopmental tests. The neurodevelopmental battery included tests of motor control and coordination, balance and station, tactile sensation and perception and laterality relationships. These tests were taken from a number of published test batteries. They were randomized, administered and scored carefully and systematically.

Visual scanning tests. The visual scanning tests were modified after Doehring (1968). They were cancellation tests in which the child was required to mark off all of the target items in a practice series with a felt-tipped pen. When he showed that he understood the task he was required to carry it out as fast as he could in a larger series. The target items he was to mark were embedded among similar items on a page. They were chosen to permit systematic investigation of the child's ability to perceive visual features involved in reading. The test was timed.

Statistical Procedures

Statistical analyses were carried out 1) to identify the variables which were significantly different for the normal and language impaired group of children and 2) to determine to what extent such variables were related to level of functioning and degree of impairment in language. The univariate analyses employed for intergroup comparisons included parametric and nonparametric t tests and X^2 analyses. Children who did not take a particular subtest because they had failed to meet criterion level on a preceding subtest were arbitrarily assigned the lowest score of any child (from either group) who did take the subtest. Polynomial regression analyses and analyses of covariance on age were carried out and also some correlational analyses. Multivariate statistics were employed in a second analysis phase. These included discriminant function analysis and stepwise multiple regression analyses. These multivariate analyses were carried out to determine 1) which variables best classified the normal and language impaired children in the study and 2) which variables were most highly correlated with the dependent variables of level of language functioning in both groups and with degree of language deficit in the language impaired group.

Results

It will only be possible in this paper to give an overview of the results of the project. Intergroup comparisons indicated that the language impaired children were inferior to the normal children in perceptual processing across a number of modalities and also in cross modal integration. In addition, these comparisons indicated that the language impaired children were inferior to the normal children in their rate of movement on repetitive and sequencing movement tasks. It was possible to distinguish the language impaired from the normal children with a high degree of accuracy on the basis of these lower level deficits. In addition, auditory processing variables were found to correlate highly with the level of receptive language functioning in the language impaired children. Articulation skill, visual and tactile processing and rate of movement variables as well as auditory processing variables correlated highly with their level of expressive language functioning.

Experimental Sensory and Perceptual Tests

The results of the experimental sensory and perceptual testing are summarized in Tables 1 and 2. Table 1 is based on the performance of the children who were able to take the subtests indicated. In Table 2, the scores of the children who were able to take each subtest, and of those who were assigned an arbitrary score because they could not, are included. All of the children included in the study were capable of understanding the nature of the tasks that they were required to perform. When the stimuli employed in the experimental tests were of sufficient duration (250 msec. tones) and were presented with sufficiently long interstimulus intervals, the performance of the language impaired group was not significantly different from that of the normal children.

126

Takers Only 5-8 1/2 Years Old t Test

VERBAL ITEMS

Auditory Items	Association	Sequencing	Serial Memory	Rapid Rate Sequencing
4. 40 msec ba/da	.001	NS	.02(M3)	NS
5. 80 msec ba/da	.001	NS	N/A	NS
6. real ba/da	NS	.01	N/A	NS
9. 40 msec bae/dae	.05	NS	N/A	N/A
17. 80 msec bae/dae	.01	NS	N/A	N/A
15. Concept Gen./Seg-mentation	.02	NS	N/A	.01
Non-Auditory Items				
21. Visual letter (e & k)	NS	.01	.05(M3)	NS

NONVERBAL ITEMS

Auditory Items	Association	Sequencing	Serial Memory	Rapid Rate Sequencing
1. 250 msec tones	NS	.02	.01(M5)	.05
2. 75 msec tones	NS	.001	.02(M4)	.05
Non-Auditory Items				
18. Cross-modal	NS	.01	.001(M3)	.001
19. Visual hues	NS	.05	.01(M3)	.01
20. Visual non-sense letters	.05	.02	.01(M3)	.01

Table 1.

Significance of difference in number of errors made by the normal and language-impaired children on verbal and nonverbal auditory and nonauditory test items only. Only the scores of the children in both groups 5 years of age or older who were actual test takers were included.

The language impaired children performed at a significantly lower level than the normal children on the tests of nonverbal auditory processing (see tables 1 and 2). The difference between groups was most marked when the stimuli to be processed were presented in a shorter period of time, either by decreasing the duration of the stimuli or by decreasing the duration of the intervals between the stimuli. The performance of the language impaired children was also affected by the number of items in the series of stimuli presented, that is, on serial memory subtests. The language impaired children also had difficulty in processing verbal (speech-like) auditory stimuli, that is, CV syllables, that incorporated rapidly changing spectra (see tables 1 and 2).

These auditory processing deficits in the language impaired children appeared to be developmental in nature. The performance of both groups of children improved with age, but the performance of the language impaired children was inferior to that of the normal children at each age level. This finding may suggest a developmental lag in the language imparied children with respect to auditory processing.

A higher level cognitive test was also administered in the auditory modality (Tallal et al. 1980). The children were asked to classify six different CV syllables (/ba/, /be/, /bi/, /da/, /de/, and /di/) as having an initial "b" or an initial "d". The language impaired children were less well able than the normal children to carry out this concept formation or concept generalization task. Those children, both language impaired and normal, who reached the criterion level on the concept generalization task were then presented with these same syllables in pairs, first with a 500 msec. interval in a sequencing task, and then with no interval, except that imposed by a natural stop gap, in a rapid-rate processing task. In this latter condition the stimulus pairs formed the real words daddy, baby, Debbie, and body. Thus, the children were, in fact, being asked to segment these words into their component syllables (Tallal et al., in press). The language impaired children who had progressed to this point had more difficulty with this segmentation task than the normals. Thus, these results indicated that, at the whole word level, the language impaired children continued to demonstrate the same pattern of impaired performance as was observed in their processing of nonsense syllables. That is, as a group they showed impairment in discriminating and categorizing stimuli which incorporate rapidly changing acoustic spectra. In addition, those language impaired subjects who were able to discriminate and categorize such stimuli in an association or concept generalization task, and to sequence such syllables when presented with long interstimulus intervals (500 msec.) were nevertheless impaired in their abilty to sequence the syllables when presented rapidly (with shorter interstimulus intervals) or to segment real words made up of such syllables. These results suggest that a basic impairment in temporal processing affected the ability of the language impaired children to discriminate rapidly changing cues in speech sounds, and also their ability to process real words incorporating such cues.

Takers plus Nontakers 5-8 1/2 Years Old t Test and CHI Square Analyses

VERBAL ITEMS

Auditory Items	Association	Sequencing	Serial Memory	Rapid Rate Processing
4. 40 msec ba/da	.001	.001	.001(M3) and (M4)	.001
5. 80 msec ba/da	.001	.001	NA	.001
6. real ba/da	NS	.02	NA	.001
9. 40 msec bae/dae	.01*	NS	NA	NA
17. 80 msec bae/dae	.01	.02	NA	NA
15. Concept Gen.Segmentation	.01*	NS	NA	.01
Non-Auditory Items				
21. Visual Letter (e & k)	NS	.05	.001(M4)	.05*

NONVERBAL ITEMS

Auditory Items	Association	Sequencing	Serial Memory	Rapid Rate Processing
1. 250 msec tones	NS	NS	.01(M4)	.05 (ISI's 10 and 70 msec)
2. 75 msec tones	NS	.001*	.02(M3) .001(M4)*	.001*
Non-Auditory Items				
18. Cross-modal	NS	.01	.02(M4)	.01
19. Visual hues	NS	NS	.02(M4)	.01 (10 msec ISI)*
20. Visual non-sense letters	NS	NS	.001(M4)	.01 (70 msec ISI)

Table 2.

Significance of difference in number of errors made by the normal and language-impaired children on verbal and nonverbal auditory and nonauditory test items. The scores of the children in both groups who were and were not actual test takers are combined. Results of Chi square analysis are reported except where an asterisk appears, indicating that a parametric t test was employed instead.

129

The results reported thus far substantiated the earlier findings of Tallal and Piercy (1974). They also provided further information with respect to word processing in language impaired children. The data appeared to strengthen the implicatons of the original findings with respect to possible relations between basic auditory rate processing and language acquisition.

It was also found, however, that the language impaired children were inferior to the normal children in their processing of visual and crossmodal stimuli. Most of the visual and crossmodal stimuli presented were nonverbal in nature. The language impaired children performed at a lower than normal level on the rate processing and serial memory subtests given with these stimuli. They also showed inferior performance on the sequencing subtest when crossmodal (tone and light) and verbal visual (grapheme) stimuli were presented (see tables 1 and 2). There were no significant differences between groups with respect to oral or manual stereognosis.

The findings with respect to visual and crossmodal stimuli are in contrast with those of Tallal and Piercy (1974) who reported that language impaired children did not show impairment in the processing of rapidly presented visual stimuli. It is possible that the difference in the results of the earlier study and of the present larger project relates to the age of the subjects included (Tallal et al., in press). Visual processing of brief-duration and rapidly presented stimuli appeared to become more accurate with age in both the normal and the language impaired group of children in the present project. The processing of such visual stimuli may show greater improvement in accuracy with increasing age in the language impaired children than the processing of rapidly presented auditory stimuli. The same may be true for serial memory for visual as opposed to auditory stimuli. If so, differences in ability with respect to visual stimuli might not be picked up in older language impaired subjects. The findings of the present project, however, indicate that perceptual processing deficits in language impaired children are not specific to the auditory system but are present in other sensory modalities also. It is possible that a generalized neurological immaturity or developmental delay is implicated rather than dysgenesis of, or lesion to, a specific area of the central nervous system.

Neurodevelopmental Testing

The subtests of the neurodevelopmental examination on which the normal and language impaired subjects were found to differ are shown in table 3. (See also Johnston et al., in preparation.) A parametric t test was used except where the distribution of scores was found to be nonnormal, in which case a nonparametric t test was used.

Control and coordination. Significant differences between groups were found for overflow movements (p <.001) and spooning of the left hand when the arms were maintained in an outstretched pronated posture (p <.05) (Touwen and Prechtl 1970). No such differences were recorded for the right hand.

130

NEURODEVELOPMENTAL TEST	NORMAL	LANGUAGE IMPAIRED	SIGN LEVEL
1. MOTOR TESTS			
a) CONTROL AND COORDINATION			
SPOON OBV L	1.53	4.16	.05
DURATION MOVEMT OBV L	1.92	4.91	.001
ONSET MOVEMT OBV L	12.50	6.97	.01
FINGER OPPOSITION TOUCHES R	22.95	20.06	.05
TRIAL 1 TOUCHES L	23.97	20.48	.01
TRIAL 1 TOUCHES R	24.35	20.64	.01
TRIAL 2 TOUCHES L	24.92	21.39	.01
DIADOCHOKINETIC TRIAL 2			
CYCLE R	16.32	14.67	.05
TRIAL 1 CYCLES L	15.89	14.55	.05
TRIAL 2 CYCLES R	17.03	14.97	.01
TRIAL 2 CYCLES L	16.78	14.91	.02
TRIAL 2 COINS BOX	14.62	13.15	.02
b) BALANCE AND STATION			
1. # HOPS R	39.05	33.45	.05
2. # HOPS L	37.76	30.70	.02
c) SENSORY TESTS			
Double Simultaneous Stimulation (DSS)			
1. DSS # MISL R	0.12	0.48	.02
2. DSS # MISL L	0.08	0.39	.02
Graphesthesia			
3. GR A # ERR R	2.24	3.09	.01
4. GR B # ERR R	1.51	2.21	.05
5. GR B # ERR L	1.62	5.55	.01
Finger Localization			
6. Two fingers touched # ERR R	1.05	2.15	.001
7. Two fingers touched # ERR L	1.43	2.24	.01
d) LATERALITY RELATIONSHIPS			
R-L DISCRIMINATION (DIS)			
1. DIS SINGLE # ERR	0.32	1.15	.01
2. DIS SINGLE REACTION TIME IN SECONDS	0.05	6.88	.01
3. DIS DOUBLE CROSSED DIS DCR # ERR	0.76	2.12	.001

Table 3.

Mean scores obtained by the normal and the language impaired children on those neurodevelopmental tests where their performance was significantly different.

Significant differences between groups were also found on a timed Finger Opposition Test (Touwen and Prechtl 1970). The normal children made significantly more contacts in 15 seconds between the thumb and

131

fingers than did the language impaired children. The differences were present both for the right hand (p <.05; p <.01 for two different trials) and for the left hand (p <.01 on one trial). However, the number of errors made in finger opposition was not significantly different for the language impaired and the normal children, nor was the incidence of overflow (mirroring) movements made with the fingers of the opposite hand on this task. There were no significant differences between groups on a Finger-to-Nose Test performed with the eyes closed.

Significant differences between groups were also found on a timed Diadochokinetic Hand Movement Test. The normal children executed a greater number of cycles of alternating hand movement (supination and pronation) in 15 seconds than did the language impaired children. The differences were present for the right hand (p <.05, p <.01 for two different trials) and for the left hand (p <.05, p <.02 for two different trials). However, the number of errors made in alternating hand movements was not significantly different for the language impaired and the normal children, nor was the incidence of overflow (mirroring) movements made with the *opposite* hand on this task. In addition, the normal children were able to place more of 20 coins in a box (Doll 1946) in 15 seconds than were the language impaired children (p <.02). Overflow of the hands while protruding the tongue was not made significantly more often by children in either group. Asymmetrical posturing of the arms was not noted significantly more often in children in either group when they were told to run as fast as they could.

Balance and station. The two groups of children did not differ with respect to their ability to maintain balance during bipedal or unipedal stance nor in their ability to walk along a straight line board 6 cm. or 4 cm. in width. They did not differ with respect to the time during which they could maintain balance while hopping on one foot. The normal children, however, were able to execute more hops within a 15 second period with the right foot (p <.05) and with the left foot (p <.02) than were the language impaired children.

Sensory tests

The language impaired children made more errors of mislocation and of extinction combined on a Double Simultaneous Stimulation Test (Kraft 1968) involving touches to the face and hands (p .02 for the left and right side). There were also significant differences between groups in the number of errors made in a series of subtests of Graphesthesia (Ayres 1972). These subtests took two different forms. On the first subtest, the child had to respond to the tactile sensation provided by the examiner. The examiner drew on the back of the child's hand while the child was blindfolded. The child responded by copying the same figure on the back of his own hand. On a second subtest he was required to point to a printed version of the figure that was traced on the back of his hand from a number of alternatives. The differences were significant at the .01 level for the right hand on the first subtest and at the .05 level for the right hand on the second subtest. For the left hand, the differences were nonsignificant on the first subtest and significant at the .01 level on the second.

A number of Finger Localization Subtests were given with the child's hands shielded from his vision (Kinsbourne and Warrington 1962). On two subtests the child was required to point to the one or two fingers touched on his right or his left hand. On a third subtest the child was required to point to the finger touched on a drawing of two hands in the supine position on a flat surface. On a fourth subtest, which was thought to be a higher cognitive level than the others, the child was to say how many match-boxes were being inserted between the outstretched fingers of the right or the left hand. The language impaired children made significantly more errors than the normal children on the second Finger Localization Subtest in which they had to identify two fingers touched simultaneously by the examiner. These differences were significant at the .001 level for the right hand, the .01 level for the left hand. The language impaired children did not differ from the normal children in their performance on the remaining Finger Localization Subtests.

Laterality. The two groups of children were not found to differ from one another with respect to lateral dominance. There were no differences in hand, foot, or eye dominance. "Mixed dominance" was not encountered more often in the language impaired than the normal children.

With respect to right-left discrimination, the language impaired children made more errors than the normals in carrying out commands such as "Show me your right ear" (p <.01). They also showed longer latencies before attempting to execute these tasks (p <.01). Moreover, they made significantly more errors than the normal children on a Double Crossover Right-left Discrimination task on which they were given such commands as "Touch your right ear with your left hand" (p <.01). Latencies were not significantly different for the two groups on this task. It is not clear to what extent difficulties with these right-left discrimination tasks are linguistic in nature and to what extent they were related to a true right-left discrimination problem. On a more difficult confrontation task "Point to my left hand" the two groups of children did not differ significantly in number of errors made.

In summary, the results of the neurodevelopmental testing indicated that the language impaired children as a group were consistently and significantly *slower* than the normal children on all timed task administered. They hopped, performed alternating hand movements, touched finger-to-thumb and placed coins in a box all at a significantly slower rate than the normal children. This rate of movement effect was observed for both gross and fine movements regardless of which side (right or left) was used or of hand or foot preference. The language impaired children also showed more choreiform/athetotiform movements on the left side but not on the right than the normal children when asked to hold their arms outstretched, the hands pronated. Unlike the other soft signs, these movements did not appear to decrease with age in the language impaired children studied. The language impaired children had more difficulty than normals in responding to tactile stimulation on the right and the left side of the body. In particular, they showed poorer finger localization ability when two fingers were touched simultaneously than the normal children. The language impaired children had greater difficulty than the normals with right-left discrimination. It was thought that this difficulty might be in part a linguistic one. The language impaired children were not different from the normals in balance and station, finger-to-nose opposition, running, associated movements on a tongue protrusion or eye following task, nor in lateral dominance.

Speech and Motor Battery

The Speech Motor Battery included tests of Isolated and Sequenced Volitional Nonspeech Movement, (Yoss and Darley 1974) tests of Diadochokinetic Rates of Movement for the syllables /pa/, /ta/, /ka/, and /pataka/ combined (Fletcher 1972), and a Rapid Word Production Test in which multisyllabic words, for example "cafeteria," had to be produced three times as rapidly as possible.

Performance on the Isolated Volitional Movement test was not significantly different for the two groups. However, the normal children made significantly fewer errors than the language impaired on the Sequenced Volitional Movement Test (p <.05), t test. The normal children also made significantly higher scores than the language impaired on all of the tests of diadochokinetic rates (/pa/ at the .05 level, /ta/ at the .01 level, /ka/ at the .01 level and the /pataka/ at the .05 level, nonparametric t tests). Performance on the Rapid Word Production Test was assessed by first transcribing in broad phonetic transcription the children's attempts to produce the words rapidly three times each. This task was carried out with satisfactory reliability by two trained listeners. The child was then given one point for each syllable spoken correctly in the Rapid Word Production Test. Thus, misarticulations or omissions of phonemes occurring when the child was under pressure to speak at a rapid rate would cause him to lose points. The language impaired children made a significantly lower score than the normal children on this task (p <.001, nonparametric t test).

Visual Scanning Test

On almost every visual scanning test the language impaired children made a significantly lower score than the normal children. The difference between groups was significant at the .01 level for the first control test in which the children were merely required to check every item (black rectangles) upon the page. Therefore, the basic rate of movement at which the children performed a simple marking task was significantly different for the two groups. The difference in rate of movement in marking the page may have affected the outcome of all of the subsequent visual scanning tests. On the second control task, however, the difference between groups was not significant. On this test, scanning for a black versus a white rectangle was required. The task was a relatively easy one for the children in both groups.

Almost all of the scores obtained by the language impaired children fell between the extremes of the scores obtained on scanning for black versus white rectangles and the scores obtained on a difficult test of scanning for two-letter alphabetic sequences.

Discriminant Function Analysis

A stepwise discriminant function analysis procedure was employed to determine which of the many test variables best classified the normal and language impaired children into their respective groups. Sixteen different classes of independent variables were entered into these analyses. These classes included neurodevelopmental variables, demographic variables, discrimination variables, speech motor variables and so on. They were set up by the experimenters according to the original testing plan. Individual variables could appear in more than one of these classes. A final composite discriminant function analysis was then carried out. All of the variables that were significant or that approached significance in the 16 separate equations were entered into this final analysis.

In summary, the results indicated that 98.3% of all subjects were correctly classified into their appropriate groups based upon an eight variable equation. These variables were, in order of relative importance:

1. Rapid Word Production (production of test words in triplets as rapidly as possible, Speech Motor Battery).
2. Two Finger Identification, number of errors, right hand (from the Neurodevelopmental Test Battery).
3. Discrimination of /ba/ versus /da/ with 40 msec duration formant transitions (Association Subtest of Repetition Method).
4. Rate Processing Subtest with cross modally tone and light flash presented stimuli (Repetition Method).
5. Rate Processing Subtest with real letters "e" versus "k" (Repetition Method).
6. Sequencing Subtest with cross modally presented stimuli (Repetition Method).
7. Scanning for "b" among easily confused letters (Visual Scanning Test).
8. Scanning for the words "hand" and "sing" among other single words (Visual Scanning Test).

Importantly, *all* of the language impaired subjects originally selected were correctly identified as language impaired and all but one normal subject were identified correctly as normal, using the above eight variables (see Procedures Section for complete description of test variables).

Discrimination between groups was thus made on the basis of variables that assessed relatively low levels of nonverbal perception and of nonspeech as well as speech motor skills. That is, virtually all of the subjects were correctly classified as language impaired or normal without the need to assess any higher level linguistic skills (semantics, syntax, pragmatics). Correct identification was made on the basis of basic perception and production tests. Importantly, all eight of the tests which proved to have high predictive validity involved rapid rate perceptual processing or rapid rate of repetitive or sequenced movements. These data strongly support our original hypothesis that an inability to process information at a normal rate is critically involved in the language disorder of language impaired children. The data also expand our original findings to include deficits in rate of movement as well as processing of rapidly presented material in a variety of sensory modalities.

In summary, although almost all of the independent variables entered into the equations represented lower-level sensory, perceptual or motor functions, they were nonetheless able to discriminate normal from language impaired children with a remarkably high degree of accuracy. Thus, these results demonstrate that it may not be necessary to consider higher level variables such as semantic, syntactic and pragmatic capabilities for the purpose of correctly classifying children as language impaired or normal.

Discussion

Interpretation of Results

The results reported thus far indicate that perceptual and motor deficits were highly characteristic of the language impaired children in this study. The perceptual deficits involved sequencing and rapid rate processing of, and serial memory for, a variety of stimuli. These deficits were not confined to the auditory modality as was expected on the basis of previous findings, but extended to the visual modality also and to cross modal (auditory plus visual) stimulus pairs. Tactile perceptual deficits were also indicated by the responses of the language impaired children on tests of simultaneous tactile stimulation (sensory extinction). It could be hypothesized that the auditory processing deficits of these children may be especially detrimental to the acquisition of spoken language because speech is characterized by rapid changes in and rapid succession of its elements.

The motor deficits manifested by language delayed children were in the rate of production of simple repetitive movements, the rate of production of sequences of movements and the ability to sequence oral movements which were not timed. The results for the sequencing of movements are particularly interesting considering recent studies by Ojemann and Mateer (1979), and Kimura (1976). Ojemann and Mateer have shown in studies of electrical stimulation of the exposed cortex that degradation of performance in consonant discrimination and in sequencing of oral volitional movements results from stimulation of the same cortical sites. Kimura (1976) and Mateer and Kimura (1977) studied the ability to perform sequences of movements in aphasic adults. They found that aphasic adults were inferior to normal adults in their performance on both manual and oral sequenced volitional movement tasks. As a result of these findings it has been suggested that, in the evolution of language in the human, cortical sites were taken over for the purposes of language operations which, at an earlier stage of evolution, were dedicated to the management of sequences of voluntary movements, particularly those involved in tool use.

Subsequent analyses from the present project have indicated a strong relationship between the auditory processing variables included in the project and level of receptive language abilities in language impaired children. Level of receptive language in the normal children on the other hand was related to higher level cognitive processing of the kind involved in the visual scanning tests. Level of expressive language ability in both the normal and the language impaired children was correlated with a variety of variables including auditory processing variables, visual processing variables, rate of hand movements, finger localization and right-left discrimination. In addition, it was found that in the language impaired but not in the normal child, the level of expressive language was highly correlated with a measure of speech articulation skill. Other variables correlating highly with the level of expressive language deficit in these children were derived from the visual scanning tests, auditory processing tests and neurodevelopmental tests.

Implications for Remediation

These findings suggest that basic perceptual and motor deficits were characteristic of the language impaired children and were related to higher level language processing skills in these children. It is important, however, to stress that these relationships are not necessarily causal in nature. None of the findings of the present study would permit such an assertion. The basic motor and perceptual deficits and the language deficts of the language impaired children may all be related to another, quite different, set of variables that were not included in the present study. In addition, the findings of the present study should be replicated with a larger group of language impaired children before a new theoretical framework is constructed.

What, then, are the implications of these findings for remediation of language disorders in children? The lack of any evidence that there is a causal relationship between basic perceptual and motor deficits and language disorders in these children should give rise to caution in considering the implications. It would be naive to suggest that treatment aimed directly toward remediation of the perceptual or the motor deficits found to be characteristic of language impaired children in the present study is likely to effect an improvement in their language skills. Such treatment might achieve modest gains in basic perceptual or motor functioning. However, if the goal of remediation is to improve language skills then the language skills should be treated directly.

A number of different approaches have been recommended for the purpose of improving language skills in language impaired children. These include natural language stimulation, facilitation of steps presumed to be taken in normal language development, behavior modification approaches, the use of play situations and interactive routines, and others (Longhurst 1974; MacDonald et al. 1974; Muma 1971; Rees 1972). As the language impaired child acquires a knowledge of the structure and the rule system of the language spoken in his environment, he will be able to use that knowledge to compensate for basic auditory processing deficits such as poor phoneme discrimination. Blesser (1973) has estimated that for most adult speaker-listener exchanges, phoneme perception is used only a relatively small proportion of the time. The adult listener is able to infer the phoneme content of running speech from his knowledge of the topic that is being discussed and his predictions as to what the listener is likely to say. In making such predictions in conversational speech, the listener is able to take advantage of the highly redundant nature of the speech signal. Redundancies are present at all levels — phonemic, semantic, and syntactic — for the listener who has sufficient mastery of the language spoken. The situation may be very different in the case where formal instruction is being received in a relatively unfamiliar subject area or when one is listening to an imperfectly learned foreign language. For the language impaired child it is very important to introduce unfamiliar materials in short, simple sentences, or even with the aid of headings, before any elaboration is attempted.

In helping the language impaired child to achieve a sufficient level of mastery of language it would be foolish, however, not to take into account the perceptual or motor deficits which he may have. Shorter utterances and/ or slower utterances having normal prosody might be processed more easily by a given language impaired child than longer or more rapidly spoken utterances. If so, it would be sensible to observe these differences in ability while also observing the level of language complexity which he is able to process. Similarly, if it is found that a given language impaired child has difficulty in sequencing articulatory gestures in speaking, he may be helped if he is taught to perform these gestures more slowly as he learns new words, new word forms, or new constructions. One of the benefits of the phoneme synthesis approach advocated by Katz (this volume) may be the reduction of speaking rate which results as the child attempts to synthesize phonemes.

The findings of the present study also have implications for remediation of learning disorders in language impaired children. It has frequently been recommended in the past that learning disabled children with auditory processing disorders should receive specific auditory training to aid them in learning tasks. Such training would be designed to strengthen or improve the child's greatest weaknesses as a preparatory step toward improved learning. An alternate strategy, that of teaching the child to compensate for his auditory perceptual weaknesses by utilizing a stronger input modality or more fully developed skills may be more effective, as has

138

been pointed out by Johnson (this volume). Compensatory strategies which enable the child to rely on visual memory for graphemes, for example, may be more useful to him than drills in phoneme identification. The success of such a strategy in treating language impaired children reported by Johnson (this volume) and Weeks (1974) may be attributable to superior visual spatial perception in the children they describe.

Redundancy of cues and of information may also be capitalized upon in the education of language impaired children. When new topics are introduced through the auditory modality, they should be presented first by means of key words and phrases. These words should be provided with reference to visual materials or ongoing experience of the topic area. The concepts to be taught in these areas may be elaborated visually, through motor activities such as drawing, modeling, writing, or verbally depending upon the abilities of the child. In this manner the child may be given an opportunity to take advantage of redundancy and repetition. For example, if the topic of instruction were to be the use of the yellow pages, the actual experience of making a purchase may be more helpful than verbal instruction alone. Verbal instruction designed to take advantage of repetition and redundancy should accompany the practical exercise.

Finally, if the language impaired child has a deficit in the rate or the sequencing of motor movements, speed of performance of motor activities should be de-emphasized in the classroom or introduced only very gradually. The children in the present study did not, as a group, manifest lack of motor coordination or of precision of the components of a movement pattern. Clinical experience suggests, however, that some children with speech articulation and expressive language deficits do manifest such motor problems. These children may also form a subgroup of learning-disabled children (Doehring 1968; Rourke and Finlayson 1978). Some of them appear to have normal receptive language functioning. It may be that the treatment procedures recommended by Ayres (1972), on the basis of her tests of sensormotor integration, effect improvement in precision and coordination of movement in this subgroup of children. If so, the improvement is likely to change the attitude of parents and teachers toward the child and to have a beneficial effect upon the child's self esteem and overall motivation. It would be difficult, however, to justify the assumption that improvement in motor control would lead directly to improvement in auditory language skills.

The evidence for basic perceptual and motor deficits in language impaired children which has been presented in this paper derives from group data. Not all of the language impaired children in this study were found to have all of the deficits described. Thus, it is important before embarking upon a course of remediation to discover each language impaired child's profile of strengths and weaknesses through careful and detailed testing. Level of functioning in visual temporal (visual rate processing), visual spatial, and auditory temporal (auditory rate processing) and sequencing of motor performance should all be determined in these children prior to treatment. Secondly, children who are functioning below age level in language skills, but at the same level in visual spatial and visual motor skills as in language skills, should probably not be considered as specifically language impaired. Such children may need special educational placement, but are not likely to benefit from specific language remediation.

In summary, remediation for children with language impairment should be designed to meet their individual needs. These needs should be determined in part on the basis of assessment of more basic motor and perceptual abilities. Such an assessment provides information about the child's relative strengths and weaknesses in these abilities as well as in areas related to language. If the child's levels of skill are observed in the treatment plan, frustration may be avoided and greater progress made. If the child experiences success, he may find it more rewarding to pay attention to language than before.

It may be objected that these are merely common sense suggestions. However, until there is a greater understanding of the relationship between basic motor and perceptual deficits and language processing, the best strategy may be to apply current knowledge in a common sense way. The outcome of such treatment, like that of any other, should be evaluated critically and continuously.

References

Ayres, J. 1972. *Southern California sensory integration tests.* Los Angeles: Western Psychological Services.

Blesser, B. 1973. Perceptual and cognitive strategies. In *Sensory capabilities of hearing impaired children,* ed. R.E. Stark. Baltimore: University Park Press.

Doehring, D.G. 1968. *Patterns of impairment in specific reading.* Montreal: McGill University Printing Services.

Doll, E. ed. 1946. *Oserestsky tests.* American Guidance Service, Inc.

Fletcher, S.G. 1972. Time-by-count measurement of diadochokinetic syllables rate. *J. Sp. Hear. Res.* 15:763-70.

Johnston, R.B., Stark, R.E., Mellits, E.D., and Tallal, P. *Neurological status of language impaired and normal children.* In preparation.

Kimura, D. 1976. The neural basis of language qua gesture. In *Studies in Neurolinguistics* (vol. 2), eds. H. Whitaker and H.A. Whitaker. New York: Academic Press.

Kinsbourne, M. and Warrington, E.K. 1962. A study of finger agnosia. *Brain* 85:47-59.

Kraft, M.D. 1968. The face-hard test. *Dev. Med. Child Neur.* 10:214-19.

Longhurst, T.M., ed. 1974. Functional language intervention (Vol. I and II). New York: MSS Information Corporation.

MacDonald, J.D., Blott, J.P., Gordon, K., and Hartman, M.C. 1974. An experimental parent-assisted treatment program for preschool children. *J. Sp. Hear. Dis.* 39:395-415.

Mateer, C. and Kimura, D. 1977. Impairment of nonverbal oral movements in aphasia. *Brain Lang.* 4:262-76.

Muma, J. 1971. Language intervention: ten techniques. Language, speech and hearing services in the schools. *ASHA* 5:7-17.

Ojemann, G. and Mateer, C. 1979. Human language cortex: localization of memory, syntax, and sequential motor-phoneme identification systems. *Science* 205:1401-3.

Rees, N.S. 1973. Auditory processing factors in language disorders: the view from Procrustes' bed. *J. Sp. Hear. Dis.* 38:304-15.

Rees, N.S. 1972. Bases of decision in language training. *J. Sp. and Hear. Dis.* 37:283-304.

Rourke, B. and Finlayson, M. 1978. Neuropsychological significance of variations in patterns of academic performance: verbal and visual spatial abilities. *J. Abnor. Child Psychol.* 6:121-35.

Stark, R.E. and Tallal, P. 1980. Sensory and perceptual functioning of young children with and without delayed language development. Final Report NS-5-2322.

Stark, R.E. and Tallal, P. 1979. Analysis of stop consonant production errors in developmentally dysphasic children. *J. Acoust. Soc. Am.* 66:1703-12.

Stark, R.E. and Tallal, P. Selection of children with specific language deficits. *J. Sp. Hear. Dis.* In press.

Tallal, P. and Piercy, M. 1974. Developmental aphasia: rate of auditory processing and selective impairment of consonant perception. *Neuropsychologia*, 12:83-93.

Tallal, P. and Piercy, M. 1973a. Defects of non-verbal auditory processing in children with developmental aphasia. *Nature* 242:468-69.

Tallal, P. and Piercy, M. 1973b. Developmental aphasia: impaired rate of non-verbal processing as a function of sensory modality. *Neuropsycholog.* 11:389-98.

Tallal, P., Stark, R.E., and Curtiss, B. 1976. Relation between speech perception and speech production impairment in children with developmental dysphasia. *Brain Lang.* 3:305-17.

Tallal, P., Stark, R.E., Kallman, C., Mellits, D. 1980. Perceptual constancy of phonemic categories: a developmental study with normal and language impaired children. *App. Psycholing.* 1:49-64.

Tallal, P., Stark, R.E., Kallman, C., Mellits, D. A re-examination of non-verbal perceptual abilities of language impaired and normal children as a function of sensory modality. *J. Sp. Hear. Res.* In press.

Touwen, B.C.L. and Prechtl, H. 1970. *The neurological examination of the child with minor nervous dysfunction.* Philadelphia: Lippencott.

Wechsler, D. 1974. *Wechsler intelligence scale for children — revised (WISC-R).* New York: The Psychological Corporation.

Wechsler, D. 1963. *Wechsler preschool and primary scale of intelligence (WPPSI).* New York: The Psychological Corporation.

Weeks, T. 1974. *Slow speech development of a bright child.* New York: Lexington Books.

Yoss, K.A. and Darley, F.L. 1974. Developmental apraxia of speech in children with defective articulation *J. Sp. Hear. Res.* 17:399-413.

Acknowledgment

This work was supported by an NINCDS Contract, No. NS-5-2323.

Questions and Answers

Q: How could you be certain that the language-disordered children in your study were "free" of any neurologic insults (perinatal asphyxia, etc.)?

A: A medical history was obtained from the parent(s), and questions about such insults were asked specifically. In addition, a classical neurological examination was carried out.

Q: What tests were used to determine expressive and receptive language levels in the children you studied?

A: The language tests employed were as follows:

Receptive Tests: Test of Auditory Comprehension of Language (Carrow); Northwestern Syntax Screening Test, Receptive portion (Lee); Token Test (modificaton described by Whitaker and Noll); ITPA, Auditory Reception Subtest; ITPA, Auditory Associaton Subtest.

Expressive Tests: Spontaneous language sample (analyzed by means of the DSS Procedure, Lee); ITPA, Grammatic Closure Subtest; Northwestern Syntax Screening Test, Expressive portion (Lee); Vocabulary Subtest of WPPSI or WISC-R.

Q: Could you give an example of how you instructed subjects in the sensory-perceptual testing in a nonverbal manner?

A: As a stimulus was presented, the examiner demonstrated the required reponse (pressing the appropriate panel). She/he then indicated to the child that he should do the same. The demonstration was provided as often as was required for the subject to learn that response by imitation. The same procedure was followed in training the child to push the second of two panels in responding to the second stimulus of each stimulus pair.

Q: In your study, was task learning (accommodation) accounted for in the improved scores that appeared to occur with CA?

A: The study was a cross sectional one, not longitudinal. Thus, performance appeared to be better in the older than in the younger children in the normal group. There was some opportunity for task learning or accommodation to occur over the 12 weeks of testing. However, the tests were given in random order to correct for this effect.

Q: To what degree can your results be explained by assuming that language-delayed children are slower at recovering appropriate labels for the test stimuli in the sequencing task?

A: It is possible that less efficient verbal mediation is a factor, even though our stimuli were designed in such a way that many of them could not readily be labeled by normal or language-impaired children. A subsequent study of young adults has indicated that failure to recognize our speech (verbal) auditory stimuli as speech and low scores on the association and sequencing subtests are correlated quite highly with one another. It is not clear with respect to that finding which of the problems of the low-scoring adults came first, the difficulty in recognizing the stimuli as speech, or the difficulty in assigning them to a category.

Q: Were error patterns of normal and disordered children similar on the perceptual test battery, i.e., were differences between groups primarily quantitative or qualitative?

A: The error patterns in general were similar, in that the rapid rate processing and serial memory subtests with all stimuli were harder for all children than the association or sequencing subtests. The differences between groups were thus primarily quantitative.

Q: If a child can understand a spoken sentence or information in context, what difference does a short stimulus interval make?

A: A child may understand a spoken sentence or information in context because he/she has acquired a knowledge of the structure of the language, i.e., a productive rule system. The child may succeed in acquiring that system by making use of the relatively long-duration, steady-state portions of the speech signal, or of redundancy at the acoustic-cue level. Also, he/she may make use to some extent of lip read cues in that process. In situations where ambiguity arises, however, or where the material being presented is unfamiliar, reliance upon acoustic cues may normally be much greater. In such situations, which probably occur more frequently in the classroom than in casual conversation at home or at play, the child having an auditory rate processing or a serial memory problem may be at a disadvantage.

Q: What are the implications of your findings in terms of therapy for severely language-impaired children, specifically the use of total communication (sign language). I refer to children who are not developing any verbal skills.

A: I believe that it would make sense to teach sign language to such children. The children in Tallal's original study were being taught the Paget (British) sign language system. The use of sign and speech as in total communication might be contraindicated in some severely affected children. That could be determined only by very careful testing.

143

Q: What is your opinion of using the Ayres battery as a diagnostic tool rather than as a remedial procedure?

A. I believe it is very important to employ such tests as those in the Ayres battery carefully and systematically. I believe that other neurodevelopmental tests are needed also, and that these, too, should be given most carefully. What is needed is normative data for a complete neurodevelopmental battery. Even then, interpretation of the results may not be an easy matter.

Q: With a maximum of 15 minutes of time available per child, what tasks would you choose for screening "bright-normal" (i.e., advantaged, suburban) kindergarten children to identify possible language and learning difficulties? Usefulness of the information obtained in terms of implications for planning instruction should be a criteria for selection.

A: I don't believe one can do more than screen for language problems in 15 minutes. I would not plan language instruction or remediation on the basis of a screening test. For screening purposes I might use the Northwestern Syntax Screening Test and a naming test (for example, the Boston Naming Test).

9

Phonemic Synthesis: Testing and Training

Jack Katz, Ph.D. and Cornelia H. Harmon, M.S.

Numerous children in our schools have learning disabilities which range in degree from mild to severe. Undoubtedly, there are many etiological factors and associated disorders in this constellation of problems; however, speech and language problems frequently accompany reading and spelling problems. It is indeed difficult to separate scholastic difficulties from those of speech, language, hearing and auditory processing disorders. Therefore, speech-language pathologists and audiologists have shown a growing interest in learning disabilities (LD). Moreover, the training and professional interests of these professionals make them uniquely qualified to serve as members of diagnostic teams. By working closely with the classroom teacher and the parents they can help evaluate and manage the child who has learning disabilities.

Phonemic Synthesis and Reading, Spelling, Speech and Language

Although auditory processing is a broad topic, today we will focus on just one important skill called phonemic synthesis (PS). In a PS task (sometimes called sound blending) the individual phonemes of a word are spoken separately with a pause between each. The examiner, using either live voice or a tape recorder, presents the phonemes at the rate of 1 per second or slower. Each sound must be produced in isolation, without coarticulation. For example, the word "man" would be pronounced, /m/, /æ/, /n/. When the sounds are coarticulated to produce /m æ n/ during ordinary conversational speech, the vowel /æ/ acquires a nasal quality which is missing in the PS presentation.

By presenting the sounds in this way, we introduce several forms of distortion into the speech signal. First, all of the sounds are stressed and the continuants are prolonged; second, the pauses between the sounds replace the transients which ordinarily occur between consonants and vowels; third, the overall duration of the word far exceeds its normal length.

Because these distortions present a considerable challenge to many individuals who have auditory processing problems, PS is a diagnostic procedure; as well as an extremely valuable therapeutic procedure. This discussion will review the literature which relates poor performance in PS to deficiencies in reading, spelling, articulation and language, consider studies dealing with training strategies using Phoneme Synthesis, and offer a basis for understanding phonemic synthesis.

Monroe (1932) tested a large sample of reading disabled children and control subjects. She found that about half of the youngsters who had reading problems had difficulty with a sound blending task; their raw scores were typically 1/3 to 1/2 those of the normal control subjects.

Mulder and Curtin (1955) compared the performance of 63 fourth grade pupils on a sound blending task involving monosyllabic nouns with their performance on the Iowa Every Pupil Test of Basic Skills. The correlation of .44 with reading was statistically significant at .01 level of confidence. They concluded that poorer readers were deficient in their ability to combine phonemes into meaningful words.

Katz and Allam (1958) studied the performance of 35 children who had articulation disorders on three auditory tasks and on the Gilmore Oral Reading Test. There was a significant correlation at the .05 level (r = 0.31) between phonemic synthesis and word accuracy on the reading test.

Connors, Kramer and Guerra (1969) tested 75 LD children and 75 control subjects in grades 1 through 6 on an auditory synthesis task. The test words varied in length from 2 to 10 phoneme groups, e.g., gra - ss for grass and t - ra - n - s - p - or - t - a - t - ion for transportation. The differences between the experimental and control subjects were highly significant at each grade level with the greatest differences occurring in children who were in grades 4-6.

Bannatyne and Wichiarajote (1969) compared performance on written spelling tests with results on the subtests of the Illinois Test of Psycholinguistic Abilities (ITPA). They found that performance on the auditory tasks of the ITPA correlated highly with spelling ability, and that among the auditory tasks the sound blending subtest showed the highest correlation.

In the area of articulation, Van Riper (1963) has said, "Case after case shows a marked inability in synthesizing a series of isolated sounds to make a familiar word...." He presented a 10-item test which he referred to as a crude one, "...in the hope that someone will investigate this very important area of perception."

Mange (1955) found that phonemic synthesis performance was related not only to the number of articulation errors but also to the type of errors. This study and two others (Mange 1953; Katz and Allam 1958) support the notion that children who have / r / problems are likely to have difficulty with auditory discrimination and synthesis.

In 1960, Mange tested 35 children who had / r / misarticulations and 35 control subjects. He used three tests of sound discrimination from the Seashore Measures of Muscial Talents, a flutter-fusion test to determine their ability to identify rapid changes in the auditory stimulus, and an auditory synthesis test. The results having the highest correlation with articulation performance were those from the synthesis task (.58), which was significant at the .01 level.

Beasley et al. (1974) and Stovall, Manning, and Shaw (1977) tested normal speaking children and those who had articulation errors in grades 1, 2 and 3. During the sound blending task the investigators presented meaningful and non-meaningful CVC stimuli while they varied the presentation rate of the phonemes. They found that the difficulty of the task increased as the interval between the phonemes became longer (100 msec. to 400 msec.) and that the children who had poor articulation performed worse than the normals when responding to "real word" stimuli. In the Stovall, Manning and Shaw study, there was a direct relationship between articulation ability and phonemic synthesis ability. Children who had the greatest difficulty in articulation had the poorest auditory synthesis, children having mild articulation problems were better, and the normal children were the best.

Katz and his colleagues (1969) studied 183 children from public and parochial schools who had learning disabilities. They evaluated the children's performance on speech, hearing, language and auditory perceptual tests. These investigators found that 57% of the children had speech problems, 55% had language disorders, 33% had a peripheral hearing loss, while a surprising 77% had auditory processing problems on the phonemic synthesis test.

Some of the results of the above study and of another study (Katz et al. 1970) are assembled in table 1. The investigators used the 67 item Templin-Darley Articulation Test (T-D) to evaluate forty kindergarten children and thirty-two 7-13 year-old children all of whom had learning disabilities. The children in the two age groups who had no articulation problems were matched in sex and age with those who had articulation errors. Then, all of the children were given language tests (Peabody Picture Vocabulary Test [PPVT] and the Utah Test of Language Development [UTLD]) and auditory processing tests (30-item, Phonemic Synthesis Picture Multiple Choice Test, Speech-in-Noise Test [S/N], Same-Different Discrimination Task [S/D] or the Phonemic Synthesis List 2A [PS-2A]).

The language test results are recorded as median performance age levels above (+) or below (-) the median chronological age. The results for the auditory processing tests are shown as the median number of correct responses; the normal ranges are listed at the top of each column.

The kindergarten children who had good articulation had median language performance which was roughly 6 months above chronological age and normal median scores on the three auditory processing tests. Despite their articulatory errors, the other kindergarten children had a median score showing normal language performance. However, they had difficulties with the three perceptual tasks, particularly with phonemic synthesis and speech in noise.

The results from the older LD children who had no articulation errors were comparable to those of the corresponding younger group for performance on language tests: median scores were average or better. However, their

147

	Median C.A.	Language Tests[1]		Auditory Tests[2]			
		PPVT	UTLD	PS PICT. (normal range = 16-24)	S/N (28-32)	SD (15-19)	PS-2A (13-18)
KINDERGARTEN Good Articulation No Errors on the Templin-Darley (T-D) Test N=20	5 yrs. 11 mos.	+5.0 mos.	+8.5 mos.	17	30	16	
Articulation Disorders Median No. of Errors on T-D Test = 14 Range = 4-23 N=20	5 yrs. 9 mos.	+3.5 mos.	+1.5 mos.	11	23	14	
7-13 YEAR OLDS Good Articulation No Errors on the T-D Test N=16	8 yrs. 8 mos.	+8.0 mos.	0.0 mos.				11.5 (equivalent to 30 on PS PICT.)
Articulation Disorders Median No. of Errors on T-D Test = 9 Range = 5-51 N=16	8 yrs. 8 mos.	− 10.0 mos.	− 13.0 mos.				6.0 (equivalent to 23 on PS PICT.)

[1] Median no. of mos. that performance age was above (+) or below (−) median chronological age.

[2] Median number of correct responses

Table 1.

Performance of learning disabled children on language tests and on auditory processing tests.

148

scores on the PS-2A test were slightly lower than average. The median score of 11.5 on the PS-2A is equivalent to a score of 30 on the PS PICT test.

The 7-13 year old LD children who had articulation errors presented quite a different picture. Their median language performance was about one year below their chronological age and they had extremely poor sound blending performance. Their score of 6 on the PS-2A test is equivalent to 23 on the PS-PICT test. Therefore, these children performed better than the younger children who had articulation disorders, but their score of 6 on the PS-2A task indicates that they had poor PS performance when compared to children of their own age.

If we regroup the children and examine the PS-PICT scores of those who did not have articulatory problems, we see that the equivalent median scores for the older group (30) is almost double that of the young children (17). Interestingly, there is a similar ratio for the children who had articulation disorders: the equivalent median score of the older children was 23 while the median score of the younger children was 11. In other words, scores on the phonemic synthesis task almost doubled as both groups of children became older, but language performance did not keep pace with chronological age for the children who had articulatory deficiencies.

Table 2 shows the language test results and the phonemic synthesis results of 7-14 year old children who were grouped according to specific learning difficulty (Katz et al. 1969). The children who had math difficulty but no significant reading, spelling or emotional problems were well within normal limits on phonemic synthesis and above the normal range on both

| | | Language Tests | | Auditory Test |
		PPVT	UTLD	PS 2A (normal range = 13-18)
DEFICIENCIES		Performance Age		Correct Responses
	Median C.A.			
Math (N = 13)	11 yrs. 9 mos.	13 yrs. 11 mos.	12 yrs. 0 mos.	15.0
Reading (N = 19)	10 yrs. 1 mo.	9 yrs. 10 mos.	9 yrs. 2 mos.	12.0
Reading & Math (N = 9)	9 yrs. 7 mos.	10 yrs. 7 mos.	9 yrs. 5 mos.	9.5
Reading & Spelling (N = 4)	11 yrs. 4 mos.	9 yrs. 4 mos.	8 yrs. 11 mos.	6.5
BEHAVIORAL-EMOTIONAL DISORDERS (N = 6)	12 yrs. 7 mos.	11 yrs. 2 mos.	10 yrs. 11 mos.	12.5

Table 2
Performance of children who had various learning deficiencies or behavioral-emotional disorders on Language and Auditory Processing Tests.

149

language tests. The group that had reading problems alone is just below the normal range in their median performance on phonemic synthesis and is almost one year behind on the Utah Test of Language Development. When children had both reading and math difficulties they were quite deficient in phonemic synthesis but performed normally or better on the language tests. However, the children who had reading and spelling problems were very low in phonemic synthesis and 2 to 2½ years behind in their language development. They had the poorest PS scores and the poorest language results of the five groups. It is inconceivable that vocabulary had a significant influence on their phonemic synthesis performance because the words were *eat, shoe* and *dog*, with the most difficult being *child, ghost* and *bank*. These results demonstrate the close relationship between phonemic synthesis and language skills in learning disabled children who had reading and spelling problems. The results for children who had emotional problems are shown for comparison. As a group, they were very slightly below the normal range in PS ability and about 1½ years behind in language development.

Phonemic Synthesis Training

The foregoing studies were presented to show the close relationship between phonemic synthesis and four very important skills — reading, spelling, articulation and language. It is our feeling that to simply diagnose an auditory processing problem in a learning-disabled child is to merely confirm what the parents and teacher already knew. Recommending a remediation program, or better yet, initiating therapy provides a far more valuable service. Thus, the following section will be devoted to an examination of various auditory training techniques which increase phonemic synthesis ability. Such techniques are important not only because the children improve in their sound blending skills, but because frequently they improve in other related skills as well. However, phonemic synthesis training should not be given in lieu of reading, spelling, speech, language or other appropriate therapies; it should be integrated into a complete management program.

Over 40 years ago, Samuel Orton, the famed neurologist, intensively studied the etiology and remediation of learning and communication disorders. He observed that children who had reading disorders and problems in speech perception also had difficulty with sound blending, and he concluded that they required systematic therapy (Orton 1937). His therapeutic techniques relied heavily on "phonetic synthesis" training to remediate auditory disorders. Furthermore, he demonstrated that children who received P.S. training for their reading problems often improved in their articulation ability even though they had not received speech therapy.

In her classical book on aphasic children, Mildred McGinnis (1963) supports the use of sound blending in remediation procedures. She advocates a sound-by-sound strategy in the early phases of therapy.

In 1971, Katz and Burge reported on their work in the diagnosis and remediation of auditory processing problems. The records of 43 children who had previously received auditory training provided the data for this study. The 33 boys and 10 girls ranged in age from 5 to 15 years with a mean age of 8 years 10 months.

Eight auditory training programs in phonemic synthesis were devised and recorded on a high quality reel-to-reel tape recorder. The programmed lessons progressed from extremely easy to very difficult tasks. The child responded to the standard PS presentation by pointing to one of two pictures which were before him during the first lesson. The stimuli were familiar two and three phoneme words such as *two* and *book*. The final lesson contained more difficult words such as *spill* and *clocks* in an open set response format. If a child's speech was unintelligible when he responded he was asked to repeat, to use the word in a sentence or to tell what the word meant.

Therapy sessions were held once or twice a week for 30 minutes. The tapes were played at a comfortable listening level in a sound treated room from a tape recorder placed one to two feet in front of the child. The clinician did not reveal to the child whether or not his responses were correct because we were interested in teaching a *skill*. If the answers had been given we would not have known if the improvement was due to the child's ability to memorize a response or to his newly developed phonemic synthesis ability. "Training" consisted of showing the child how to blend the sounds together and how to respond to the tapes. After each program was over the child was permitted to plot his performance (number correct) on a graph.

There were sufficient test-retest results available to report on 29 of the children. Table 3 shows their performance on the phonemic synthesis tests. Seven children were given the phonemic synthesis multiple choice picture test (PS-PICT) because of their age or the severity of their problem. After therapy these children more than doubled their mean score (+ 48%) on this 30 item test. Their pre-therapy score was poor (2 sd's below the mean) while

Katz & Burge: Subjects received P.S. training.			Metzl (1969): Subjects received no P.S. training between tests.	
	PS Pict.[1] (N = 7)	PS-2A[2] (N = 22)		PS-2A[2] (N = 30)
Pre-therapy	10.9(36%)	10.8(43%)	1st Test	15.8(63%)
Post-therapy	25.8(84%)	18.1(72%)	2nd Test	17.9(72%)
Difference	14.4(48%)	7.3(29%)	Difference	2.1(8%)

[1] 30 item test; normal range = 16-24.
[2] 25 item test; normal range = 13-18.

Table 3
Phonemic Synthesis ability of learning disabled children before and after P.S. training compared with children who received no P.S. training.

their post therapy result was above average. The twenty-two children who were given the 25 item PS-2A test showed a 29% improvement. They went from a mean score that was below average to a mean score at the upper limit of normal. These results were not submitted to further statistical analysis because there was no overlap in the scores. Improvement ranging from 2 to 19 points was noted. For comparison, Metzl's (1969) normative results indicate that the expected retest improvement for children who receive no PS training is only 2 points. Interestingly, children under 8 years of age demonstrated more improvement per repetition of a program than older children. Nevertheless, all age groups showed consistent improvement.

Because this investigation was not conducted as part of a school program, we were not able to determine how the improved PS skill might have influenced school performance. However, the informal reports were excellent. Typically, progress was reported in listening ability, in spelling and in word attack skills in reading. The clinicians were also aware of the children's spontaneous improvement in articulation and general speech clarity.

The above study was followed by one in a public school setting (Katz and Medol 1972). Twenty-five children were divided into two similar groups based on PS pretest scores, age, articulation errors, IQ, etc. Thirteen children were assigned to the "phonemic synthesis training" or experimental group and 12 to the control or "traditional therapy" group.

The experimental group was given live voice training in phonemic synthesis instead of their regular speech therapy sessions. The control group continued to get the type of therapy that the clinician typically provided which closely resembled the nine-steps program recommended by Van Riper (1963). Care was taken to avoid giving the experimental group standard therapy and the control group any phonemic synthesis training.

The PS therapy was conducted in a manner similar to the programmed instruction described previously. In general, the phonetic content of the words followed the sequence from vowel-consonant, to consonant-vowel, consonant-vowel-consonant and then to words containing consonant blends.

Eleven experimental and nine control subjects completed the study. Table 4 shows the test-retest results on the PS-2A and the Goldman-Fristoe articulation test. The experimental group improved by approximately seven points on the phonemic synthesis test much like the LD children in the previous study. The traditional therapy group improved by four points which is only two points above that which is normally expected from test to retest (Metzl 1969). The improvement of the PS group was significant at the .01 level of confidence while the control group change was significant at the .05 level.

We were interested in seeing if the children would improve not only in their phonemic synthesis ability but also in their articulation ability even though thet had not received any speech therapy. On the Goldman-Fristoe Articulation Test the PS group had a mean of 12.7 errors before the training. At the end of the therapy period they had an average of 2.9 errors, a

	Experimental Group (PS Training) N = 11		Control Group (Conventional Speech Therapy) N = 9	
	PS-2A Median correct responses	G-F Artic. Test Median errors	PS-2A Median correct responses	G-F Artic. Test Median errors
Pre-therapy	9.8(39%)	12.7	8.1(32%)	11.2
Post-therapy	16.8(67%)	2.9	12.1(48%)	4.9
Difference	**6.9(28%)**	**9.8**	**4.0(16%)**	**6.3**

Table 4
Articulation errors and phonemic synthesis abilities of children who
received P.S. training compared with the performance of children who received
conventional speech therapy.

mean improvement of 9.8 responses in the three month period. This change was far more than we could expect to occur spontaneously in such a short period of time. The speech therapy group had 11.2 mean errors on the pretest and 4.9 on the post test for an average improvement of 6.3 responses. One-third of the controls made no improvement at all in articulation compared to 9% of the experimental group who did not improve. The improvement shown by the experimental group was statistically significant at the .01 level of confidence while the change for the control group was not statistically significant at the .05 level.

The results from the articulation test were quite remarkable. In fact, 64% of the children in the phonemic synthesis group were dismissed from therapy compared to the dismissal of 44% who had received traditional speech therapy. The authors cautioned that "...this should not be interpreted to mean that phonemic synthesis training should replace traditional speech therapy." Indeed, there was good articulation improvement and many dismissals in the traditional therapy group. These results support the use of an auditory training procedure in remediating auditory processing problems and provide evidence that phonemic synthesis training can carry over into other skills. Further clinical research is needed to evaluate the differences between live voice and tape recorded PS therapy programs, and to evaluate the effects of a combined speech therapy and phonemic synthesis training program. We presume that this dual approach would yield better results than either of the two approaches by themselves.

Presently, we are developing a new PS program which is based on the previous tape recorded program. These materials consist of 15 lessons plus extra training and practice materials for those phonetic combinations which are usually difficult. It is much easier to synthesize a consonant-vowel-consonant (CVC) word than to synthesize a consonant blend plus a vowel.

For example, the word *ski*, /s k i/ is more difficult than the word *seek* /s i k/. Therefore, extra instruction is provided on the tape to help the child learn this task.

Harmon used the recorded program with seven children who had either reading or speech-language problems. Four children were also tested as controls. She used the Lindamood Auditory Conceptualization (LAC) Test as the criterion for improved auditory functions and the Phonemic Synthesis Test, list 3A, to evaluate any changes in sound blending skills (Harmon 1974). As in the two previous studies the children who had PS training improved in their sound blending skills: they increased from a median score of 4 to a score of 23 (at the 95 percentile). They also improved their auditory skills: the median pretest score of 44 (equivalent to the first half of first grade level) on the LAC increased to a median of 82 on the post test (about equal to the last half of the 4th grade level). The program continued for a 6 month period because vacations, illness and other minor catastrophies intervened. Nevertheless, the improvement which was equivalent to about three years of development certainly represents an impressive change. Control subjects showed far less change.

From our initial studies we have developed some guiding principles regarding auditory training in phonemic synthesis. Although these represent common sense we feel that they are worth repeating. Use high quality recordings or live voice for the best results. We cannot expect a child to improve in the articulation of specific sounds if the training signal is poor. Start at a level that is below the child's ability and help him to improve. The pretest will give you an idea of what the youngster is able to do. When in doubt, go to a lower, not a higher level. Proceed slowly with lots of repetition. Phonemic synthesis training should be fun. If it is not, be creative.

A Brief Explanation of What Phonemic Synthesis Is and Why

Although we do not fully understand how phonemic synthesis ability or traning works, we do know that PS relates to critical academic and communication skills and that through PS training communication skills improve. Our rationale for attempting PS remediation is based primarily on the work of Luria (1970) and the work of Tallal and Piercy (1973, 1974, 1975).

Luria (1970) noted in his work with hundreds of patients who had traumatic brain lesions that the middle-posterior portion of the temporal lobe is important for the reception, elaboration, and discrimination of speech. Luria points out that this region of the brain serves three important functions: 1. analysis, 2. synthesis, and, 3. memory. If this is so, then it would appear that a test of phonemic synthesis would be well suited to challenge the phonemic zone. That is, phonemic synthesis requires careful analysis in the unsophisticated listener because of its inherent distortion. It certainly requires synthesis because the patient must combine each phoneme with the others to be successful. Finally, its relationship with auditory memory was established by the Katz et al. 1969 study which demonstrated a correlation of .47 between PS and the memory portion of the UTLD.

In addition, Luria (1970) identified important articulation, spelling and reading regions in the brain that surround the phonemic zone superiorly, anteriorly and posteriorly with close neural links. In fact, the articulation and phonemic zones overlap one another. Obviously, the connection between PS and receptive language is easy to establish anatomically because the posterior temporal lobe is considered part of Wernicke's area.

Baru and Karaseva (1972) help us to link the posterior temporal region with the ability to analyze rapid signals. In their study they obtained puretone thresholds at 1000 Hz for 1200 msec. signals and compared this with threshold for 1.2 msec. signals. Normal listeners required about 20 dB more intensity to be able to identify the presence of the brief tone. Patients who had peripheral or central lesions in areas other than the middle-posterior portion of the temporal lobe performed like the normal subjects or required even less of a difference between brief and longer signals. The patients who had lesions to the auditory cortex could not identify brief tones until the stimuli were about 10 dB greater than those required by normals. This research suggests that without the posterior temporal region we would not be able to make the rapid sound analyses required for speech.

The work of Tallal (1976, 1980) and of Tallal and Piercy (1973, 1974, 1975) helps us understand the relationship between auditory processing, LD and language disorders. They found that brief speech and non-speech cues could not be discerned by children who had delayed language. However, slowing down the transition in the speech signals from 43 to 250 msec. (or even 95 msec.) permitted the children to respond normally. The work of Tallal and Piercy, Luria, Baru and Karaseva explains why the posterior temporal region is sensitive to rapid signals and to phonemic analysis. While Tallal (1978) points out that many patients who have language problems have disorders of higher linguistic processes, she says that we cannot rule out that "...cognitive or linguistic deficits could result from a more primary perceptual problem, such as a difficulty in detecting a signal change, in discriminating temporal or spectral features, or in integrating different aspects of complex signals over time" (p. 73). She further says that until a disorder of the primary perceptual mechanism can be ruled out, it would be difficult to indicate precisely what the child's language problem is and what should be done about it.

We can now attempt to explain why phonemic synthesis training might be so effective. First, the child receives positive reinforcement from his general speech improvement.

Second, the child who has a defective auditory system develops a clearer understanding about the sounds of speech because the stimuli are clear, prolonged and repeated. The use of individual phonemes gives the auditory system time to process the acoustic information and provides consistent stimuli which help the inefficient system establish the engrams of speech. Furthermore, the "idealized" neutral phonemes are likely to be processed more centrally than co-articulated ones; the improved engrams can help the child establish phoneme boundaries which are important for processing co-articulated sounds. As the youngster responds more accurately to speech he learns to retain an accurate concept of the sounds.

Third, the child learns that words are made up of discernable units and that these units can be manipulated. Knowing how words are constructed helps the youngster synthesize co-articulated sounds; eventually he processes a complete word. Moreover, his previously inefficient and confused strategies for phoneme storage and word retrieval become organized and successful.

Fourth, the child who has become a good "processor" applies his newly developed skills to decoding new words, which leads to his improvement in spelling and in reading.

Summary

In this paper we have tried to develop a rationale for using Phonemic Synthesis training with children who have reading, spelling, articulation and/or language disorders. The literature supports the connection between these skills and PS. Results suggest that the child who improves in his phonemic synthesis abilities will also improve in articulation and in other related language skills. Finally, we have proposed an explanation of how PS affects the child's auditory processing and language skills.

References

Bannatyne, A.D. and Wichiarajote, P. 1969. Relationship between written spelling, motor functioning and sequencing skills. *J. Learning Disabil.* 2:6-18.

Baru, A.V. and Karaseva, T.A. 1972. *The brain and hearing.* New York: Consultants Bureau.

Beasley, D.S., Shriner, T.H., Manning, W.H., and Beasley, D.C. 1974. Auditory assembly of CVC's by children with normal and defective articulation. *J. of Communicat. Dis.* 7:127-33.

Conners, C.K., Kramer, K., and Guerra, F. 1969. Auditory synthesis and dichotic listening in children with learning disabilities. *J. of Spec. Ed.* 3:163-69.

Gardner, H., Albert, M.L., and Weintraub, S. 1975. Comprehending a word: the influence of speed and redundancy on auditory comprehension in aphasia. *Cortex* 11:155-62.

Harmon, C.H. 1974. Collection and analysis of normative data on two tests of auditory perception: Phonemic synthesis #3 and same/different discrimination #4. Unpublished thesis, Central Missouri State Univesity.

Katz, J. and Allam, N. 1958. Unpublished study.

Katz, J. and Burge, C. 1971. Auditory perception training for children with learning disabilities. *Menorah Med. J.* 2:18-29.

Katz, J., Chubrich, R.C., Davis, R.E., Gallaway, K.C., and Illmer, R. 1969. Speech, hearing, language and auditory perceptual functions in children with learning disabilities. Unpublished paper.

Katz, J., Davis, R.E., Johnson, M.G., Struckmann, S., and Illmer, R. 1970. Early identification of exceptional children. Unpublished study.

Katz, J. and Illmer, R. 1972. Auditory perception in children with learning disabilities. In *Handbook of clinical audiology,* 1st ed., ed. J. Katz. Baltimore: Williams and Wilkins, Co.

Katz, J. and Medol, I. 1972. The use of phonemic synthesis in speech therapy. *Menorah Med. J.* 3:10-18.

Katz, J. and Pack, G. 1975. New developments in differential diagnosis using the SSW test. In *Central auditory processing disorders*, ed. M. Sullivan. Omaha: University of Nebraska Press.

Luria, A.R. 1970. *Traumatic aphasia: its syndromes, psychology and treatment.* The Hague: Mouton and Co.

Mange, C. 1960. Relationship between selected auditory perceptual factors and articulatory ability. *J. Speech Hear. Res.* 3:367-74.

Mange, C. 1955. Relationships between selected auditory factors and articulation ability. Unpublished dissertation, Pennsylvania State University.

Mange, C. 1953. A study of speech sound discrimination within words and within sentences. Unpublished thesis, Pennsylvania State University.

McGinnis, M.A. 1963. *Aphasic children: identification and training by the association method.* Washington, D.C.: A.G. Bell Association for the Deaf.

Metzl, M.N. 1969. Measurements of sound synthesis ability in second, fourth, and sixth grade children and adults. Master's thesis, Hunter College, New York.

Monroe, M. 1932. *Children who cannot read.* Chicago: University of Chicago Press.

Mulder, R.L and Curtin, J. 1955. Vocal phonic ability and silent reading achievement: a first report. *Elementary School J.* 56:121-23.

Orton, S.T. 1937. *Reading, writing and speech problems in children.* New York: W.W. Norton and Co.

Stovall, J.V., Manning, W.H., and Shaw, C.K. 1977. Auditory assembly of children with mild and severe misarticulations. *Folia Phoniat.* 29:162-72.

Tallal, P. 1980. Auditory temporal perception, phonics, and reading disabilities in chilren. *Brain and Lang.* 9:182-98.

Tallal, P. 1978. Implications of speech perceptual research for clinical populations. In *Speech and language in the laboratory, school and clinic*, eds. J.F. Kavanah and W. Strange. Cambridge, Mass.: MIT Press.

Tallal, P. 1976. Rapid auditory processing in normal and disordered language development. *J. Speech Hear. Res.* 19:561-71.

Tallal, P. and Piercy, M. 1975. Developmental aphasia: the perception of brief vowels and extended stop consonants. *Neuropsycholog.* 13:69-74.

Tallal, P. and Piercy, M. 1974. Developmental aphasia: rate of auditory processing and selective impairment of consonant perception. *Neuropsycholog.* 12:83-93.

Tallal, P. and Piercy, M. 1973. Developmental asphasia: impaired rate of non-verbal processing as a function of sensory modality. *Neuropsycholog.* 11:389-98.

Van Riper, C. 1963. *Speech correction: principles and methods.* Englewood Cliffs, New Jersey: Prentice Hall.

Questions and Answers

Q: Which language tests did you use in your studies?

A: Just about all of the children got the PPVT and the Utah Test of Language Development. The ITPA and the LLAT were used less frequently.

Q: What was your rationale for using the Peabody and the Utah as measures of "language functioning" for your adolescent population? Wouldn't the vocabulary section of the WISC have been more realistic?

A: I am not clear why you feel that the vocabulary subtest would be more realistic than the PPVT and the UTLD. The UTLD was our best single test in correlating with all of the other speech, language, and auditory processing tests. The PPVT was also highly correlated and, like the section of the WISC, it is a measure of vocabulary. In addition, very few of the children were adolescents. The oldest in most of our studies was 13 years.

Q: Discuss how phonemic synthesis relates to other auditory skills including the SSW test.

A: In the various studies that we did we found small correlations between PS and memory. In a few cases the correlations reached statistical significance. We have used standard tests of memory for digits, for sentences, and for speech sounds. Logically, a bit of phonemic synthesis is auditory memory; a bit more of PS seems to be speech sound discrimination. That is, the correlations with same/different discrimination tasks have been higher than with memory tasks.

The correlation between PS and the SSW is probably even higher. The SSW measures a broad range of central and peripheral functions including the individual's difficulty in hearing clear information.

I imagine that the relationship between the SSW and PS is fairly substantial with correlations of about .4 and .5. We talked about the high correlation between PS and the Utah Test of Language Development. The correlation is way up there in the .6s, so that is quite a healthy relationship with this broad language measure. The correlation with PPVT is about .5.

Q: Have you done anything with phonemic *analysis*? For example, ask the child to say the sounds of *cat, nose, baby*, etc?

A: I have relatively little experience with phonemic analysis, although in our present PS program we have incorported some of these items. In general, I think that the analysis task requires more sophistication than the synthesis task. It may not be as necessary for very basic reading or basic spelling; however, having this ability must be a significant help to the youngster.

Q: If auditory perceptual problems (e.g., phonemic synthesis) are the basis of linguistic defects, how do you account for the children who have normal language and problems with phonemic synthesis.

A: Auditory perception and language skills are highly correlated but by no means identical. Let us say that the correlation between PS

158

and the UTLD is .7, which means that PS accounts for only half of the variance. This means that half of what the UTLD measures is something other than PS. Needless to say, language is extremely complex. I presume that we are able to compensate for lack of auditory processing abilities of one sort with other auditory or non-auditory language skills. When we lack this flexibility, then it is likely that language deficits will show up. In the data that we have presented, there are no populations that showed a great discrepancy between PS and language function.

Q: How do you utilize information obtained from a central test battery in a remedial program?

A: Depending on the youngster's problems and performance on auditory processing tests, we recommend various forms of management and counseling for the child and his family. We have developed programmed instruction materials which we hope to make available soon. One can provide specific programs depending on the types and the severity of the problems. In addition to training in phonemic synthesis, in same/different discrimination and in speech-in-noise skills, we can work on memory and sequencing tasks. Recommendations should be made to the classroom teacher to minimize the adverse effects of environmental noises on the child's ability to learn. Knowing the results of the central tests can also aid in making proper referrals to other specialists.

10

Language Processing Disorders: Factors in Diagnosis and Remediation

Katharine G. Butler, Ph.D.

Those of us who work in the clinical "vineyard" of language-disordered children have found ourselves searching diligently for information among the groves of Academe, in the laboratory of the experimental psychologist, on the terraces of psycholinguistic endeavor, on the mountains of memory, and in the valleys of research on attention and effort. I suspect that most of us also reside in the city of Frustration, where each open boulevard gradually seems to narrow to smaller streets, ending in seldom-trod paths and blank walls. Only occasionally do we manage to attain an insight which reveals new vistas in this most complex of tasks: the analysis of language processing disorders and the restoration of communication skills.

While my major area of clinical research is that of language-processing disorders among young children, I have been increasingly interested in the influence of auditory strategies on language learning and in the parameters of the so-called auditory processing skills which may have some bearing on the attentional and language deficits of high-risk children. Attentional, perceptual and linguistic behaviors are defined in divergent ways in the literature; it is my intent to focus on some of these definitions and then to relate them to assessment and intervention.

In looking at auditory language-processing within the framework of information processing, we might adopt Dominic Massaro's (1975) definition of language processing as "the abstraction of meaning from an acoustic signal or from printed text." He further notes that language processing might be viewed as a sequence of processing stages or operations. Such stages or operations occur between the stimulus, or sound wave pattern, and the assignment of meaning to that stimulus. In particular, we wish to examine the processing of acoustic stimuli: selective attention mechanisms; pattern identification; short-term memory; coding procedures; long-term memory and recall; and retrieval strategies from both short and long-term memory. The parameters of language processing provide a framework in which we may then consider disorders of language comprehension and expression (Butler 1979).

Attention

There are many ways to look at "attention." There is the global attitude frequently taken by parents, teachers, and specialists who deal with language-disordered children. For them, "attention" is generally equated with "following directions," or even more ambiguously with "paying attention to the speaker." Kahneman (1973) notes that some types of information-processing activities need only an input of information, while others require attention or effort. Since effort and attention have limitations, either external or internal to the child, one way to identify disorders of attention is to monitor the level of interference from concurrent activities.

We should remember, however, that there may well be simultaneous processes working, "performing bottom-up, data driven analyses as well as top-down, conceptually driven ones" (Norman 1976). If one espouses the bottom-up, top-down mode of attentional processes, then the major limitation may be dependent upon how many of the resources are used. As Norman indicates, this focuses upon matters other than the location of attentional "bottlenecks" in the various stages of processing. It has been noted that well-learned tasks, those which are "rote" or "automated" require little conscious effort and attention; thus it is possible to perform more than one well-learned task simultaneously. The introduction of less well-known information changes the picture dramatically. As if our desire to define and to measure the components of attention were not already stretched beyond current assessment capabilities, we are also attempting to measure various aspects of the incoming auditory signal (a bottom-up process), in contrast to emphasizing cognitive processing and linguistic concepts (a top-down process).

To examine the role of attention in information-processing, Geffen and Sexton (1978) asked children to divide their attention between two stimuli or to focus their attention on one stimulus while rejecting the other stimuli. These authors found that children as young as seven have different strategies for focusing and dividing attention, and that such strategies become increasingly differentiated with age. Interestingly enough, they also found that resistance to distraction did not improve with age for *focused attention* tasks; however, for the *divided attention* tasks, there was improvement in resistance to distraction between the ages of seven and ten.

A number of authors hypothesize that older children use "selective attention," while younger children tend to divide attention. Geffen and Wale (1979) report that seven-year-olds can divide attention when given sufficient time, and can focus attention on more speeded tasks when required. These authors also report that socioeconomic differences in REA (Right Ear Advantage) studies may indicate that middle-class children adopt strategies which maximize their performance, while lower-class children do not.

Perhaps another important concept is that of listener "set." Hiscock and Kinsbourne (1980) note that children have difficulty in processing verbal material and attending simultaneously to the left. Since many studies in selective listening and attention use dichotic listening tasks, and since so many of the newly developed audiological evaluation techniques provide for dichotic tasks, it is important to note that dichotic REA may actually be a right-side-of-space advantage, rather than a right ear advantage

(Hiscock and Kinsbourne 1980). Two factors may be at play. First, information from an unattended channel may be processed if the physical, phonetic and/or semantic features of the unattended message matches the child's expectations, i.e., his listening set. Second, children may experience difficulty in attending to the left during linguistic processing if the instructions have been given on the right side; this is, again, a listening set.

Normal children age eight and above demonstrate an ability to inhibit intrusion from distracting stimuli, although there appears to be data that resistance to distracton is possible as early as the kindergarten year. Children of this age, who have received perceptual pretraining on concept tasks, may be able to generalize control strategies in a variety of learning situations. This writer is currently exploring the ability of pre-school children to resist distraction in a competing message paradigm. We have observed some four year old children who are able to consciously control the intrusion of distracting stimuli in this difficult task. However, little is currently known about the effect of fatigue, the level of difficulty, the degree of attention and effort, and the semantic-perceptual factors, etc., which affect the performance of young children and which prevent children from developing a variety of listening strategies.

Those of us dealing with young pre-school children must recognize that the child's affective behavior and his linguistic behavior are important. It is difficult to differentiate between a child's ability to perform a language-processing task and the child's abilities to attend to and to perceive the task which precede his performance. Similarly, the clinician who is attempting to measure language processing will have difficulties in differentiating the auditory processing abilities from the attentional and perceptual abilities. Lovrinic (1979) warns of difficulties in using present audiological tests such as the Willeford Battery, or the SSW, to identify auditory processing problems. She notes that studies conducted with these instruments often do not account for list effects, order effects, and ear effects.

As Bregman (1978) points out, the sensory systems must evolve ways of sorting out the input so that a "descripton" of each source can be recovered. In judging auditory information, the individual must use some general information regarding the "parsing" of all signals and in addition, utilize knowledge, skills and a variety of intentions concerning specific types of signals (Bregman 1978). We speak of attention as though it were a single act when, in reality, it is a series of judgments about a variety of acoustic events.

Other Factors of Language Processing

Having looked briefly at attention and at the difficulties one might encounter in trying to evaluate it (audiologically or linguistically), let us turn our attention to other factors involved in language processing.

While there are any number of such definitions, Massaro (1975) notes that language processing can be divided into four processes or functional components. These are (1) feature detection, (2) primary recognition, (3) secondary recognition, and (4) recoding. Massaro refers to feature detection as the sensory stage, and primary recognition as the perceptual stage. The feature detection process is that which transforms the sound wave pattern into acoustic features held in perceptual auditory storage. Massaro maintains that there is a one-to-one relationship between the auditory signal and the information stored at the preperceptual stage. Apparently, auditory signals must extend in time so that a complete sound pattern is present in order to provide sufficient information to the listener who can identify that sound pattern and select it from other possible alternatives. The model assumes that information is held in the so-called preperceptual auditory storage for about 250 milliseconds. At this point, primary recognition (or perception) occurs. It is estimated that performance levels off at around 250 milliseconds, which is estimated to be the approximate life of the preperceptual image (Massaro 1975).

Others have reported that the auditory image may prevail for as much as one-half a second, although much of that research is based on results from adults rather than from children. Measurement of adult performance invariably raises questions about applying that knowledge to children who are either normal or disordered. In addition, the evaluation of very young children brings with it a number of factors which increase the variability of the data gathered. In any case, the speech-language pathologist in the field has little access to instrumentation for temporal measurements, although this may change over the next decade.

It has been reported that the younger the subject, the more likely he is to ignore important aspects of auditory stimuli. He may also fail to apply mnemonic strategies, unless taught to do so. In addition, a review of protocols from various language tests indicates that older children who have language and learning disorders function at a developmentally younger age. Thus, it is not uncommon to find a ten or twelve year old learning-disordered or language-delayed child functioning at the level of normal children who are three years his junior. From this a number of questions spring to mind: (1) Are such children unable to exclude inputs which are irrelevant? (2) Do children respond incorrectly simply because they are unable to process the stimuli, reject the linguistic distractors, and respond within specified time limits? (3) What is the nature of the distractor or foil? Is it verbal or nonverbal, linguistic or non-linguistic? (4) Does the semantic context of the background provide motivational attributes? (5) Is the foreground message important enough to be recognized? (6) Are the two sets of stimuli (the intended signal and the distracting signal) sufficiently distinct?

Memory

Those who attempt to construct language tests should recognize that some children recall information more slowly and some require more than one trial to demonstrate memory. How can we measure the difference between a child who has forgotten a message which he cannot retrieve and

163

a child who can retrieve the information if he is given sufficient time or additional cues? The literature suggests that children's strategies for remembering change over time and that we should examine the interdependency of comprehension and memory.

Thus, those of us who are interested in language and language processing are, perforce, students of memory. As Estes (1976) notes, short term memory is thought to encompass intervals ranging from a few hundred milliseconds to twenty or thirty seconds. As he states, short term memory and primary memory refer to the same concept (p. 5). Long term memory and secondary memory are similar concepts. He reports that investigators agree that the original stimulus is transformed in successive stages and that it is removed from its original modality-bound form. In general, what is retrieved from memory is not the original input, but rather a transformation which is a product of that input and the individual's memory system.

Those who monitor the memory output of language-disordered children are frequently intrigued by the seemingly idiosyntonic memories recalled. Estes points out that developmental research is handicapped because children generally have difficulty focusing on an experimental task and excluding distraction. In fact, attention to task and the exclusion of distractions are phenomena which vary "so strongly and systematically with age" (Estes, 1976, p. 12) that accurate research presents problems. Estes summarizes that research by indicating that selective attention in young children is difficult to measure and that learning disability is almost synonymous with distractibility. While this may or may not be true, particularly given today's definition(s) of learning disability, certainly there is a need to explore the responses such children make to selective attention tasks. Such responses may reveal not only the level of performance but may provide clues to the content and the manner of retrieval strategies. I suspect that more can be learned about a child's mode and level of functioning from his aberrant responses than can be learned from normal, if somewhat temporally delayed, responses.

Recently, Estes (1979) reviewed the theories of memory and noted that one of the most influential models was proposed by Craik and Watkins (1973), a so-called "levels-of-processing" interpretation. Craik and Watkins suggested that, depending upon the time available and the entire processing load, items might be processed at different levels rather than encoded as units in the perceptual systems. These "levels" have been the subject of considerable research and are still the subject of debate. Estes looked at semantic memory and explored how the meaning of a word might be interpreted in context. A word's meaning consists of a memory trace vector within its context (p. 53). He cites the example of a listener hearing not only the word "canary," but the sentence, "A canary (pointing to the canary) is a bird" (p. 54). Given this example, the output of the memory trace vector would be an input to another memory vector incorporating traces of both "canary" and "bird." A more detailed accounting of such semantic representation at various levels of abstraction may be found in Nilsson's (1979) text entitled *Perspectives on Memory Research*. Suffice it to say that the speech-language pathologist and audiologist should consider not only the levels of processing but the depths of abstraction during both evaluation and intervention.

Numerous investigators have reported that the functional properties of short-term memory (i.e., primary memory) appear to be independent of age from early childhood to adulthood. As a corollary, in a study of several hundred five-year-olds who had been identified as "high risk" at school entry, this writer found that one aspect of auditory processing which appeared to function at age level was short-term memory for digits. Interestingly, other short term memory tasks involving phonological synthesis or analysis did not fare nearly as well (Butler 1978). In general, the literature suggests that memory span is highly dependent upon active "chunking" and "temporal spacing." Children who have language disorders may demonstrate difficulties in clustering or organizing items categorically. Research by Farnham-Diggory (1972) has postulated that training in specific aspects of clustering and chunking may be beneficial. For example, she suggests cross-modal pairing, rote-linking and attention control strategies.

Changes in mnemonic ability appear to be related to the development of rehearsal, organizational and retrieval strategies. While successful in the specific, various types of training designed to assist children to organize or cluster items in relation to categorical retrieval cues are less than successful in general. There is some thought that such organizational and retrieval skills are felt to be a by-product of formal education, but how this occurs has not yet been defined. As educators change curricula and classroom facilities from structured to unstructured (or vice versa), from closed to open, from modality-specific to multi-modality, the variations in educational fashion further complicate selecting subjects for controlled studies to evaluate the effect of specific pedagogical procedures on learning.

Over the past decade, there has been an increased emphasis on self-paced learning and a de-emphasis on rote instruction. Gone are the days of memorizing nursery rhymes, Mother Goose tales, and Aesop's fables, or of interpreting poetry. Today's self-paced learning may be subject to future modification, since, as one educator informed me, "We have discovered that with college students, there is not so much self-paced learning as there is self-slowed learning." It would appear that there is a need, after all, for the extrinsic motivation that can be supplied by a clinical educator or speech-language pathologist.

Motivation

While not yet clearly seen on the educational horizon, a re-examination of the educational baby in the amorphous bathwater may yet occur. Having tossed out the more highly structured procedures and embraced a turbulent stream of experiential and experimental techniques, control of undesirable or unwanted behaviors among children has been achieved through behavior modification techniques, and more recently, through a humanistic approach. Berry addresses some of these issues in her language teaching program, which is described in *Teaching Linguistically Handi- capped Children* (Berry 1980). The global-ontogenic teaching program she advocates includes an initial unit on phonology and phonation. This is fol- lowed by a unit which stresses a perceptual-semantic component, includ- ing organizing, categorizing, and sequencing information temporally, and finally, generalizing information. Berry stresses that "in language learning, motivation, attention and memory form a troika of interdependent sub- strates" (p. 79). She addresses the need to develop attention in language- disordered children and provides practical classroom suggestions.

Zajonc (1980) explores the impact of motivation upon attention and memory within an information-processing model. Although most com- temporary theories consider affect to be postcognitive, he hypothesizes that affective judgments may, in fact, precede perceptual and cognitive opera- tions. He concludes that cognition and affect are systems which influence each other, while they independently affect information processing. With- out writing "a model for affect and for the various ways that it interacts with cold cognition," he includes three processes — affect, recognition and fea- ture identification — related to representations in memory. While sensory processes have the earliest onset time, "affective reaction always directly follows the sensory input" (p. 171). Clinicians involved in assessing and treating children who have language-processing disorders may wish to look more closely at the impact of affect and motivation on performance.

The importance of the school environment to the child's practice and development of information-processing skills appears to increase as he gets older. Children who study successfully use attentional strategies, verbali- zations and mnemonics to retain information in both short and long term memory. It has been thought that older children may increase performance not only through increased memory and rehearsal strategies, but also by the acquisition of cultural and educational ground rules. Children develop conscious planning skills as they recognize the need to respond to school- related tasks. Rehearsal strategies are developed as the child sees a purpose in learning. As Wiig and Semel (1980) report, "problems with memory — either short or long term — can show up in problems with processing lan- guage and producing it" (p. 282). Language production depends on more than memory, of course. It is affected by the child's experiential past, by his momentary feelings, and by the environment for communication. Sim- ply stated, processing the structure of a sentence depends on short-term memory, while interpreting the meaning depends on long-term memory.

Unknowingly, parents, teachers and clinicians place cultural de- mands on children and expect performance to follow. In speech and lan- guage discrimination tasks, for example, the question is often asked, "Are these (two items) the same or different?" Nickerson (1978) points out that the act of comparing one thing with another and of "determining whether they are instances of the same thing must be a very fundamental type of perceptual activity" (p. 77). Researchers have found that it takes less time to determine the similarity than it does to determine the differences between two stimuli. Nickerson speculates that judgments of sameness and of difference may depend on partially different processes, rather than being two sides of the same coin, as we might imagine. He raises the question as to whether or not the "sensitivity to the similarities between specific stimuli in one's environment is more adaptive than sensitivity to the differences between them." Thus, assessing a child's ability to judge auditory stimuli might well reveal a differing reaction time (RT) between items which require a "difference" judgment. We will return to the matter of reaction time and the retrieval of information from memory later in this paper. It is sufficient to note here that specific strategies to address such issues as reaction time differential between same-different responses among language-disordered children are yet to be developed.

Clearly, those who work with language and learning handicapped children must carefully explain the rules of the "language game" that we all play. Age and experience typically expand our repertoire of linguistic behaviors, but rarely is it recognized that it takes time, training, and practice, even among normal children, to quickly and accurately respond to narrowly defined semantic tasks. Flavell (1979) addresses the issue of metacognition and cognitive monitoring, and reports on studies which indicate that older children are more aware of the amounts of time and of practice which are needed for recall tasks. When older children are given a memory task and sufficient time to study, they know when they are ready to recall the information perfectly. On the other hand, younger children would study and say that they were ready for the recall test when they were not. In a study where elementary school children were asked to help the experimenter evaluate the adequacy of verbal instructions by indicating omissions or ambiguities, the young children thought they could follow the instructions although, in truth, the instructions were filled with omissions and obscurities. Flavell suggests that young children are limited in their knowledge and understanding about cognitive phenomena and they do relatively little monitoring of their own comprehension, memory, etc. Cognitive monitoring research is now being related to language, oral comprehension, reading, and language acquisition.

Flavell indicates that metacognitive strategies are necessary to regulate or to monitor cognitive strategies. He notes a study in which educable retarded children were taught self-testing strategies and much later used such strategies when confronted with the same tasks, and again, with different tasks. Indeed, the teaching of cognitive monitoring strategies may well help both normal and handicapped children, including the language disordered. Practical applications of metacognitive and cognitive enhancement procedures may be found in Kauffman's (1980) recent work. As O'Leary (1980) notes, however, one must not become over-optimistic about what training in cognitive strategies may accomplish. She concludes that self-instruction is effective, while self-assessment "is not useful with clinical populations unless it is accurate and accompanied by external reinforcement, and unless the task is easy for the child to perform." (p. 93).

Children who have language-processing problems may not be able to cope with many acoustic and linguistic features at one time. For example, if a child attends to the number of sounds, he may ignore the pauses, and vice versa. The child may utilize both important and unimportant features of a word or an object, thus obscuring the essential correspondence that is being sought. Language tests frequently differ significantly in the range of responses which are deemed "correct." On some verbal tasks, all answers within a relatively broad range may be considered acceptable and credit is given for even partially correct responses. On other tests, responses must be exactly the same as the ones identified in the manual. Again, the examiner must know how to score the test and but also must evaluate how the responses are affected by the difficulty of the task.

The degree to which a child with a language-processing disorder participates in the tasks during an evaluation may reflect not only his momentary attention but may also reflect his reaction to the activity. An increase in the requirements of the task usually increases the level of effort and attention. But it need not always be so. The child may "choose" not to attend and may mask that choice so that the adult assumes that the task is misunderstood. For all of us, child or adult, how hard we work and when we work may depend upon the nature of the activity. As Mark Twain so gleefully reported, "Work consists of whatever a body is obliged to do.... Play consists of whatever a body is not obliged to do" (The Adventures of Tom Sawyer, 1876). Thus, some language-disordered children may reject the obligation to respond.

Even among normal children and adults, inattention causes a deterioration of performance. It is difficult to ascertain the degree to which language handicapped children monitor their surroundings auditorially in contrast to investing auditory effort in the primary task at hand. While we know that attention is withdrawn from perceptual monitoring of the environment when attention to the primary task is increased, it is also true that auditory interference can and does occur even when the information load on the system is far below its total capacity. Usually, however, the amount of interference is generally an increasing function of load. Before we leave this matter of short-term memory load, it might be well to reiterate that it is of particular importance in both diagnostic and therapeutic activities to monitor the role that time and time pressure play in the processing, retention and retrieval performance of language-disordered children. Short term recall implies that the rate of the activity must be paced by the rate of decay of the stored components. Whenever there are an increasing number of items that must be rehearsed, there is a rapid build-up of time pressure. Particularly for language impaired children, this time-pressure provides additional stress which tends to decrease retention and inhibit performance.

Recall

As we have seen, it is impossible to be concerned about language processing and comprehension-expression without considering how memories are stored and retrieved. Considerable research has indicated that memory retrieval may be facilitated by altering the current context of testing or evaluation to produce an environment more like that involved in the original learning. Providing similarity between the semantic context at the time of learning and at the time of testing may be helpful. As Estes (1979) reports, an event is stored together with a representation of remaining events at the time of origination, i.e., the event is stored as an "episode." Recall of an episode is enhanced if a match between the current testing environment and the context of the original learning environment can be made.

"Cuing" may help create a context at the time of testing that is similar to that which occurred at the time of learning. This writer has been experimenting with the use of cuing in the context of language-processing tasks and has noted that, with at least some language disordered children, cuing has limited success under some conditions. While cuing procedures are reported to improve performance beyond that which is common in "free recall" (Spear 1976) among normal adults, language disordered children respond less satisfactorally, at least under competing message conditions. Among children three to five years of age, the cuing process may lengthen the temporal duration of the linguistic tasks and may even heighten what some observers have referred to as auditory fatigue.

Recognition accuracy may also be impaired during testing if items are read in a different voice from that heard for the original presentation. The impact of vocal quality, intonation and pattern has not been systematically investigated by speech-language pathologists or audiologists, although both utilize a number of live-voice and audio-taped tests and training programs. There may be a different response to adult voices and to children's voices, a matter of concern to those constructing competing message or auditory figure-ground tests or training tasks. The listener is thought to attend to the sexual characteristics of the speaker's voice by a process called filtering. Filtering refers to the selection of a stimulus for attention because that stimulus possesses a single feature that is absent from irrelevant stimuli. The filtering process is felt to be more rapid than other types of processing (pigeonholing, for example), because it requires a judgment about the presence or absence of a single feature. In addition, if the listener is required to identify the sex of the voice initially, his "filtering process" may be easily disrupted by an irrelevant stimulus thereby causing him to respond incorrectly (which he would not have done had he been asked to identify a parameter other than voice.)

Shiffrin (1976) reviewed a number of studies which suggest that when two classes of stimuli are insufficiently distinct, or when a target stimulus is not easily distinguished from distracting stimuli, all stimuli may be processed in a limited, perhaps serial, fashion. Thus, the listener may miss

a target simply because too much time is used to process or to check distractors. Before that target stimulus can be checked, new stimuli arrive, and
the listener stops processing the earlier information and begins processing
the new information. However, when the targets are distinct from the distractors, e.g., when tones are targets in a speech background, then the targets are located and processed efficiently, since the decison does not depend on the background task. Shiffrin points out that in such cases,
"attentional deficits" are not seen.

I would like to raise the possibility that children who have language
processing and attention disorders may well differ in degree, if not in kind,
in their performance of tasks which require them to distinguish between
target tones and a linguistic background. There is some clinical evidence
that young children have significantly more difficulty in processing foreground tones or non-linguistic stimuli when the background distractors are
linguistically attractive and meaningful, and are within the childrens' experiental environment. Among the many processing tests and programs, not
nearly enough attention has been paid to the differences between the wanted
message or speaker and the distractors or foils. Frequently, the distractors
appear to have been chosen because of their acoustical and phonemic
properties regardless of their semantic, pragmatic and psychological
properties.

Reaction Time

While the reaction-time of disordered children (either using motor or
verbal responses) to langage stimuli has been noted to be somewhat slower
occasionally than that of normal chilren, most audio-taped instruments have
not been carefully reviewed to determine the appropriate temporal interval desirable between the offering of the stimulus and the required motor
or verbal response. Even less attention has been paid to the possible differential reaction time between normal and disordered populations. It has
been noted by cognitive psychologists that reaction time provides a powerful technique for examining language and language processing. However, reaction time is highly dependent upon output or production limitations. RT's and accuracy measures are almost always correlated, negatively
or positively, according to Shiffrin (1976), at least among normal subjects.

The entire concept of reaction time, accuracy of response and output
limitations of both normal and disordered children on language processing
tasks is in need of further investigation. The number of new instruments
for assessment and remediation is increasing rapidly. Our diagnostic ar-
mamentarium, now relatively broad and shallow in its contour, will undoubtedly take on greater precision and depth in the decade to come.

It would appear likely that assessment will best be conducted through
the utilization of computer assisted procedures which will permit the examiner to more closely identify the limitations on the perception of, or
memory for, auditory stimuli. The future use of mini-computers and mi-
cro-processors is anticipated, not only during diagnostic but in remedia-

tion activities as well. It is only by looking at performance in the millisecond range that some aspects of short-term memory and auditory attention may be determined. Shiffrin (1976) notes that "most, if not all attention limitations may be a result of search and decision processes occurring in short-term memory." (p. 194). If true, then how language is processed in terms of quantity, quality and speed is relevant. However, a caution must be mentioned: while language processing is generally considered to be a temporally-based event, there is a danger in trying to separate into stages or mechanisms the cognitive processes involved (Craik and Levy, 1976). It has been noted that "meaning" and long term memory are involved from the beginning and that "attention" involves sensory analysis, pattern analysis, meaning and long-term memory and that the so-called stages of processing, while present, need not necessarily be completed prior to the next stage or level.

Factors in Remediation

In both diagnosis and remediation, the clinician would be wise to observe the child's ability (1) to attend for a sufficient length of time to auditory information, (2) to filter out irrelevant information, either auditory or visual, (3) to resist distractions, again either auditory or visual, (4) to attach meaning to linguistic units of increasing length and complexity, (5) to predict or recognize the occurrence of linguistic information which has previously been provided, (6) to respond to unknown or new linguistic information, (7) to handle tasks which place increased load on short term memory, (8) to utilize cues to increase comprehension-expression task performance, (9) to respond to auditory tasks under varying conditions of background noise and (10) to divide attention between auditory tasks.

Because short term memory storage is thought to be largely acoustic in nature, tasks involving only a few auditory stimuli may simply provide information about what is held in the "rehearsal buffer" and processed at the phonemic level. Semantic analysis occurs in relationship to long-term storage and thus sentences or longer units of auditory information are required. It is thought that several things may contribute to the child's failure to process at the semantic level, including semantic content (the nature of the material presented), overwhelmingly complex tasks, or restricted processing capacity. Since capacity within short-term memory is inherently limited, if the child does not utilize efficient strategies of rehearsal and recall, there may be insufficient time for the child to respond appropriately to incoming auditory stimuli.

Language processing diagnosis and treatment requires that information be available regarding the child's level of ability to process information at the sensory, perceptual, cognitive, and affective levels. Obviously, phonology, morphology, syntax, semantics and pragmatics are also to be considered. Treatment rests upon the availability of such information, a most difficult task. During both testing and treatment the clinician may wish to measure the extent to which both "given" and "new" information is recalled by the child. Recent information on discourse analysis (see Rees, this volume) would be helpful.

If one of the goals of remediation is to modify language comprehension and retrieval strategies, consideration must be given to temporal, processing and task factors, as suggested earlier. For example, it is not always easy to identify whether failure has occurred because the message was somehow interrupted during the acquisition period, during the storage period, or during the retrieval period (Butler 1980). The clinician must therefore analyze remediation tasks or programs in terms of the stimulus characteristics of such tasks, i.e., input characteristics, processing characteristics, and output (response) expectations. In addition, the kind of feedback provided by either the program or the clinician is important (Witkin and Butler 1980).

Intervention programs in language-processing vary the degree of structure which is provided at any of the three stages (input-process-output). Audio-taped programs tend to be highly structured, with all the inherent assets and liabilities that "structuring" suggests. Since language disordered children exhibit highly variable responses to various auditory tasks, it may be wise to select both carefully devised audio-taped presentations and structured clinician-devised tasks. The rate of presentation of stimuli and changes in that rate are as important as the semantic content. Since semantic and syntactic rules are thought to operate at all stages of language processing (Massaro 1975), it may be difficult to localize the effects of such rules in the performance of the child. Such difficulties notwithstanding, it should be recalled that the literature suggests that children who have language processing disorders may exhibit difficulties in devising appropriate strategies for the recall and retention of linguistic information, in selective attention, and in certain auditory perceptual tasks.

Intervention may need to address several general areas of concern. These may include, but are not limited to, the following:

1. Attention-directing strategies, including focused and divided attention tasks.
2. Selective attention tasks, as well as auditory vigilance and resistance to distraction tasks.
3. Recall of immediate and short term memory tasks, emphasizing meaningful linguistic stimuli, under single and multiple trial conditions.
4. Organizational strategies, including chunking, clustering, temporal spacing, rote-linking and cross-modal pairing.
5. Rehearsal strategies utilized to maintain auditory information in short-term memory and thence, to long-term memory, as appropriate.
6. . Recall and retrieval strategies utilized in remembering and producing language.
7. Metacognitive and cognitive strategies, such as self-instruction, self-assessment and other self-controlling procedures.

8. Psychological (affective) responses to linguistic events.

This paper has attempted to address some of the issues and concerns which underlie our current attempts to deal with the conceptual and practical aspects of language-processing and its disorders. The topics of visual processing, of written and read language, and of the relationship between visual and auditory modalities in language learning have not been reviewed, due to time constraints. However, intermodality factors do indeed play a part in the intervention process, as well as in the assessment procedures. However, as Dr. Charles Van Riper was wont to say upon the close of a lecture: "Any more would be a vulgar indulgence." I leave to you that indulgence, since there is much that remains to be said about language processing and its disorders. Certainly, much remains to be known and the clouds of theoretical uncertainty are dense, broken by occasional glimpses of the sun of progress.

References

Berry, Mildred 1980. *Teaching linguistically handicapped children*. Englewood Cliffs, NJ: Prentice-Hall.

Bregman, Albert S. 1978. The formation of auditory streams. In *Attention and performance*, vol. 7, ed. J. Requin. New York: Halsted Press.

Butler, Katharine 1980. Disorders of other aspects of auditory function. In *Communication disorders: an introduction*, ed. R.J. Van Hattum. New York: MacMillan Pub. Co.

Butler, Katharine 1980. Language processing and disorders of retrieval. *Proceedings of the 18th International Congress of Logopedics and Phoniatrics*. Washington, D.C. In press.

Butler, Katharine 1979. Language processing disorders and their treatment. In *Communicative Disorders: An Audio Journal*, vol. 4, no. 5, eds. L. Bradford and R. Wertz.

Butler, Katharine 1978. Educational and social implications of auditory processing deficits. *Proceedings of the 17th International Congress of Logopedics and Phoniatrics*, vol. 2. Basel, Switzerland: S. Karger.

Craik, F.I.M. and Levy, A. 1976. The concept of primary memory. In *Handbook of learning and cognitive processes: attention and memory*, vol. 4, ed. W.K. Estes. New York: Halsted Press.

Craik, F.I.M. and Watkins, M.J. 1973. Levels of processing: a framework for memory research. J. Verb. Learn. Verb. Beh. 12:599-607.

Estes, W.K. 1979. On the descriptive and explanatory functions of the theories of memory. In *Perspectives of memory research*, ed. L. Nilsson. Hillsdale, NJ: Lawrence Erlbaum Associates.

Estes, W.K. ed. 1976. *Handbook of learning and cognitive processes: attention and memory*, vol. 4. New York: Halsted Press.

Estes, W.K. 1979. On the descriptive and explanatory functions of the theories of memory. In *Perspectives of memory research*, ed. L. Nilsson. Hillsdale, NJ: Lawrence Erlbaum Associates.

Farnham-Diggory, S. 1972. *Information processing in children*. New York: Grune and Stratton.

Flavell, J.H. 1979. Metacognition and cognitive monitoring, a new area of cognitive developmental inquiry. Amer. Psychologist 3:906-11.

Geffen, G. and Sexton, M.A. 1978. The development of auditory strategies of attention. Developm. Psychol. 14:11-17.

Geffen, G. and Wale, J. 1979. Development of selective listening and hemispheric asymmetry. *Developm. Psychol.* 15:138-46.

Hiscock, M. and Kinsbourne, M. 1980. Asymmetries of selective listening and attention switching in children. *Developm. Psychol.* 16:70-82.

Kahneman, Daniel 1973. *Attention and effort.* NJ: Prentice-Hall.

Kauffman, James M. 1980. Teaching exceptional children to use cognitive strategies. *Except. Ed. Quart.* vol. 1, in press.

Lovrinic, Jean, 1977. The nature of auditory processing problems realted to language/learning disabilities: an audiologist's view. Paper presented at the American Speech-Language-Hearing Association, Houston, Texas.

Massaro, Dominic 1975. *Understanding language: an information-processing analysis of speech perception, reading and psycholinguistics.* New York: Academic Press.

Nickerson, R.S. 1978. On the time it takes to tell things apart. In *Attention and performance*, vol. 7, ed. J. Requin. New York: Halsted Press.

Norman, Donald A. 1976. *Memory and attention: an introduction to human processing.* New York: Wiley & sons.

O'Leary, Susan G. 1980. A response to cognitive training. *Except. Ed. Quart.* vol. 1, in press.

Shiffrin, Richard M. 1976. Capacity limitations in informtion processing, attention and memory. In *Handbook of learning and cognitive processes: attention and memory*, vol. 4., ed. W.K. Estes. New York: Halsted Press.

Spear, Norman, E. 1976. Retrieval of memories: a psychobiological approach. *Handbook of learning and cognitive processes: attention and memory*, vol. 4., ed. W.K. Estes. New York: Halsted Press.

Wiig, E.H. and Semel, A.M. 1980. Understanding of words and word relationships: assessment. In *Language assessment and intervention for the learning disabled.* Columbus, Ohio: Charles E. Merrill.

Witkin, B.R. and Butler, K. Selecting intervention programs in auditory processing. Unpublished paper.

Zajonc, R.B. 1980. Feeling and thinking: preferences need no inferences. *Amer. Psychologist* 35:151-75.

11

Summary of Question and Answer Periods

Robert W. Keith, Ph.D.

At intervals throughout the symposium, time was set aside for questions from the audience and discussion among the guest faculty. Questions relating specifically to a speaker's presentation have been placed at the end of the appropriate chapter. The following is a compilation of responses to questions of a more general nature, not related to a specific presentation.

Question: Dr. Ferry, what is your opinion of the value of the Southern California Sensory Integration Battery for Diagnosis and Therapy in the remediation of language and learning disorders?

Dr. Ferry: This approach is very prevalent in our part of the country. I have reviewed the available literature on it and have talked with a number of other individuals who have reviewed this subject. In my opinion, from the neurological standpoint, there is no scientific validity or rationale for the use of this therapy. It promotes much the same theory as the Doman Delicato philosophy did several years ago. In other words, it maintains that retraining certain parts of the brain, particularly the lower brainstem, will facilitate learning. However, there is no evidence of this whatsoever.

I am also concerned that many children are taken out of language and learning classes or programs to receive sensorimotor integration therapy. While this may help them improve their coordination, (that I think would improve with time anyway), it takes them away from what they really need. As I have said, neurologically, it is of no proven validity. Until well-controlled and well documented studies have shown its effectiveness, my opinion is that it should not be used and that conventional proven techniques for remediation should be used instead.

Dr. Richardson: I would agree with Dr. Ferry. While a young child may benefit from these exercises, I would prefer that a child with a language disorder be given language therapy for that specific problem. I had one experience with a previous patient in which sensory integration therapy was done for congenital nystagmus. The child's problem had no effect on learning, and the sensory integration treatment was of no benefit.

175

Question: How can I determine if a psychologist is knowledgeable in communication disorders before I refer to him/her?

Dr. Culbertson: Dr. Ferry reminded me of a seminar I give to the pediatric residents at Vanderbilt which is entitled, "How to tell when you have a lemon." My message to them is don't be afraid to ask questions. I think you can do it in a nonthreatening way. The psychologist who is secure and open minded will be able to answer the questions nondefensively. You should ask about their area of specialty and their level of training. You should also ask about their experience with children with different types of disorders. Then, briefly give them an example of the type of child you would like to refer. I think you should also ask for samples of types of tests that the psychologist might use with the child. In order to evaluate the responses, you must know something about different types of psychological tests yourself and which ones are appropriate for children with communication disorders. I think that most psychologists would not be threatened by answering these questions, and I think it is your responsibility to ask them if you are going to refer your patients to them.

Question: What criteria do you use to refer a child to an audiologist for a central test battery?

Dr. Culbertson: Prior to my evaluation I ensure that the child's peripheral auditory abilities are alright, that the child can hear. Then, on the basis of my auditory tests, which I consider incomplete, I would look for any specific problems with auditory memory or auditory discrimination. Because I prefer an added opinion, I would use low scores on those specific measures to refer the child to an audiologist for a more complete battery.

Question: If the child scores high on the audiologist's battery and low on yours, or vice versa, which results would you use?

Dr. Culbertson: That's a loaded question. I think I would try to be open minded about including information from other professionals, particularly in the area of central auditory dysfunction where psychological testing can provide only part of the answer. However, I would also carefully evaluate the audiologist's battery to determine what the child was asked to do and how he was asked to respond. My intent would be to determine *why* there are differences in the child's responses to our respective batteries.

Question: Why do you include hyperactivity and short attention span in your list for nonreferral?

Dr. Ferry: The fact is that we simply cannot, as pediatric neurologists, see every hyperactive child or evey child who is thought to have a short attention span and still have time for youngsters with serious organic disorders like seizures and brain tumors. I do not think that neurologists should see children with these behavioral symptoms routinely. The child's pediatrician, child development specialist or psychologist, among others, should be involved in primary evaluation of these youngsters.

Similarly, a frequent and well intentioned question, but one that we often cannot answer is, "what percent of a child's behavior is organic or functional?" In most cases I do not have any idea, and it would not make much difference in the ultimate therapy. For example, it is very difficult to determine what part of a child's short attention span is due to auditory perceptual problems, memory, fatigue, hypoglycemia or whatever. The process needs careful evaluation but there are many non-neurologists who are well trained to evaluate behavioral problems such as hyperactivity and short attention span.

Question: What material would you recommend for inclusion in assessing auditory memory skills since you indicated that memory for digits is insufficient?

Dr. Butler: I believe I indicated (in informal comments) that *if* recall of digits is used, its greatest usefulness may be in determining the pattern of errors rather than in measuring "auditory memory." We have not discussed where errors occur in digit span tests, but such factors as primacy and recency play an important part in the recall of digits among normal individuals. I hope that the information presented at this Symposium will lead the listener to consider many more parameters for measuring short and long term memory within a number of contexts.

There are, of course, many instruments on the market. Each must be reviewed with an eye to its stated purpose, and its actual assessment outcome. You may be interested in a new test of auditory comprehension which was the result of an investigation by a group of audiologists in Los Angeles. It has been standardized on children with various degrees of hearing loss, and measures auditory comprehension in both noise and quiet conditions. Standardization information on the hearing impaired population is available, and it is my understanding that norms for hearing children may be available in the future. There are 10 subtests and the administration time can be lengthy with young children. One must always be aware that optimal performance from language or hearing impaired children may not be demonstrated if auditory overload and/or auditory fatigue occur.

A text which provides considerable information about language and learning disorders and the assessment thereof was identified in my presentation, i.e., Drs. Wiig's and Semel's 1980 text entitled, *Language Assessment and Intervention for the Learning Disabled.* Various language tests are described in detail as are remediation procedures in the areas of syntax, morphology, categorization, etc. In contrast, Dr. Berry's text, *Teaching Linguistically Handicapped Children,* supplies an environmental-developmental approach. Essential to Berry's approach is the presence of a skilled clinician who can take advantage of the daily activities to stimulate and enlarge the child's language repertoire.

Question: What measures would be used to evaluate children whose primary language is not English?

Dr. Culbertson: In general, most tests that are appropriate for children who are deaf or who have severe language disorders might be considered for children whose primary language is not English. Some examples would be the Leiter International Performance Scale, the Hiskey-Nebraska and The Pictorial Test of Intelligence. I must caution that using tests such as the Performance Section of the WISC-R or others such as the Columbia Mental Maturity Scale require some understanding of language. Even though they are called performance tests, they require that a child understands what you are asking him to do. So it is very important to analyze the task that you are presenting. As Dr. Johnson so aptly stated this afternoon, what we often consider as a nonverbal test is really verbal.

Dr. Johnson: With our preschool children, the Columbia has turned out to be one of the better measures for children with severe language disorders. If we can get the task across, it is one we have been able to use more often than almost any other test. With autistic youngsters our advice from others has been that the Leiter is more useful but there are more problems with picture interpretation. There are also some problems with regression toward the mean with the Columbia, I think. One really is constantly struggling with what kind of an IQ measure to use but I think it is very important that we continue to measure intelligence.

Question: Would someone comment on the state of bilingual education and testing?

Dr. Johnson: I think that we have problems with calling programs just bilingual. Until we move to bicultural programs we may not be broadening the scope of education enough. That is, if we look only at verbal behavior it is not going to be sufficient. We should also include other professions, e.g. anthropology and sociology, when searching for other measures.

Question: Dr. Katz, in light of Dr. Rees' presentation I would like to hear your comments on the relationship between auditory recall and auditory synthesis.

Dr. Katz: I would like to respond by commenting about auditory perception in general because this needs to be addressed as much or more than the relationship between auditory memory and synthesis. Dr. Rees serves a very important function for those of us who are involved in research and the theoretical study of auditory processing. She serves as a gadfly forcing us to try to do better.

However, I do not believe that her message is that clinicians should deny treatment to children. Auditory perceptual tests do indeed identify children who cannot make good use of what they hear and auditory training does appear effective in remediating some of these problems. As a clinician you cannot afford to wait until we have all of the possible answers before incorporating useful procedures. If we waited until penicillin and aspirin were completely understood before they were used, then there would be a lot of unnecessary sickness and suffering.

Question: Do you consider the Auditory Discrimination in Depth program as an effective approach to phonemic synthesis?

Dr. Katz: The ADD program by Lindamood would no doubt be an effective way of teaching sound blending. As you will recall we have data from the opposite approach. Cornelia Harmon did Phonetic Synthesis training with a small group of children. She found a substantial jump in their performance on the Lindamood test. The improvement was equivalent to about 3 1/2 years on the test. I am sure that work on the ADD program would show positive improvement on a test of PS.

Dr. Butler: We have found the LAC (Lindamood Auditory Conceptualization) test to be quite helpful. As the child or adult moves through the various subtests, the clinician can observe the examinee's processing performance which is reflected by the way in which he/she handles the small wooden blocks representing the phonemes. It is not known whether the ADD (Auditory Discrimination in Depth) program is superior to other programs, such as the SOS (Sound-Order-System), etc.

Dr. Katz: According to Cornelia Harmon, who is very familiar with the ADD program, one of the big problems is understanding how to use it effectively. She feels that once you learn how to use it then it is very effective. She also feels that it is unfortunately being used less and less because people get the materials and they don't know how to apply them. It was one of the reasons why we decided to do something that was very straightforward in working with phonemic synthesis, and we always erred on the side of making it simple.

There is certainly a general factor in auditory perception that children who are down in one area tend to be down in the others. I use a model that is based on work by Luria, the neuropsychologist. He showed that analysis of sound, synthesis of sound, and some memory information are involved in the back part of the temporal lobe. Then he showed an area where articulation is defective. It tends to be a little bit anterior and superior but overlaps the phonetic region. Reading and spelling, of course, are involved posteriorly, more around the angular gyrus. If there is a defect to the auditory analysis and synthesis area, then you can expect that, unless you have other abilities which can compensate, it should start to affect articulation. It should also affect reading and spelling. He felt that spelling, particularly, is highly auditory and this agrees with what we find. The two closest areas for this kind of discrimination would be spelling and articulation.

Dr. Keith: I was asked to address the following question. The question concerns Dr. Butler's comments that comparisons of auditory processing testing in controlled vs. non-controlled situations showed children perform better in controlled situations. Since audiologists test in controlled situations will they obtain high false negative rates? That is, will they miss children in controlled situations who have an auditory processing problem in real life? Also, are they testing appropriately by independent ear testing?

First, regarding the controlled situation, it is clear that we do miss behaviors in our artificial test situation that are observed in the classroom. One way of gaining information about auditory behavior is to use an auditory problems checklist that asks systematic questions about behavior and helps get some information about how the child behaves in other environments. Sometimes the audiologist in the artificial environment can then better relate test results to what the referring source is seeing. An example of an excellent checklist was published by Lee Fisher, who is from Grant Wood area Education Agency, 4401 West Sixth Street, Cedar Rapids, Iowa, 52404.

Are we testing appropriately when we use independent ear tests? Obviously, when we test dichotically (different signals to different ears), it is an artificial situation because people usually listen diotically (same signal to two ears), so that what we are doing is different from real-life situations. I think that it is important to keep in mind the different purposes for using the various tests. If we wish to establish neuromaturational levels of auditory function we should test each ear independently. If we wish to investigate how the child functions in his usual acoustic environment we should probably test diotically.

Question: Should audiologists include a screening procedure for central auditory dysfunction in the audiological assessment?

Dr. Keith: I feel that audiologists ought to begin thinking about disorders from the middle ear to the cortex rather than from the middle ear to the 8th Nerve. I feel that doing air and bone conduction, SRT and speech discrimination in quiet is like doing a Templin-Darley and a Northwestern Syntax Screen Test and saying that you have done a complete speech and language evaluation. While I do not claim to know what the best battery is, a screening battery should probably begin with a speech discrimination test in quiet to use as a baseline measurement. Charlotte Dempsey suggests the use of the Gardner High Frequency Word List which has a mildly distorted speech signal. Children who have poor resistance to distortion do poorly on this quick test.

Next I recommend testing speech in noise, although I think you need to do it at a favorable S/N ratio and not as a masking study. With speech at an unfavorable S/N ratio (0 or -10dB S/N) some of the acoustic signal is not available and it becomes an auditory closure task i.e., a cognitive task. When a more favorable S/N ratio is used, for example, + 9dB, the child is required to separate auditory foreground and background but he is not required to supply linguistic segments which are masked as in an auditory closure task. This resistance to distortion is a useful test of how the child functions auditorily in his normal environment.

Question: Discuss Oscar Buros and the WRAT.

Dr. Butler: Dr. Oscar Buros served as Editor of the prestigious Mental Measurement Yearbooks for many, many years. The example I cited reflected the reviews of the WRAT (Wide Range Achievement Test), an instrument which was referred to by Dr. Jan Culbertson. As the psychologists among you know, it is one of the most widely used instuments. Many professionals use it and find it valuable. However, if you read the reviews in Buros' *The Seventh Mental Measurement Yearbook*, there is considerable doubt about its minimal usefulness. This serves to illustrate that even widely used instruments may not have sufficient reliability and validity data and that many users may be unaware of the strengths and weaknesses of the instruments they use constantly.

Dr. Culbertson: I still find the WRAT useful, not so much in providing me with a grade level of functioning, but in helping me examine the style in which the child responds to the different academic tasks. I analyze what is being asked of the child; I use it descriptively often when I am talking with the teacher about what the child can and cannot do. It is like any test — the scores are not the only reason for using the test. We must also attend to the child's strategy in completing the test.

Question: Discuss the CAPT, and other tests and programs.

Dr. Butler: As I may have indicated, the CAPT (Composite Auditory Perceptual Test) and its concomitant program, TAPS (Teaching Auditory Perceptual Skills) were developed under a grant, and thus may be obtained from the local education agency which held the grant and is now reproducing the materials at cost. The CAPT has been presented at ASHA by Dr. Belle Ruth Witkin and me and studies which came out of the grant have been reported in *Language, Speech and Hearing Services in the Schools*, (Vol. VIII, No. 3, July, 1977), entitled "Auditory Processing in Children. Two Studies of Component Factors," by Witkin, Butler, and Whalen. The CAPT is a standardized test, having normative data from hundreds of children, and is applicable to elementary school children, ages 6 through 8, and to learning disabled or language disordered children in that age range and somewhat older. The basic research establishing the parameters of this instrument are reported in the *LSSHS* 1977 issue.

Question: In light of what has been presented these last few days, should we, audiologists and speech/language pathologists, look at the auditory portion of the McCarthy Scale of Children's Abilities to obtain an overview of the child's abilities? What is its youngest age norm?

Dr. Culbertson: The McCarthy has normative data for children 2 1/2 -8 1/2 years of age, although I find it less useful with children under four years because of its length. It includes measures of auditory sequential memory for digits, words and sentences. There are measures of retrieval (e.g., the child is required to recall ideas from a story read to him). I think the McCarthy samples a child's memory skills quite well, but I would not consider it an "overview" of the child's auditory perceptual abilities.

Dr. Ferry: I might add that from my experience in traveling around the country and visiting a number of long-term follow-up programs of neonatal high-risk infants, it is probably the one test for the 3-5 year olds which is being used most widely, even with its limitations. Some data will be available within the next 1 1/2 - 2 years on the follow-up programs. People seem to recognize its limitations.

Question: Where can we find information regarding test and remediation materials that are presently available?

Dr. Keith: I am reminded that Ralph Rupp has developed a 70-page catalog of commercially available *Tests and Remediation Programs on Auditory Processing* (cost $8.00). It is available by writing to him at: University of Michigan, 1111 East Catherine Street, Ann Arbor, Michigan, 48109.

Question: This question deals generally with our poor agreement on the terminology that we use. For example, we use the word "perception" with little agreement on or understanding of what it means.

Dr. Butler: You are perfectly correct. "Perception" means one thing to the neurologist, another to the psychologist, and a third to those working in language and learning disorder. In some strict sense, it probably refers to a state of physiological readiness. In a broader sense, it may mean the processing of a complex acoustic signal in which speech cues exist but must be separated from irrelevant detail. Unfortunately, to some, perception has come to stand for a series of disparate skills, such as "discrimination," "closure," "sequencing," etc. While perception does indeed involve discrimination and closure and may have temporal sequential aspects, it is not a simple concept even within various definitions. As we have indicated, perception and attention and cognition are intertwined at all levels, making assessment and remediation a challenging task.

Dr. Keith: During these discussions primary recognition was defined as "perception" and secondary recognition was defined as "conceptualization." Later Doris Johnson used a term "capacity deficit" and "strategy deficit." It would seem that these terms deserve consideration in order to sort out fundamental sensory abilities (capacity) from cognitive language based abilities (strategy). Nevertheless, there is presently poor agreement and it is likely to be a long time before we agree on terminology.

Question: In what direction is the area of central auditory abilities and language learning heading?

Dr. Katz: Up! It seem like for so many years this subject was just lying there. About a dozen years ago I could not find a single paper or session at an ASHA convention dealing with auditory perception. Now you can go to auditory processing and language learning sessions from the beginning to the end. Whatever auditory perception is, we are now studying it, we are sharing our information and we certainly know that there is a great need for further work and study. I don't think that we will find unanimity because people work differently. Unless we are in a totalitarian system, we are all going to have our own approach and our own opinions. That's okay, at least we are doing something which is more than we did before.

Dr. Keith: I would like to thank our audience for their questions and the members of the panel for their comments. It is clear that we are making great strides in the diagnosis and remediation of central auditory and language disorders in children. We are helped by a increased recognition and awareness of the many problems in these complex areas and it seems that we are beginning to ask better questions. While we have a long way to go, we appear to be moving in the right directions.

Index

storage 163;
reading 91;
short-term memory 165;
vs. speech perception
105-6;
see also Central Auditory
Function.
Auditory Perceptual
Disorders 17, 22, 23,
61, 72;
see also Central Auditory
Disorders.
Auditory Perceptual Tests,
see Evaluation of Central
Auditory Disorders.
Auditory Sequencing 94,
95, 96-104, 128;
in dysphasic children 108;
of non-speech stimuli
108-121;
spoken language
comprehension 102-4.
Auditory Strategy 63.
Auditory System
effect of immature
pathways on language
development 63;
metabolic rate 4;
neurological function 63;
neuromaturational level
xii, 181;
pre-natal development 2.
Auditory Visual
Associations 74.
Auditory-Visual-Motor
Response 74.

Bilingual Education
Programs 178.
Binaural Fusion xi, 64.
Binaural Separation xi, 64,
66-69, 95.
Binaural Synthesis 64, 95.
Body Movement Disorders
17.
Brain Development 1-2; see
also Embryology,
Neurological
Development.
Brain Function 18, 81;
effect of immature
pathways on language
development 63;

evaluation methods 3;
and language
development 5;
male/female differences 3;
metabolic activity 4;
and reading 155;
retraining 175;
speech articulation 155;
spelling 155;
see also Cerebral
Hemispheres,
Neurological
Development.
Brain Stem Lesions
ABR results 34, 35;
acoustic reflex results 32,
34, 40, 55;
and auditory
neuromaturational level
66;
case studies 34, 40;
PI (performance vs.
intensity) function 39,
40;
pure tone audiometry 30,
40;
SSI-CCM test results 39,
40, 55;
SSI-ICM results 38, 39, 40;
SSW test results 39, 40.
Brain Tumors 177; see also
Brain Stem Lesions and
Temporal Lobe Lesions.

Capacity Deficit 183.
CAPT, Composite Auditory
Perceptual Test 182.
CCM, Contralateral
Competing Message 38,
39;
see also Brain Stem
Lesions, SSI Test,
Temporal Lobe Lesions.
Central Auditory Disorders
and attention 85;
auditory tasks 95-6;
cause and effect
relationships 61, 110,
121, 137;
cognitive factors 77;
demographic studies x;
developmental lag 128;
evaluation 61, 91, 92, 95-

6, 114;
expressive language 87;
language delay 110;
and language disorders
94, 96, 128, 136;
and learning disorders 94;
neurodevelopmental tests
125, 130-34;
neurological evaluation
5-8;
neuromaturational level
xii, 181;
neuropsychological
evaluation 18-26;
peripheral speech
disorders 70, 79, 121,
123, 137;
problems in assessment
77-83, 87;
psychological evaluation
13-26, 176;
relationship to site-of-
lesion 114, 116;
remediation 74-75, 94,
110, 179, 183;
semantic aspects of
language 87;
symbolization 83;
time compressed speech
115-16;
see also Audiological
Evaluation, Auditory
Perceptual Disorders,
Evaluation of Language
Disorders, Evaluation of
Learning Disorders.
Central Auditory Function
x, 114-18, 137;
auditory language tests
72-74;
case history 61-62;
causes and effects 61, 110,
121, 137;
controlled vs. non-
controlled test situation
180;
definition ix;
evaluation 61, 91, 95-6,
114;
evaluation vs. remediation
179;
interactionist model 98;
interpretation of results
xi-xii;

189

Oral Apraxia 124.
Oromotor Deficiencies 21.
Otitis Media xii, 8, 62, 117.

Parallel Processing of
  Speech Sounds 106.
Paranoia 25.
Passive-Aggressive
  Reaction 25.
Passive Dependent
  Reaction 25.
Pediatric Audiology xii.
Pediatric Neurologists
  professional qualifications
  6-7;
  referrals to 8, 9, 177;
  role in diagnosis of
  language disorders 5;.
Pediatrician
  counselor to parents 86;
  role in diagnosing central
  auditory disorders 85-92.
Perception 87;
  defined 183;
  evaluation of learning
  disabilities 82;
  and memory 164;
  primary recognition 163,
  183;
  rapid rate processing 136;
  reductionist model of 98;
  same-different
  discrimination 166;
  see also Cognition,
  Experimental Sensory
  and Perceptual Tests,
  Sensory-Perceptual-
  Cognitive Experiences.
Perceptual Deficiencies
  language disorders 121-
  44;
  see also Auditory, Visual
  or Haptic Perceptual
  Disorders.
Perceptual Deficit
  Hypothesis x, xi, 61, 94,
  96.
Perceptual-Motor Learning,
  see Auditory-Motor or
  Visual-Motor Learning.
Perinatal Asphyxia 3, 8.
Peripheral Auditory
  Disorders 30, 62, 64, 66.
Peripheral Hearing Tests

62, 64, 66;
  see also Audiological
  Evaluation.
Perseveration 82.
PET Scan (Positron-
  Emission Tomography)
  3.
Phenytoin 12.
Phoneme
  as perceptual unit 99, 107.
Phoneme Discrimination
  Training 138.
Phoneme Monitoring Task
  98.
Phonemic Analysis
  and memory 165.
Phonemic Synthesis, see
  PS, Phonemic Synthesis.
Physical Examination 8.
  temporal lobe lesion 43.
PI, Performance vs.
  Intensity Function 62;
  brain stem lesions 39, 40,
  43;
  central auditory disorders
  38;
  rollover 38, 43;
  temporal lobe lesions 29,
  43.
Picture Interpretation 16.
Picture Test of Intelligence
  27, 178.
Pitch Pattern Test 116.
Playtest 88.
Pneumoencephalography
  40.
PPVT, Peabody Picture
  Vocabulary Test 47, 59;
  and PS performance 147,
  158.
Premature Infants 2, 11, 21.
Preperceptual Auditory
  Storage 163.
Primary Attention Deficits
  causes 86;
  types 85.
Primary Perceptual Units
  63, 97-101.
Primary Recognition 183;
  see also Perceptual
  Abilities.
PS, Phonemic Synthesis 73,
  96, 138;
  inherent distortion 145;
  and memory 165.

PS Performance
  and central auditory
  function 145-59;
  emotional problems 149;
  interstimulus interval 147;
  language development
  147, 149-50;
  language disorders 155;
  learning disabilities 147,
  155;
  math deficiency 149;
  rapid auditory stimuli
  146, 155;
  reading ability 146, 150;
  speech articulation
  disorders 146, 147, 150,
  152;
  spelling 146;
  SSW results 158;
  temporal lobe function
  180;
  vocabulary 150.
PS Training 150-54;
  and ADD Program 179;
  and aphasic children 150;
  audio-taped program 151,
  153;
  effects of 155;
  and LAC program 154;
  live-voice program 152;
  receptive language 155;
  temporal lobe function
  154.
PS-PIC, Phonemic
  Synthesis Picture
  Multiple Choice Test
  147, 151.
PS-2A, Phonemic Synthesis
  Test List 2A 147, 152.
PS-3A, Phonemic Synthesis
  Test List 3A 154.
PSI, Pediatric Speech
  Intelligibility Test 47-56,
  59;
  attention 53, 54;
  control of non-auditory
  factors 52-55;
  effect of chronological age
  51;
  effect of cognitive abilities
  52;
  effect of sentence format
  52;
  generation of test
  materials 47-49, 56, 59;

191

Index of Authors